YUNGBLUD

PRESENTS:

TWISTED TALES OF THE RITALIN CLUB 2:

WEIRD TIMES AT QUARRY BANK UNIVERSITY

PUBLISHERS Joshua Frankel & Sridhar Reddy
CFO & GENERAL COUNSEL Kevin Meek
SENIOR V.P. Josh Bernstein
V.P., PUBLIC RELATIONS & MARKETING Jeremy Atkins
V.P., DIGITAL Anthony Lauletta
EDITORIAL COORDINATOR Dominique Rosés
ARTIST LIAISON Jess Lechtenberg
PRODUCTION DESIGN DIRECTOR Courtney Menard
DESIGN DIRECTOR Tyler Boss
SENIOR DIGITAL MARKETING ASSOCIATE Rebecca Cicione

Written by
Yungblud & Ryan O'Sullivan

Art by
MinoMiyabi & Derick Jones

Colors by
Aladdin Collar

Lettering by
Justin Birch

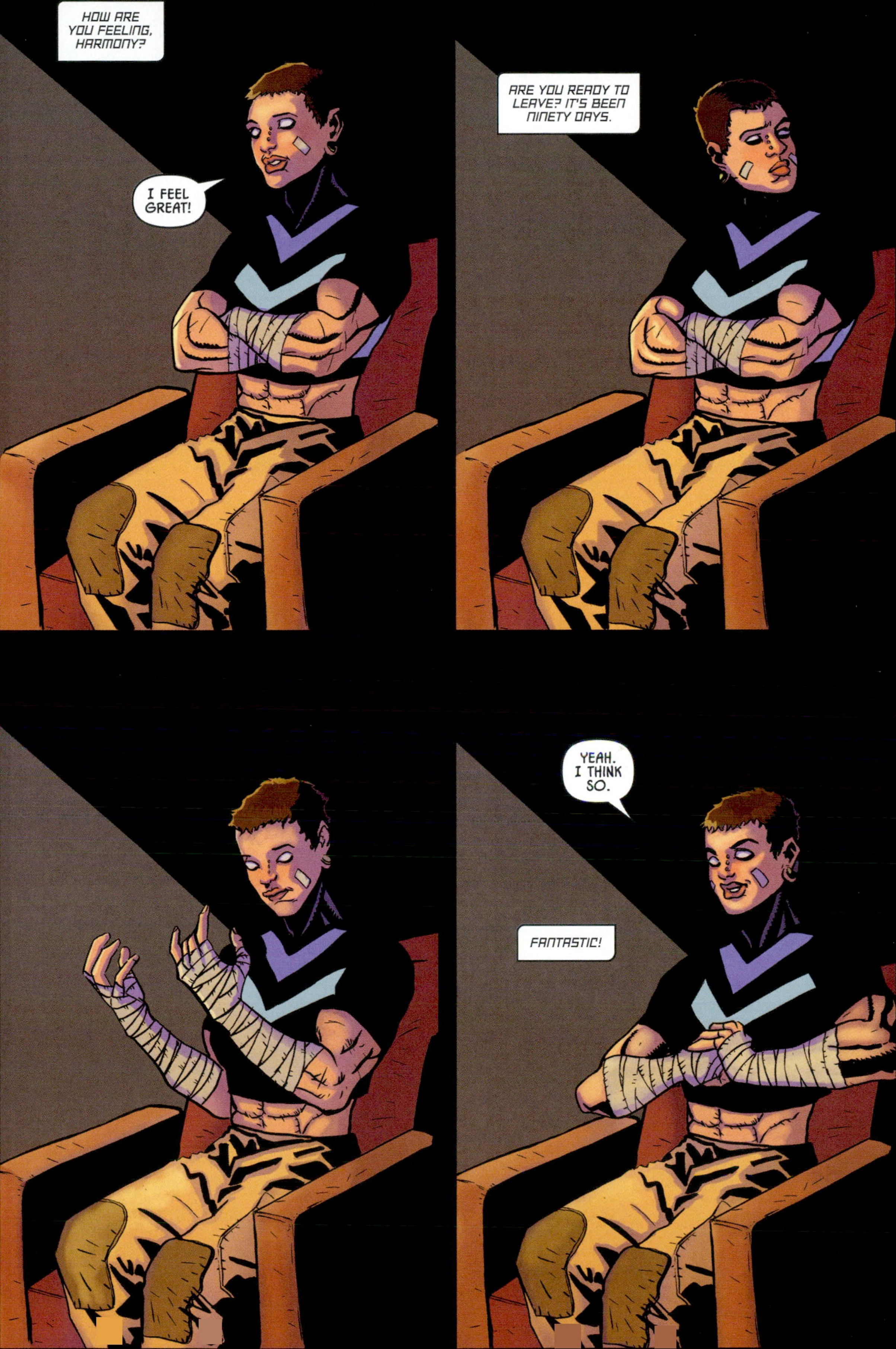
HOW ARE YOU FEELING, HARMONY?
I FEEL GREAT!
ARE YOU READY TO LEAVE? IT'S BEEN NINETY DAYS.
YEAH. I THINK SO.
FANTASTIC!

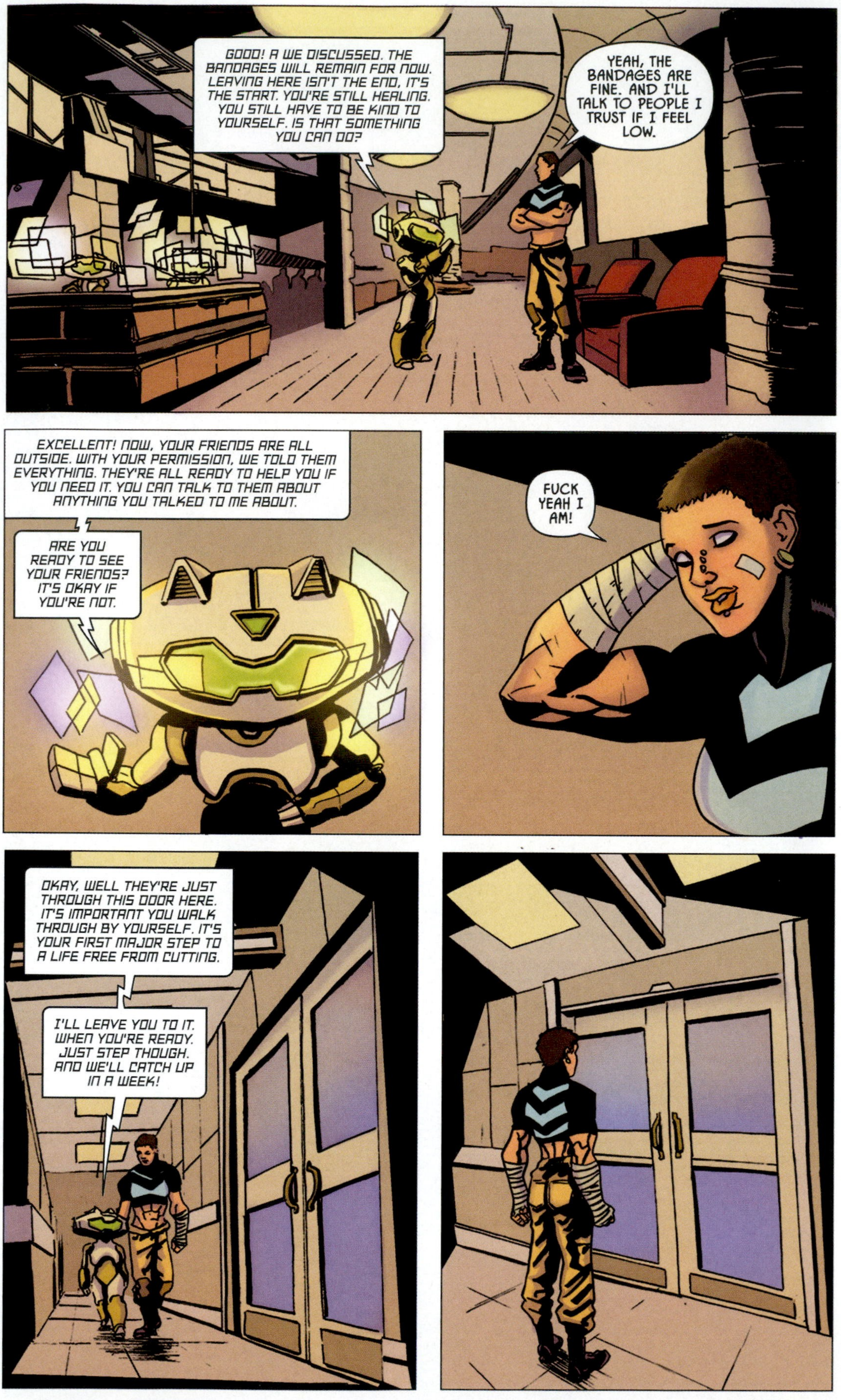
GOOD! A WE DISCUSSED. THE BANDAGES WILL REMAIN FOR NOW. LEAVING HERE ISN'T THE END, IT'S THE START. YOU'RE STILL HEALING. YOU STILL HAVE TO BE KIND TO YOURSELF. IS THAT SOMETHING YOU CAN DO?
YEAH, THE BANDAGES ARE FINE. AND I'LL TALK TO PEOPLE I TRUST IF I FEEL LOW.
EXCELLENT! NOW, YOUR FRIENDS ARE ALL OUTSIDE. WITH YOUR PERMISSION, WE TOLD THEM EVERYTHING. THEY'RE ALL READY TO HELP YOU IF YOU NEED IT. YOU CAN TALK TO THEM ABOUT ANYTHING YOU TALKED TO ME ABOUT.
ARE YOU READY TO SEE YOUR FRIENDS? IT'S OKAY IF YOU'RE NOT.
FUCK YEAH I AM!
OKAY, WELL THEY'RE JUST THROUGH THIS DOOR HERE. IT'S IMPORTANT YOU WALK THROUGH BY YOURSELF. IT'S YOUR FIRST MAJOR STEP TO A LIFE FREE FROM CUTTING.
I'LL LEAVE YOU TO IT. WHEN YOU'RE READY. JUST STEP THOUGH. AND WE'LL CATCH UP IN A WEEK!

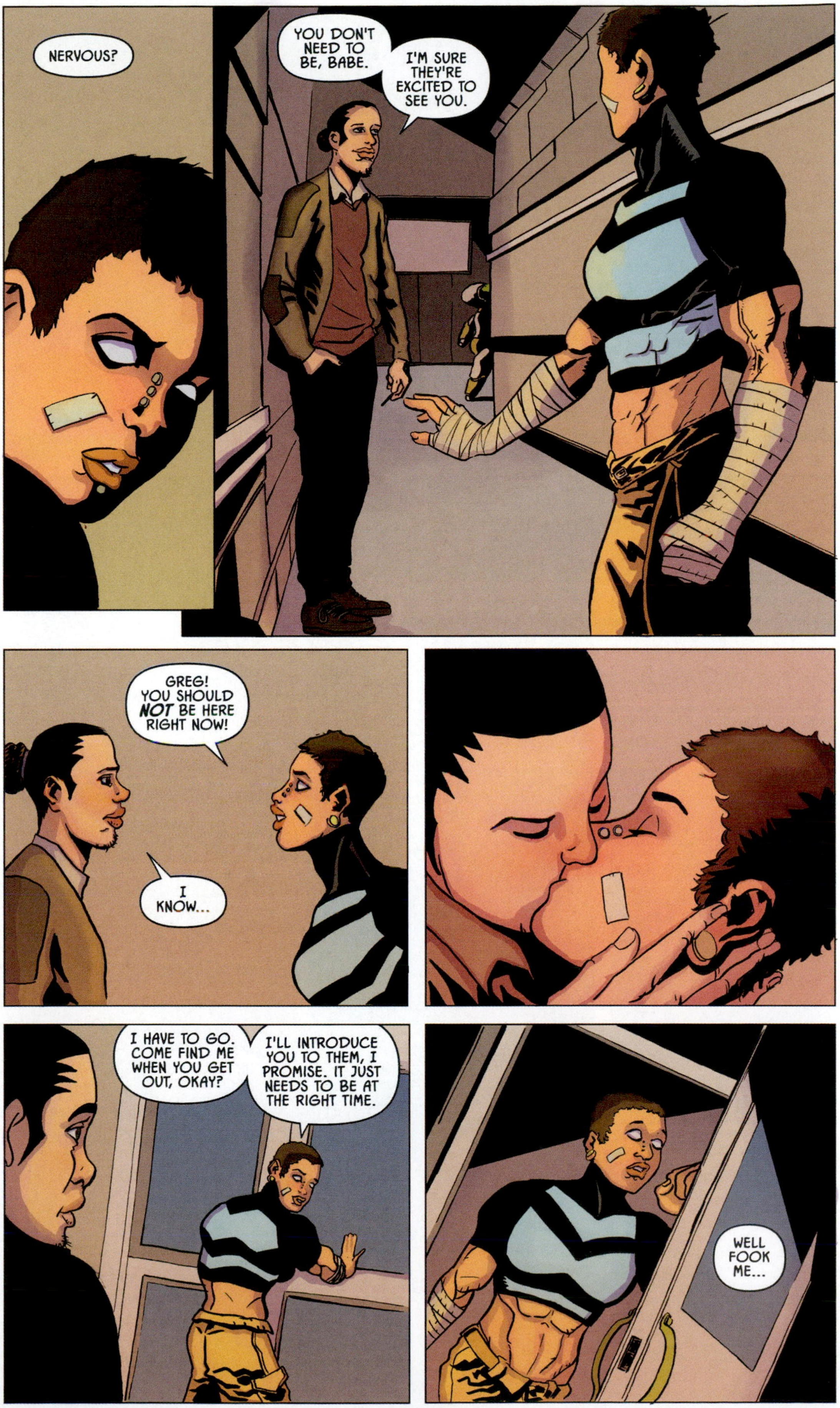
NERVOUS?
YOU DON'T NEED TO BE, BABE.
I'M SURE THEY'RE EXCITED TO SEE YOU.
GREG! YOU SHOULD **NOT** BE HERE RIGHT NOW!
I KNOW...
I HAVE TO GO. COME FIND ME WHEN YOU GET OUT, OKAY?
I'LL INTRODUCE YOU TO THEM, I PROMISE. IT JUST NEEDS TO BE AT THE RIGHT TIME.
WELL FOOK ME...

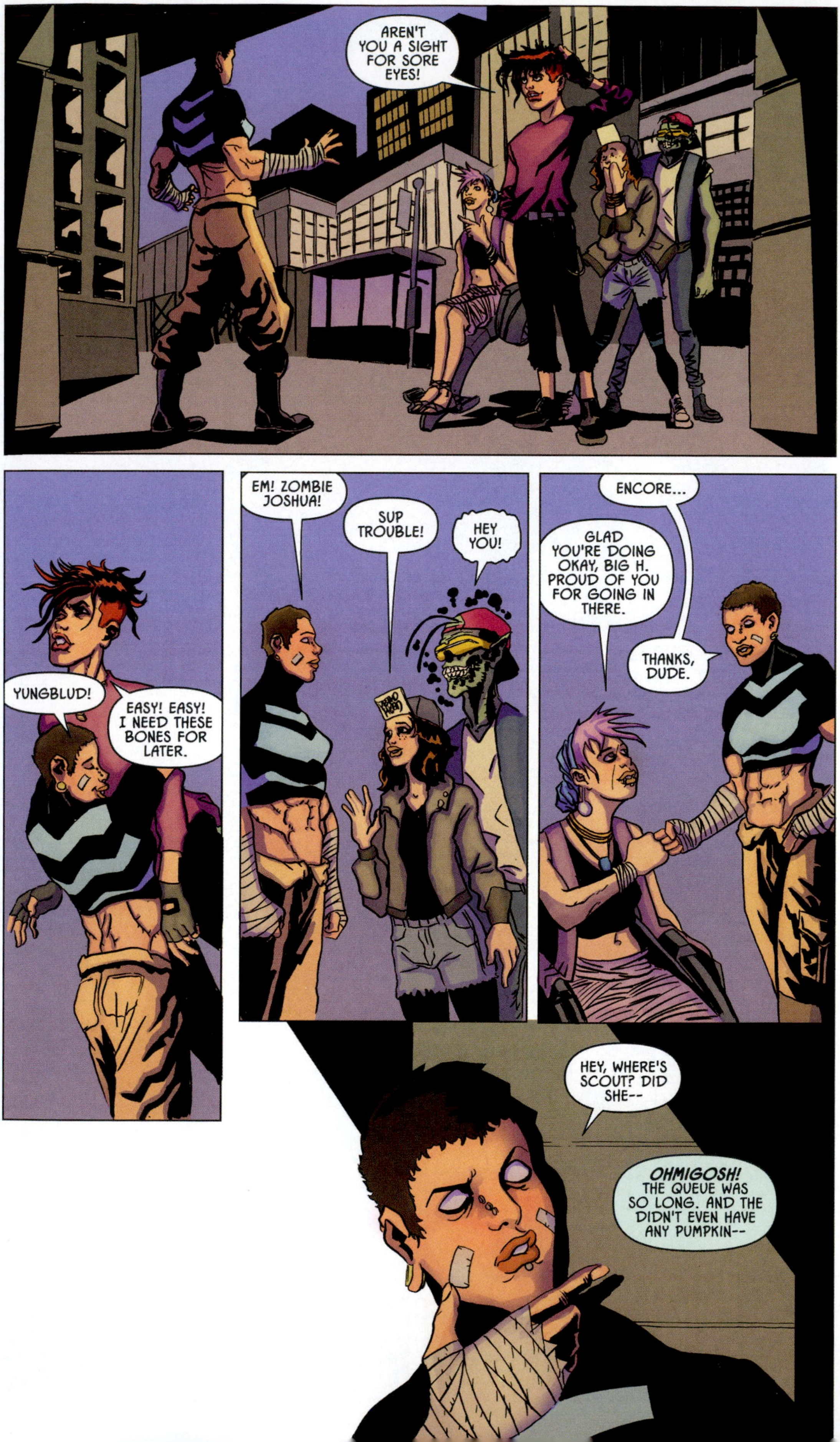
AREN'T YOU A SIGHT FOR SORE EYES!
YUNGBLUD!
EASY! EASY! I NEED THESE BONES FOR LATER.
EM! ZOMBIE JOSHUA!
SUP TROUBLE!
HEY YOU!
ENCORE...
GLAD YOU'RE DOING OKAY, BIG H. PROUD OF YOU FOR GOING IN THERE.
THANKS, DUDE.
HEY, WHERE'S SCOUT? DID SHE--
OHMIGOSH! THE QUEUE WAS SO LONG. AND THE DIDN'T EVEN HAVE ANY PUMPKIN--

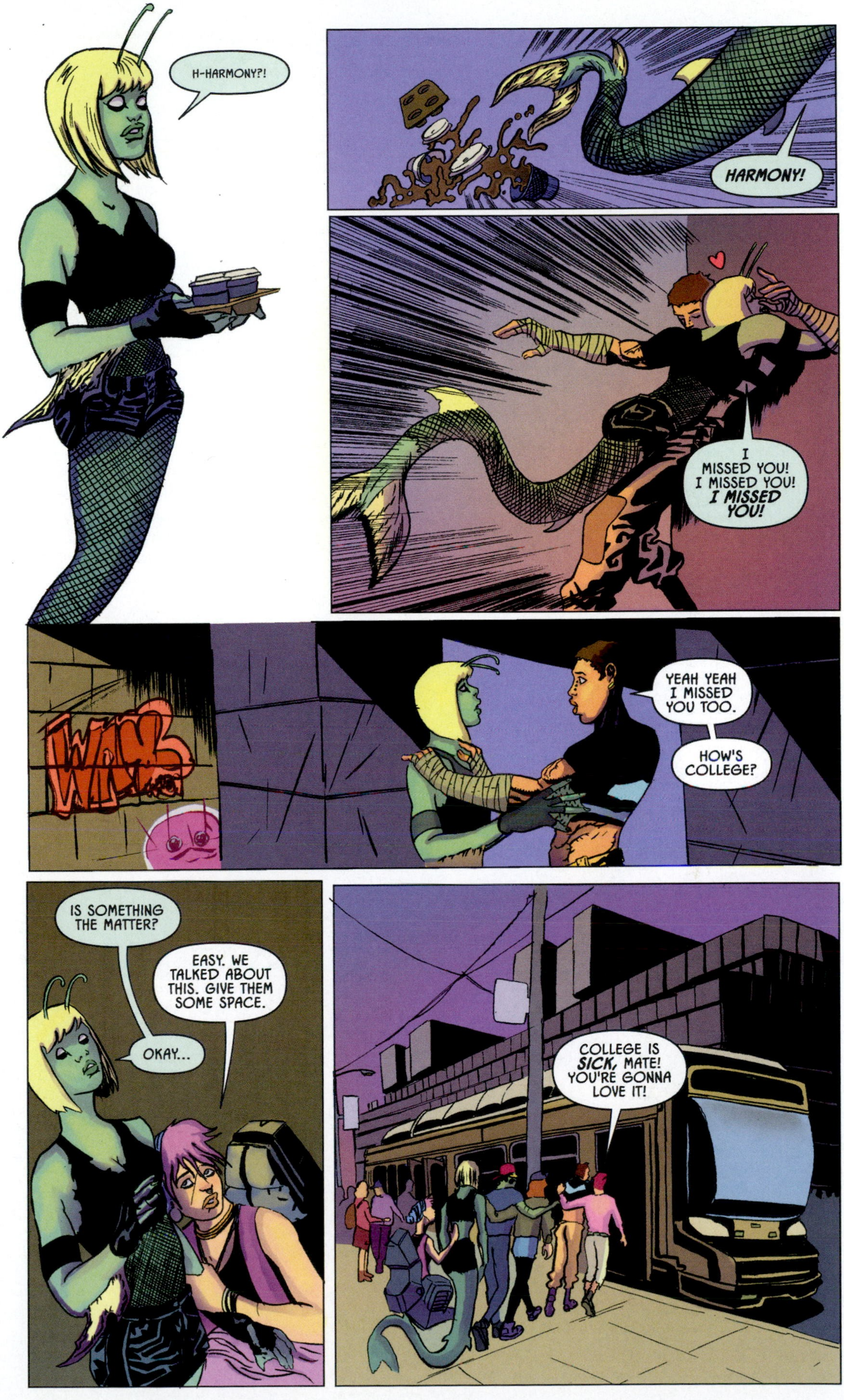
H-HARMONY?!
HARMONY!
I MISSED YOU! I MISSED YOU! I MISSED YOU!
YEAH YEAH I MISSED YOU TOO.
HOW'S COLLEGE?
IS SOMETHING THE MATTER?
EASY. WE TALKED ABOUT THIS. GIVE THEM SOME SPACE.
OKAY...
COLLEGE IS SICK, MATE! YOU'RE GONNA LOVE IT!

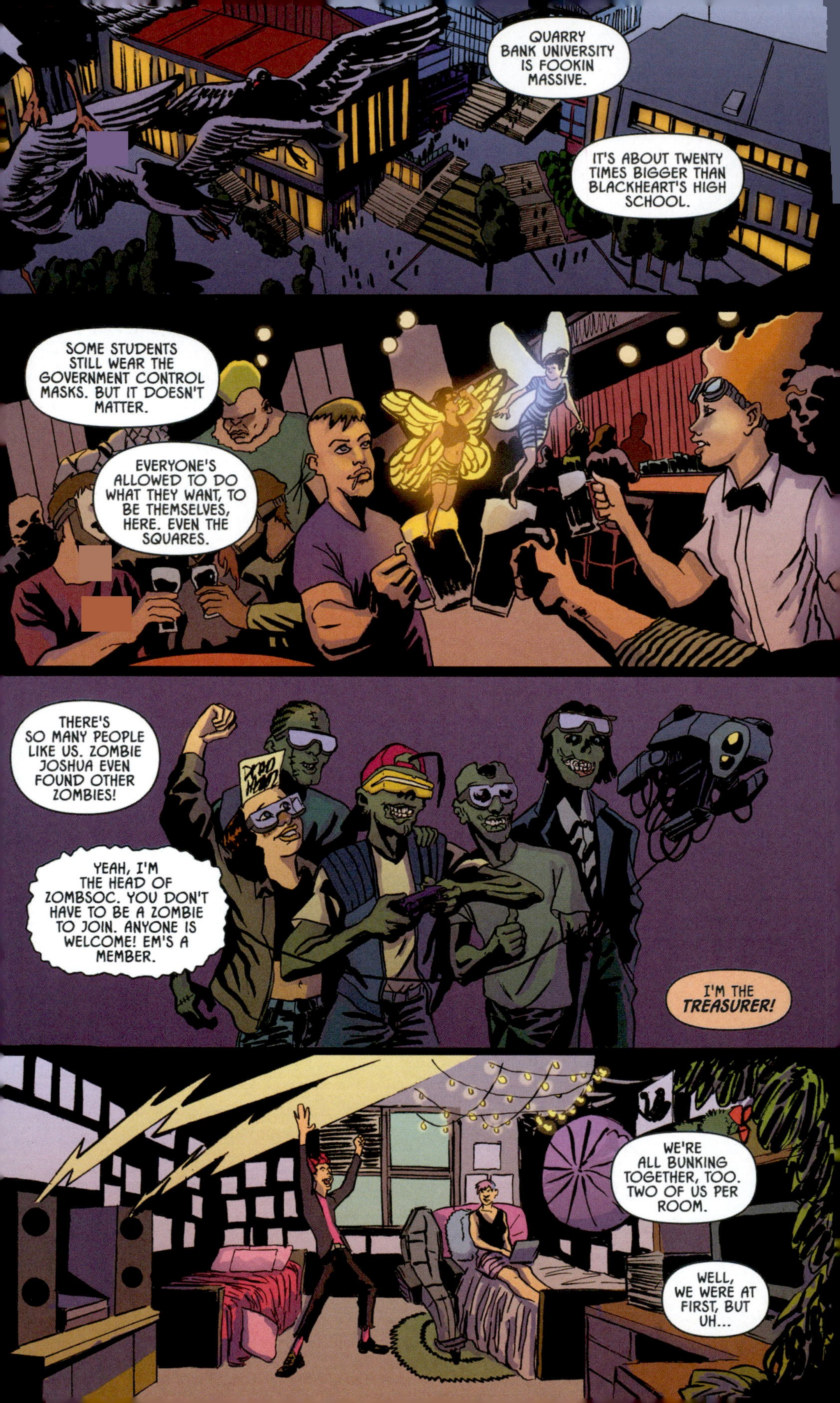
QUARRY BANK UNIVERSITY IS FOOKIN MASSIVE.
IT'S ABOUT TWENTY TIMES BIGGER THAN BLACKHEART'S HIGH SCHOOL.
SOME STUDENTS STILL WEAR THE GOVERNMENT CONTROL MASKS. BUT IT DOESN'T MATTER.
EVERYONE'S ALLOWED TO DO WHAT THEY WANT, TO BE THEMSELVES, HERE. EVEN THE SQUARES.
THERE'S SO MANY PEOPLE LIKE US. ZOMBIE JOSHUA EVEN FOUND OTHER ZOMBIES!
YEAH, I'M THE HEAD OF ZOMBSOC. YOU DON'T HAVE TO BE A ZOMBIE TO JOIN. ANYONE IS WELCOME! EM'S A MEMBER.
I'M THE *TREASURER!*
WE'RE ALL BUNKING TOGETHER, TOO. TWO OF US PER ROOM.
WELL, WE WERE AT FIRST, BUT UH...

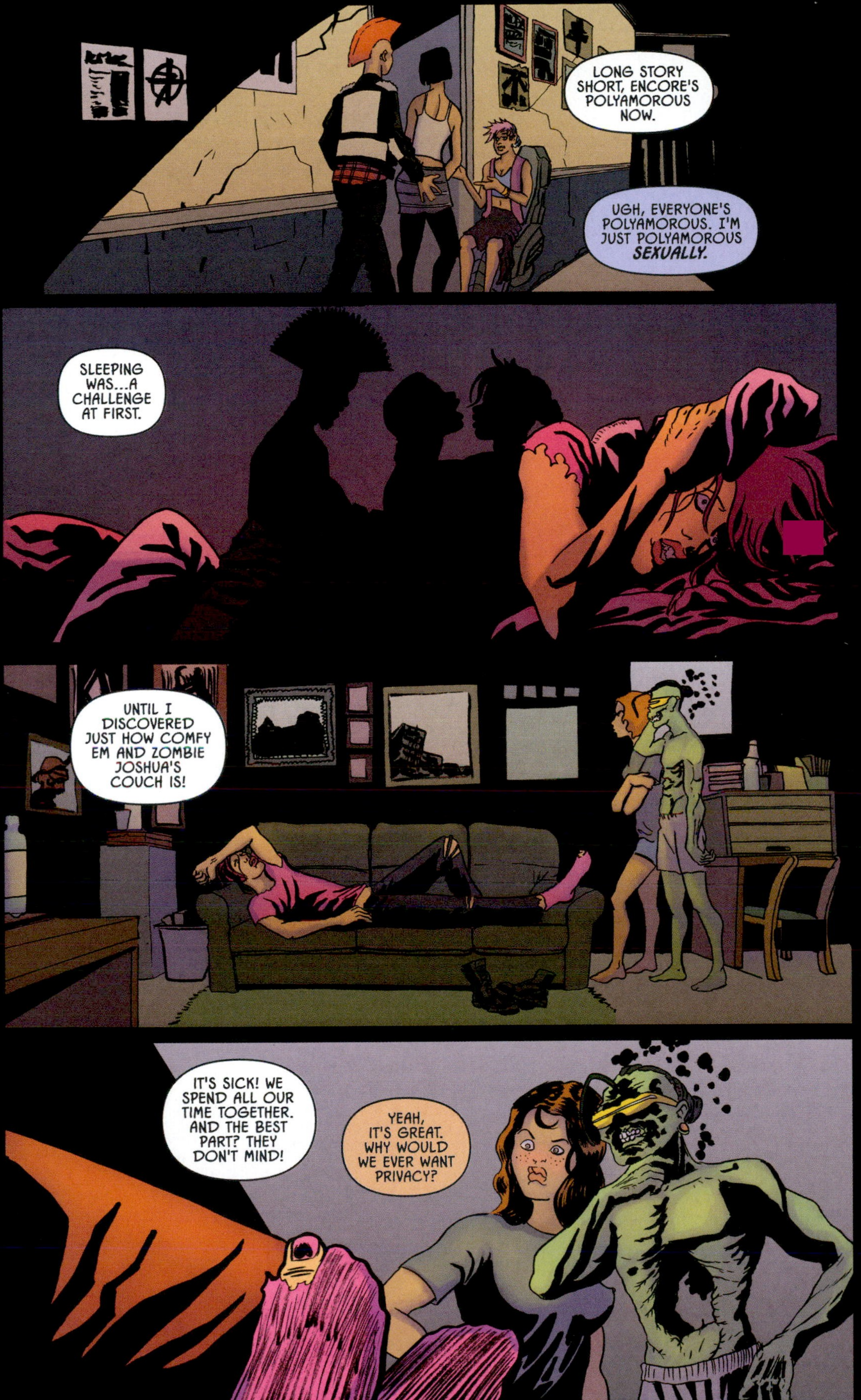
LONG STORY SHORT, ENCORE'S POLYAMOROUS NOW.
UGH, EVERYONE'S POLYAMOROUS. I'M JUST POLYAMOROUS *SEXUALLY.*
SLEEPING WAS...A CHALLENGE AT FIRST.
UNTIL I DISCOVERED JUST HOW COMFY EM AND ZOMBIE JOSHUA'S COUCH IS!
IT'S SICK! WE SPEND ALL OUR TIME TOGETHER. AND THE BEST PART? THEY DON'T MIND!
YEAH, IT'S GREAT. WHY WOULD WE EVER WANT PRIVACY?

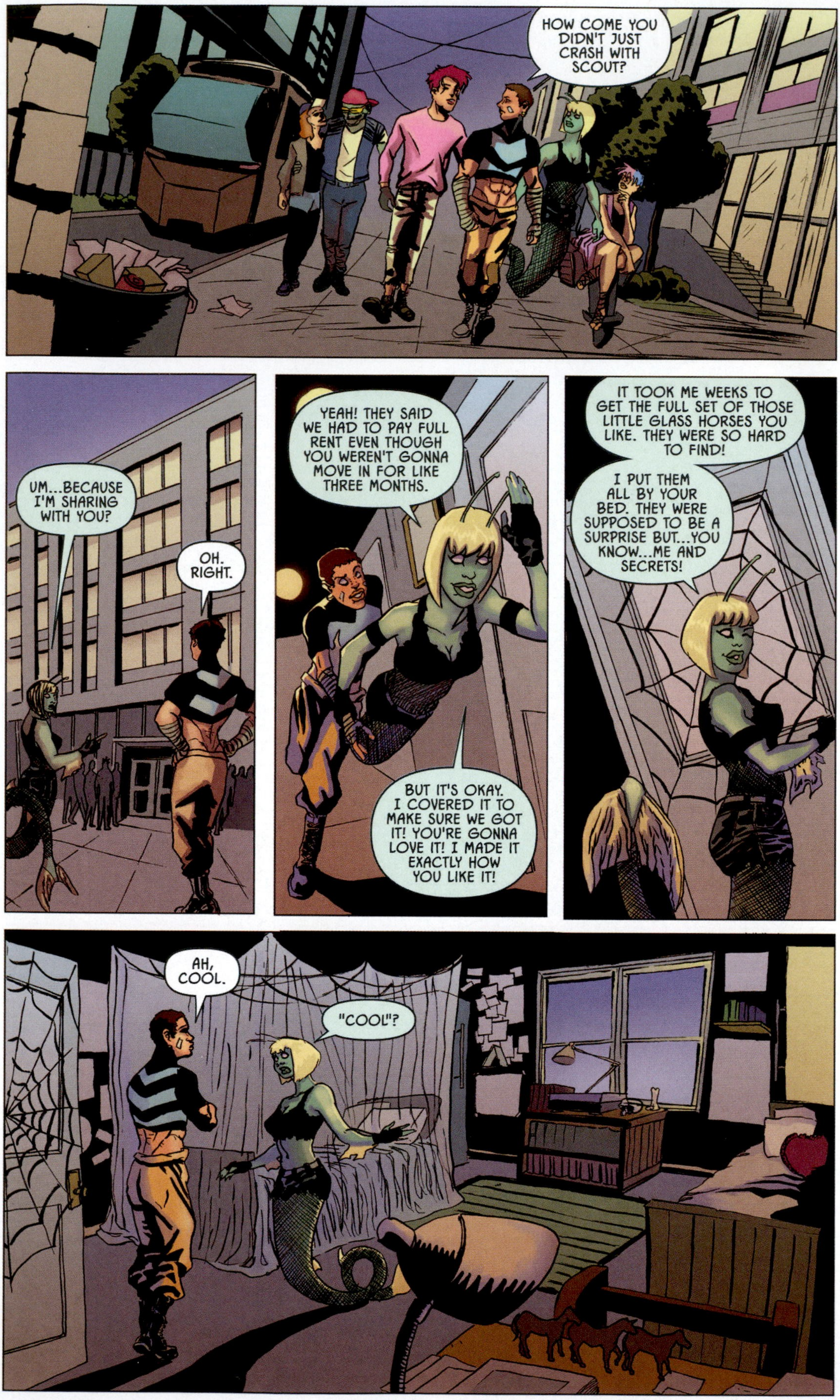
HOW COME YOU DIDN'T JUST CRASH WITH SCOUT?
UM...BECAUSE I'M SHARING WITH YOU?
OH. RIGHT.
YEAH! THEY SAID WE HAD TO PAY FULL RENT EVEN THOUGH YOU WEREN'T GONNA MOVE IN FOR LIKE THREE MONTHS.
BUT IT'S OKAY. I COVERED IT TO MAKE SURE WE GOT IT! YOU'RE GONNA LOVE IT! I MADE IT EXACTLY HOW YOU LIKE IT!
IT TOOK ME WEEKS TO GET THE FULL SET OF THOSE LITTLE GLASS HORSES YOU LIKE. THEY WERE SO HARD TO FIND!
I PUT THEM ALL BY YOUR BED. THEY WERE SUPPOSED TO BE A SURPRISE BUT...YOU KNOW...ME AND SECRETS!
AH, COOL.
"COOL"?

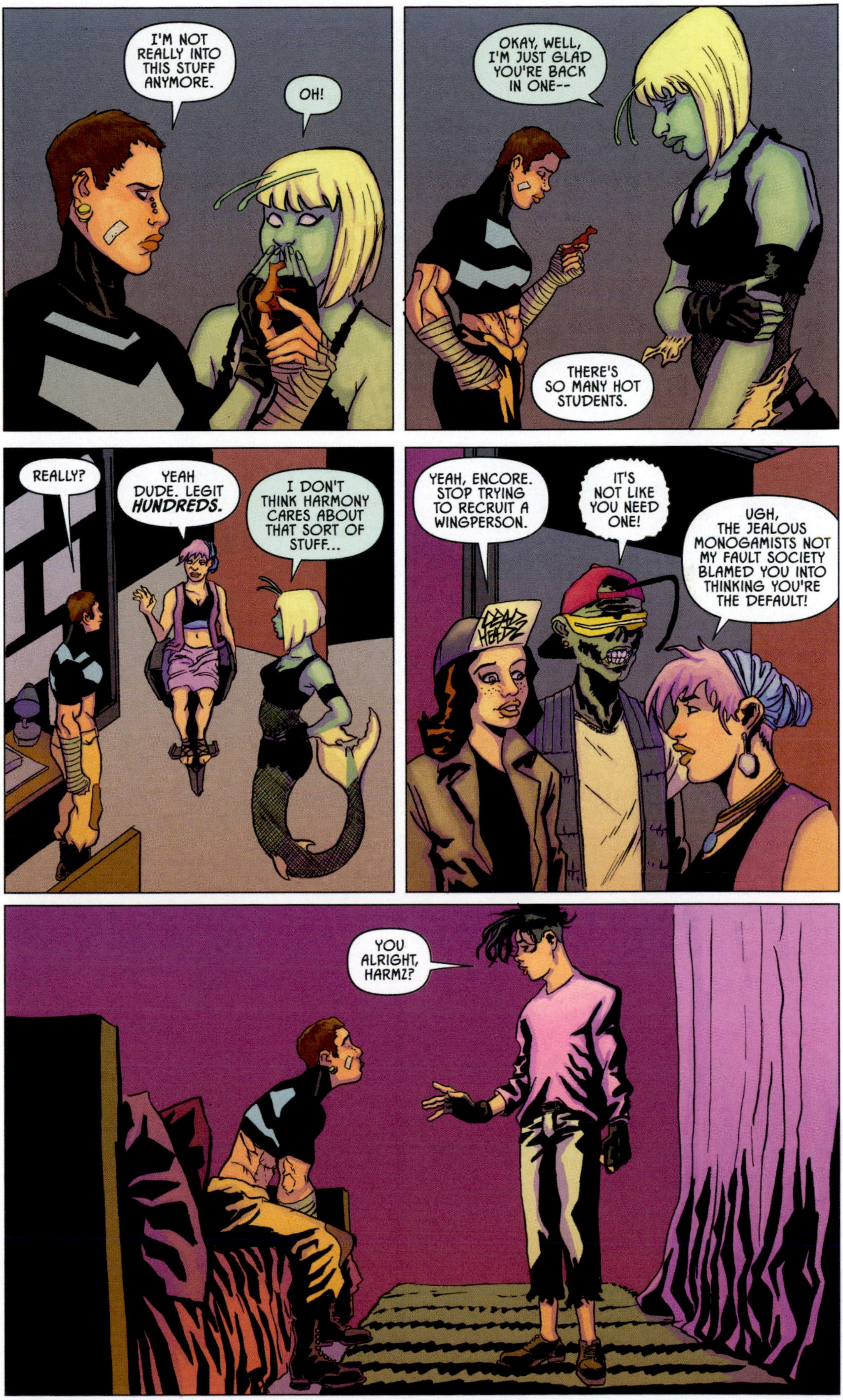

I'M NOT REALLY INTO THIS STUFF ANYMORE.
OH!
OKAY, WELL, I'M JUST GLAD YOU'RE BACK IN ONE--
THERE'S SO MANY HOT STUDENTS.
REALLY?
YEAH DUDE. LEGIT HUNDREDS.
I DON'T THINK HARMONY CARES ABOUT THAT SORT OF STUFF...
YEAH, ENCORE. STOP TRYING TO RECRUIT A WINGPERSON.
IT'S NOT LIKE YOU NEED ONE!
UGH, THE JEALOUS MONOGAMISTS NOT MY FAULT SOCIETY BLAMED YOU INTO THINKING YOU'RE THE DEFAULT!
YOU ALRIGHT, HARMZ?

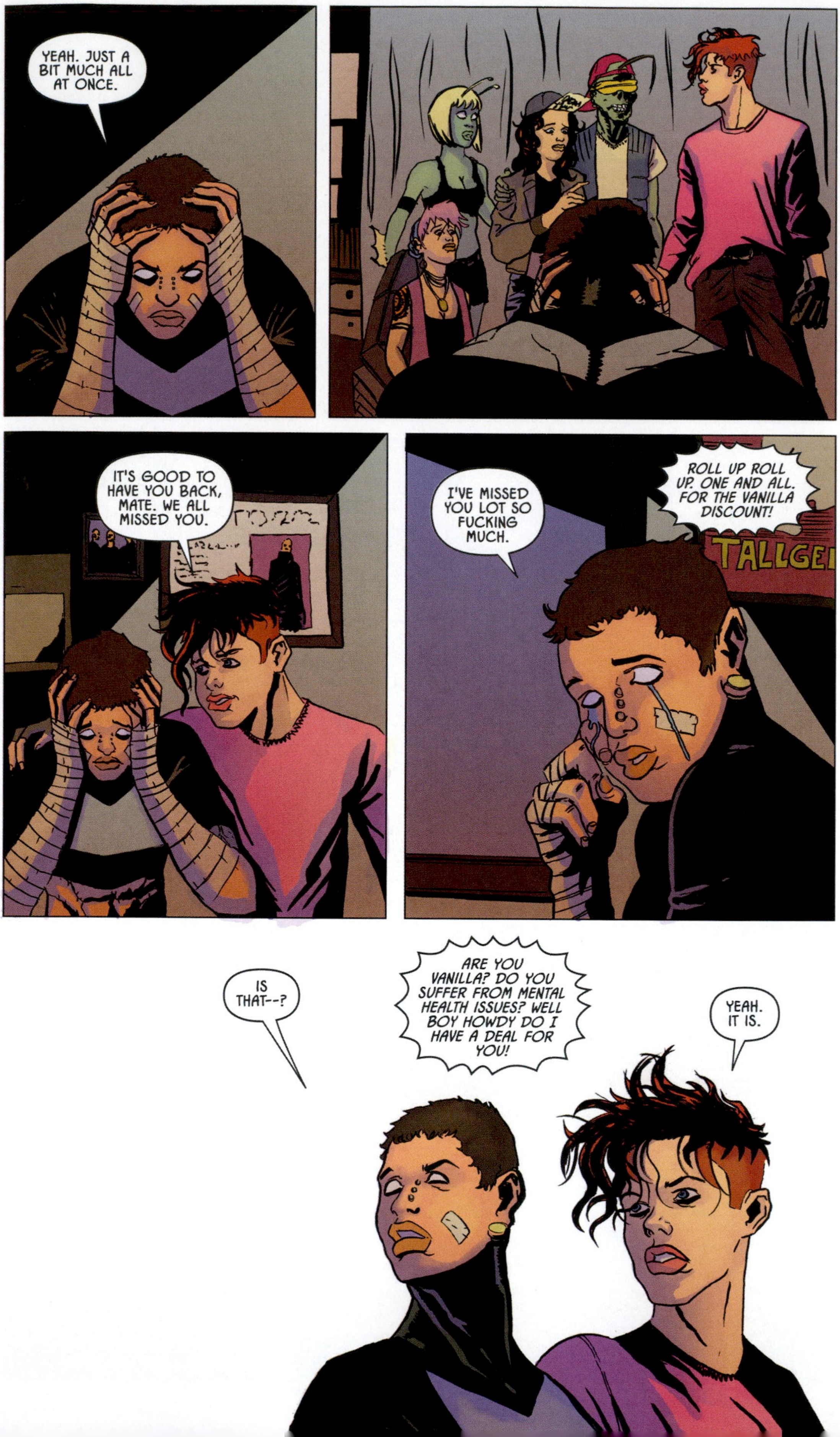
YEAH. JUST A BIT MUCH ALL AT ONCE.
IT'S GOOD TO HAVE YOU BACK, MATE. WE ALL MISSED YOU.
I'VE MISSED YOU LOT SO FUCKING MUCH.
ROLL UP ROLL UP. ONE AND ALL. FOR THE VANILLA DISCOUNT!
TALLGE
IS THAT--?
ARE YOU VANILLA? DO YOU SUFFER FROM MENTAL HEALTH ISSUES? WELL BOY HOWDY DO I HAVE A DEAL FOR YOU!
YEAH. IT IS.

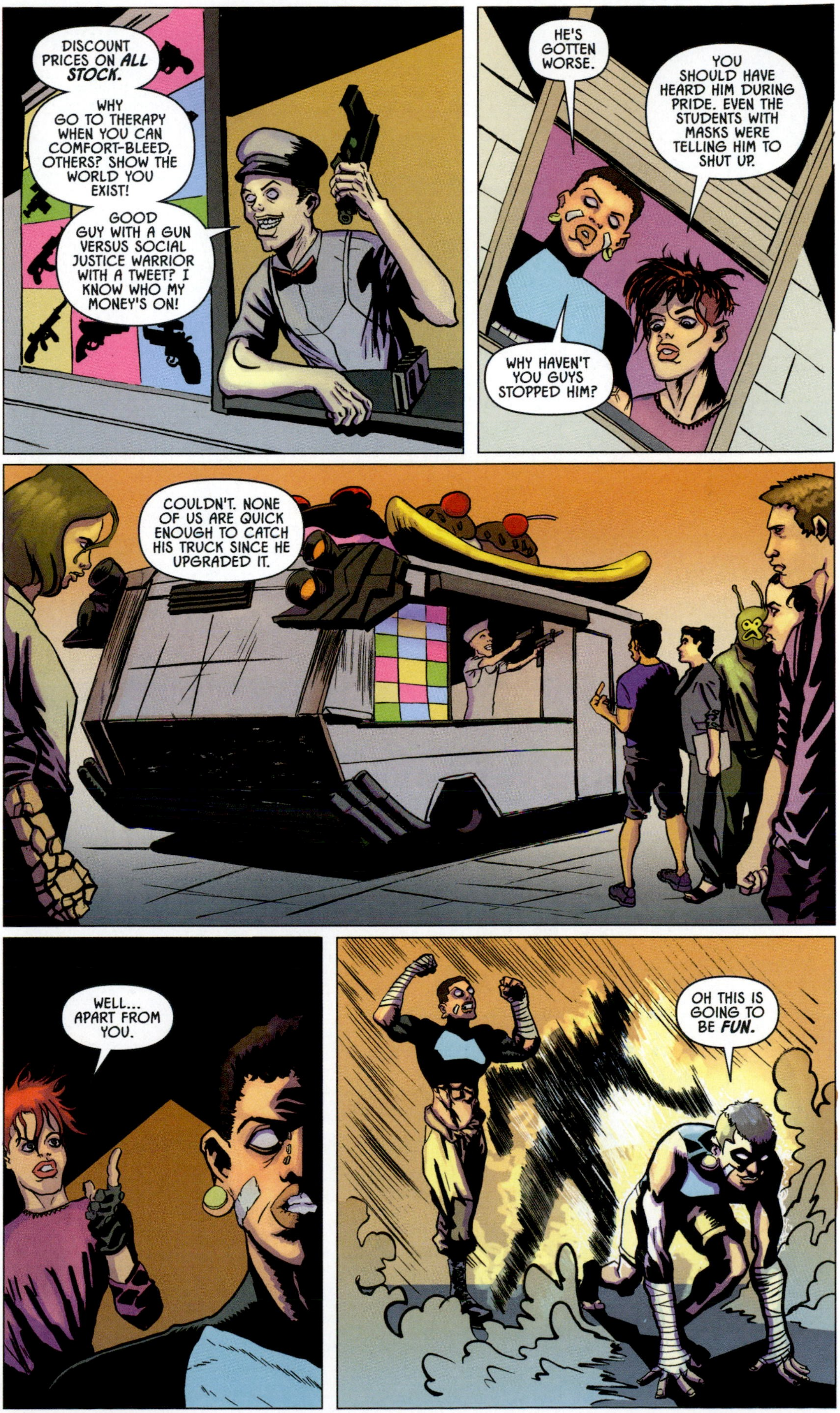
DISCOUNT PRICES ON ALL STOCK.
WHY GO TO THERAPY WHEN YOU CAN COMFORT-BLEED, OTHERS? SHOW THE WORLD YOU EXIST!
GOOD GUY WITH A GUN VERSUS SOCIAL JUSTICE WARRIOR WITH A TWEET? I KNOW WHO MY MONEY'S ON!
HE'S GOTTEN WORSE.
YOU SHOULD HAVE HEARD HIM DURING PRIDE. EVEN THE STUDENTS WITH MASKS WERE TELLING HIM TO SHUT UP.
WHY HAVEN'T YOU GUYS STOPPED HIM?
COULDN'T. NONE OF US ARE QUICK ENOUGH TO CATCH HIS TRUCK SINCE HE UPGRADED IT.
WELL... APART FROM YOU.
OH THIS IS GOING TO BE FUN.

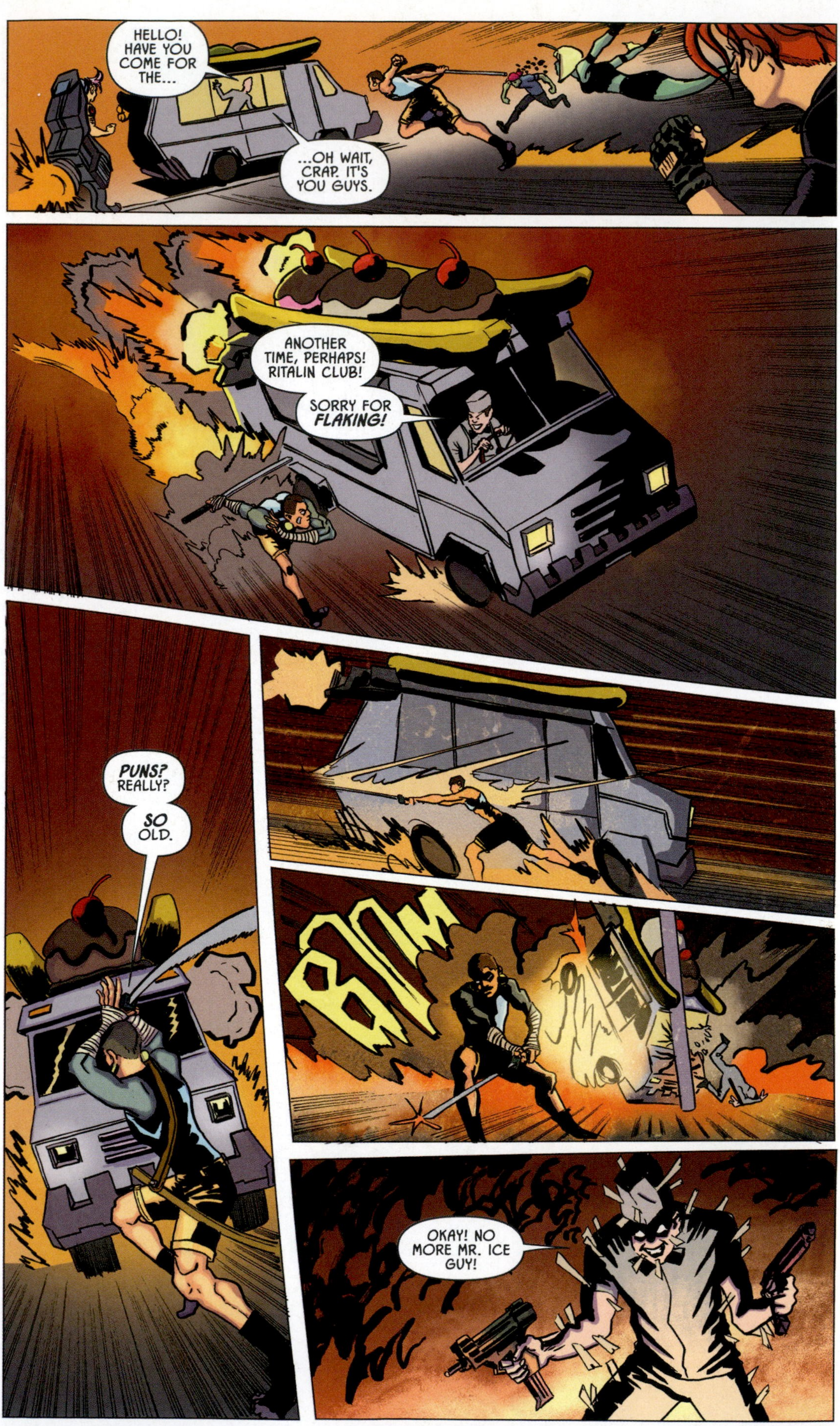
HELLO! HAVE YOU COME FOR THE...
...OH WAIT, CRAP. IT'S YOU GUYS.
ANOTHER TIME, PERHAPS! RITALIN CLUB!
SORRY FOR *FLAKING!*
PUNS? REALLY?
SO OLD.
BOOM
OKAY! NO MORE MR. ICE GUY!

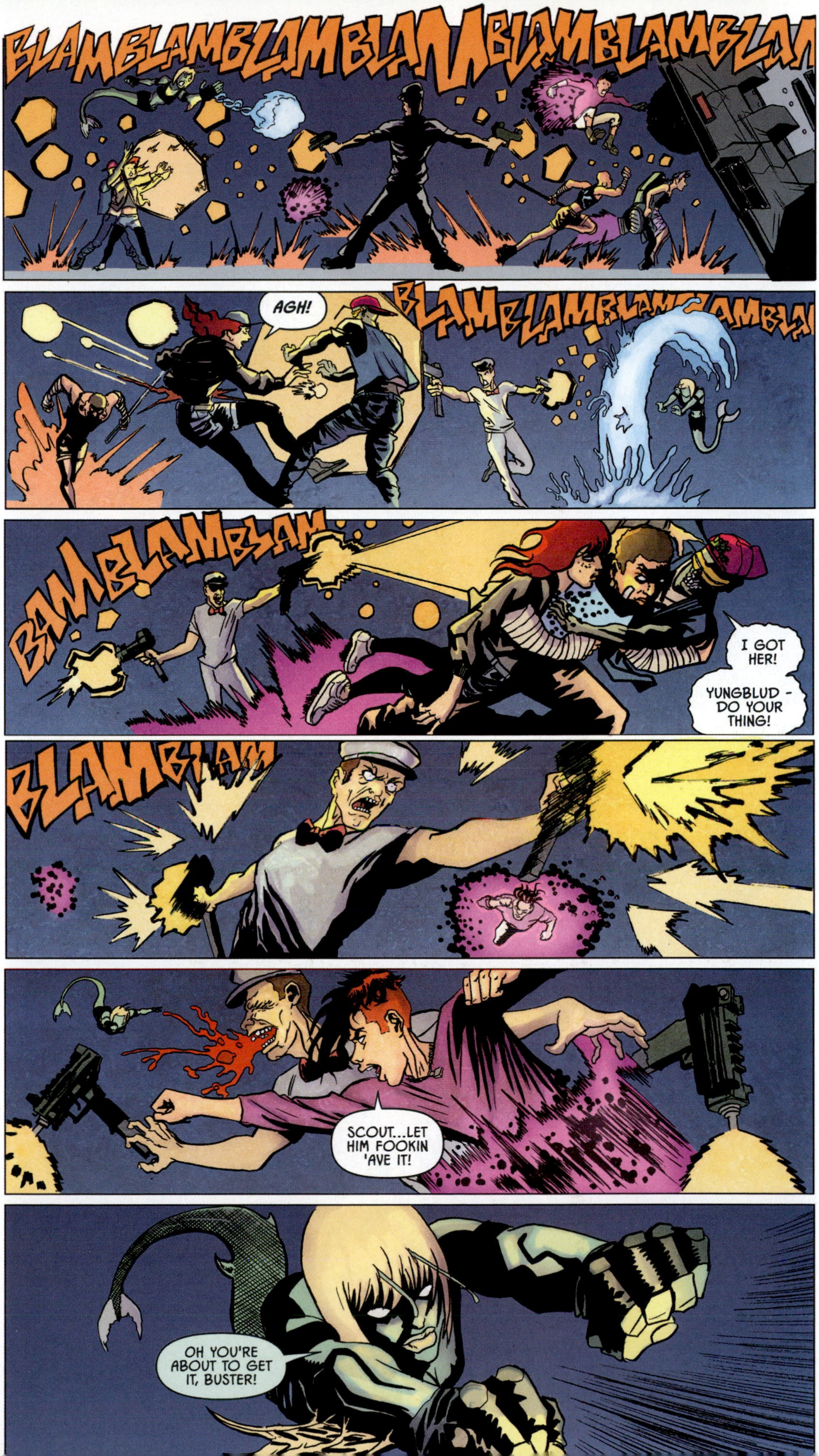
BLAMBLAMBLAMBLAMBLAMBLAMBLAMBLAM
AGH!
BLAMBLAMBLAMBLAMBLAM
BAMBLAMBLAM
I GOT HER!
YUNGBLUD - DO YOUR THING!
BLAMBLAM
SCOUT...LET HIM FOOKIN 'AVE IT!
OH YOU'RE ABOUT TO GET IT, BUSTER!

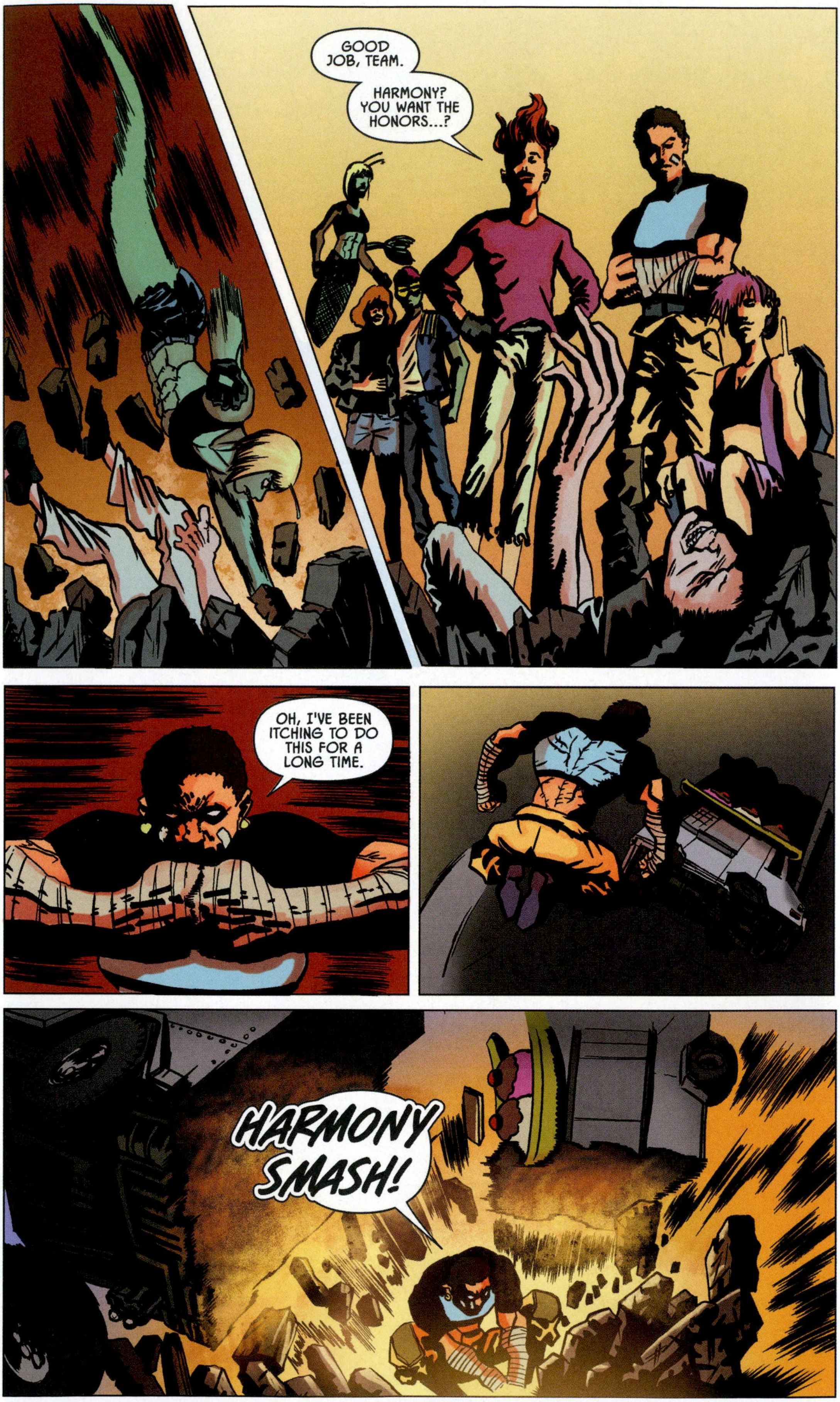
GOOD JOB, TEAM.
HARMONY? YOU WANT THE HONORS...?
OH, I'VE BEEN ITCHING TO DO THIS FOR A LONG TIME.
HARMONY SMASH!

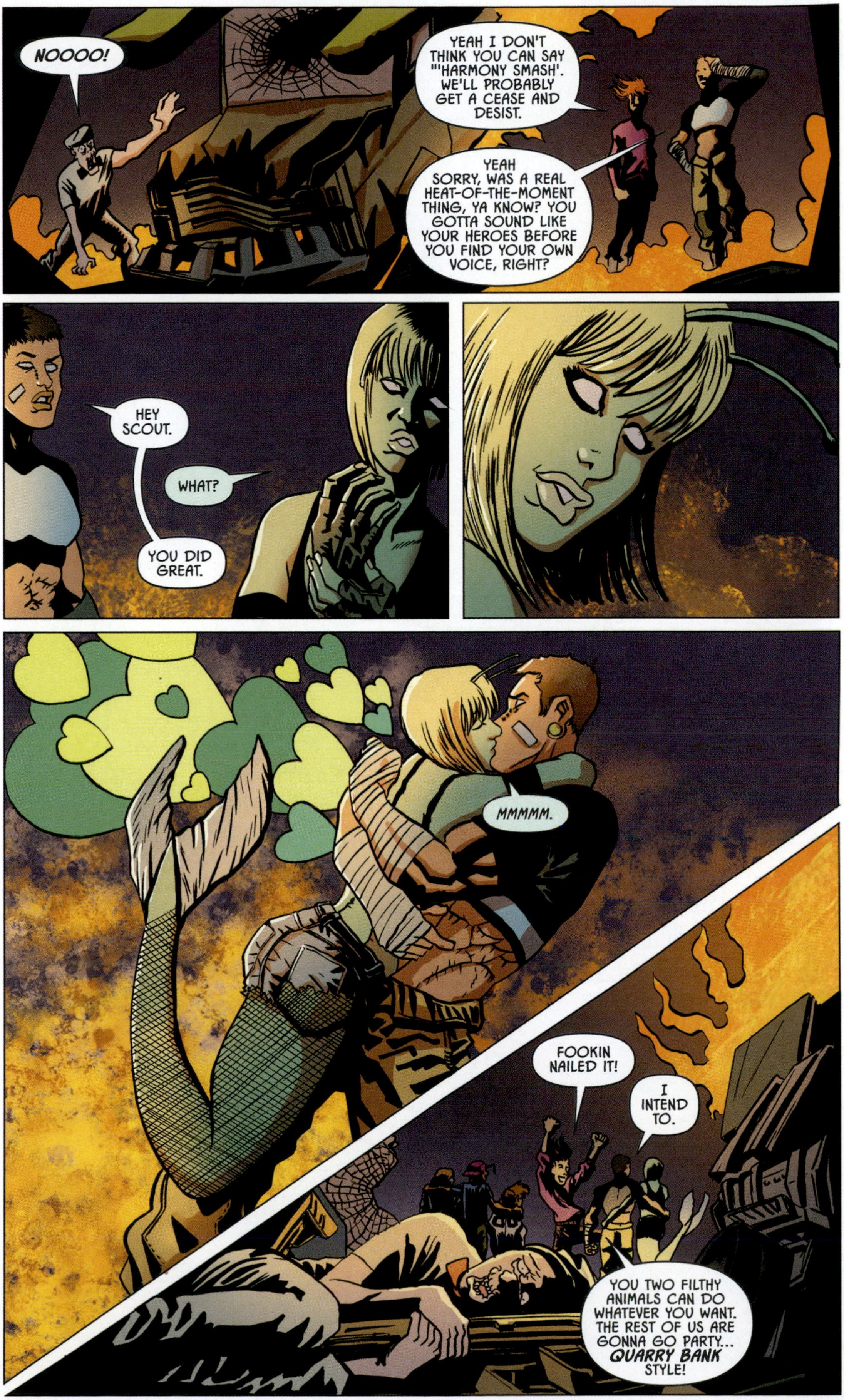
NOOOO!
YEAH I DON'T THINK YOU CAN SAY "'HARMONY SMASH'. WE'LL PROBABLY GET A CEASE AND DESIST.
YEAH SORRY, WAS A REAL HEAT-OF-THE-MOMENT THING, YA KNOW? YOU GOTTA SOUND LIKE YOUR HEROES BEFORE YOU FIND YOUR OWN VOICE, RIGHT?
HEY SCOUT.
WHAT?
YOU DID GREAT.
MMMMM.
FOOKIN NAILED IT!
I INTEND TO.
YOU TWO FILTHY ANIMALS CAN DO WHATEVER YOU WANT. THE REST OF US ARE GONNA GO PARTY... QUARRY BANK STYLE!

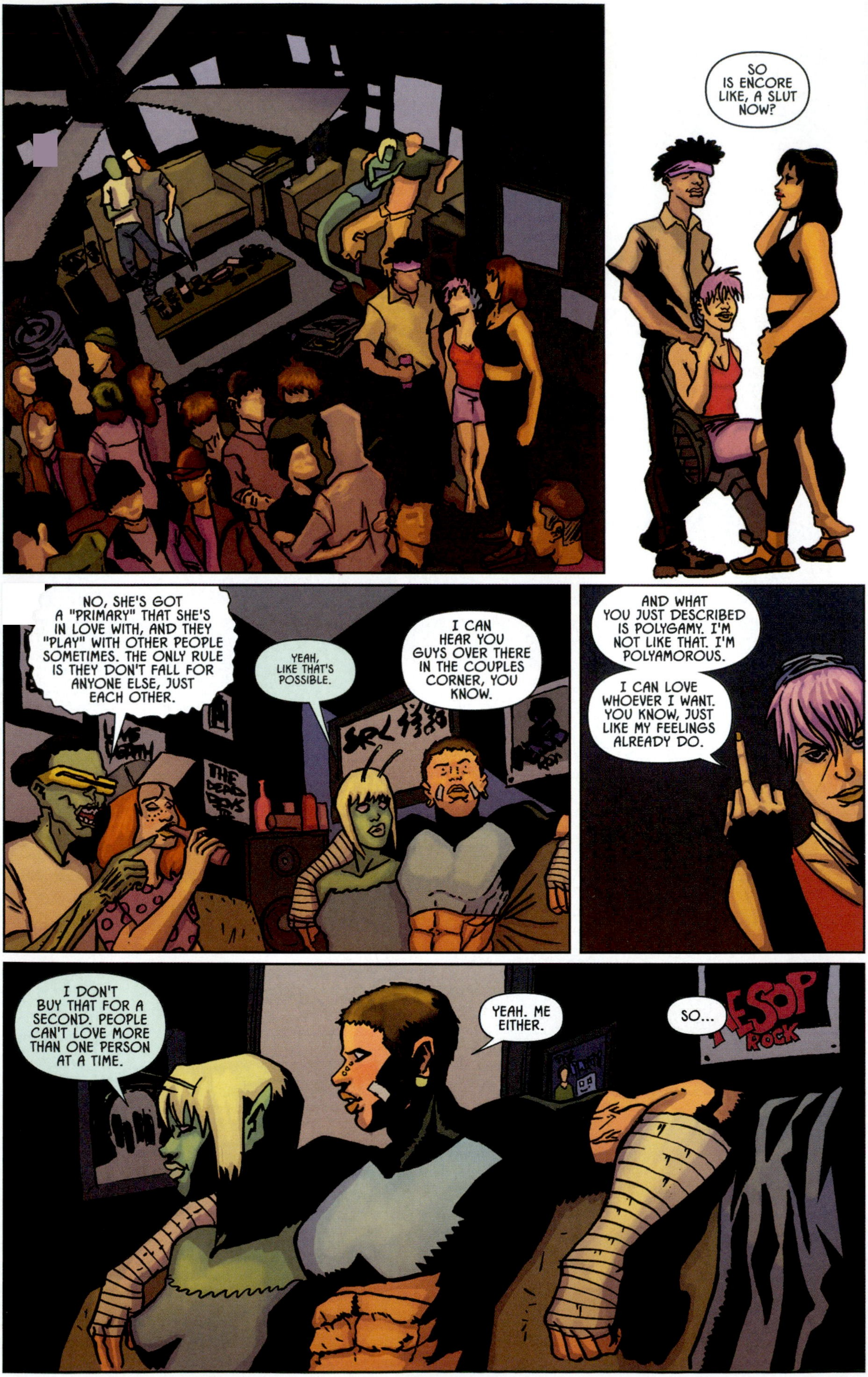
SO IS ENCORE LIKE, A SLUT NOW?
NO, SHE'S GOT A "PRIMARY" THAT SHE'S IN LOVE WITH, AND THEY "PLAY" WITH OTHER PEOPLE SOMETIMES. THE ONLY RULE IS THEY DON'T FALL FOR ANYONE ELSE, JUST EACH OTHER.
YEAH, LIKE THAT'S POSSIBLE.
I CAN HEAR YOU GUYS OVER THERE IN THE COUPLES CORNER, YOU KNOW.
AND WHAT YOU JUST DESCRIBED IS POLYGAMY. I'M NOT LIKE THAT. I'M POLYAMOROUS.
I CAN LOVE WHOEVER I WANT. YOU KNOW, JUST LIKE MY FEELINGS ALREADY DO.
I DON'T BUY THAT FOR A SECOND. PEOPLE CAN'T LOVE MORE THAN ONE PERSON AT A TIME.
YEAH. ME EITHER.
SO...

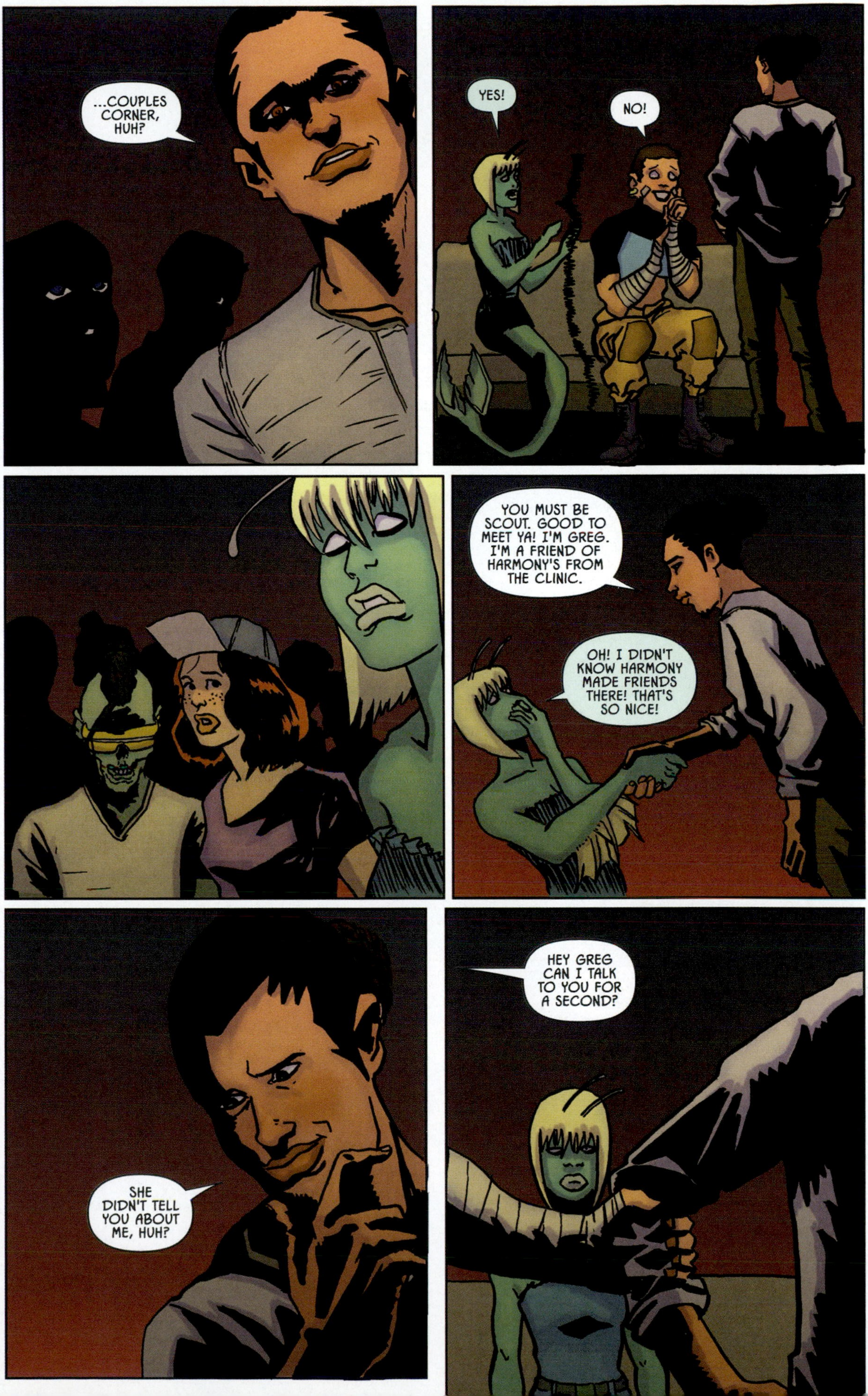
...COUPLES CORNER, HUH?
YES!
NO!
YOU MUST BE SCOUT. GOOD TO MEET YA! I'M GREG. I'M A FRIEND OF HARMONY'S FROM THE CLINIC.
OH! I DIDN'T KNOW HARMONY MADE FRIENDS THERE! THAT'S SO NICE!
SHE DIDN'T TELL YOU ABOUT ME, HUH?
HEY GREG CAN I TALK TO YOU FOR A SECOND?

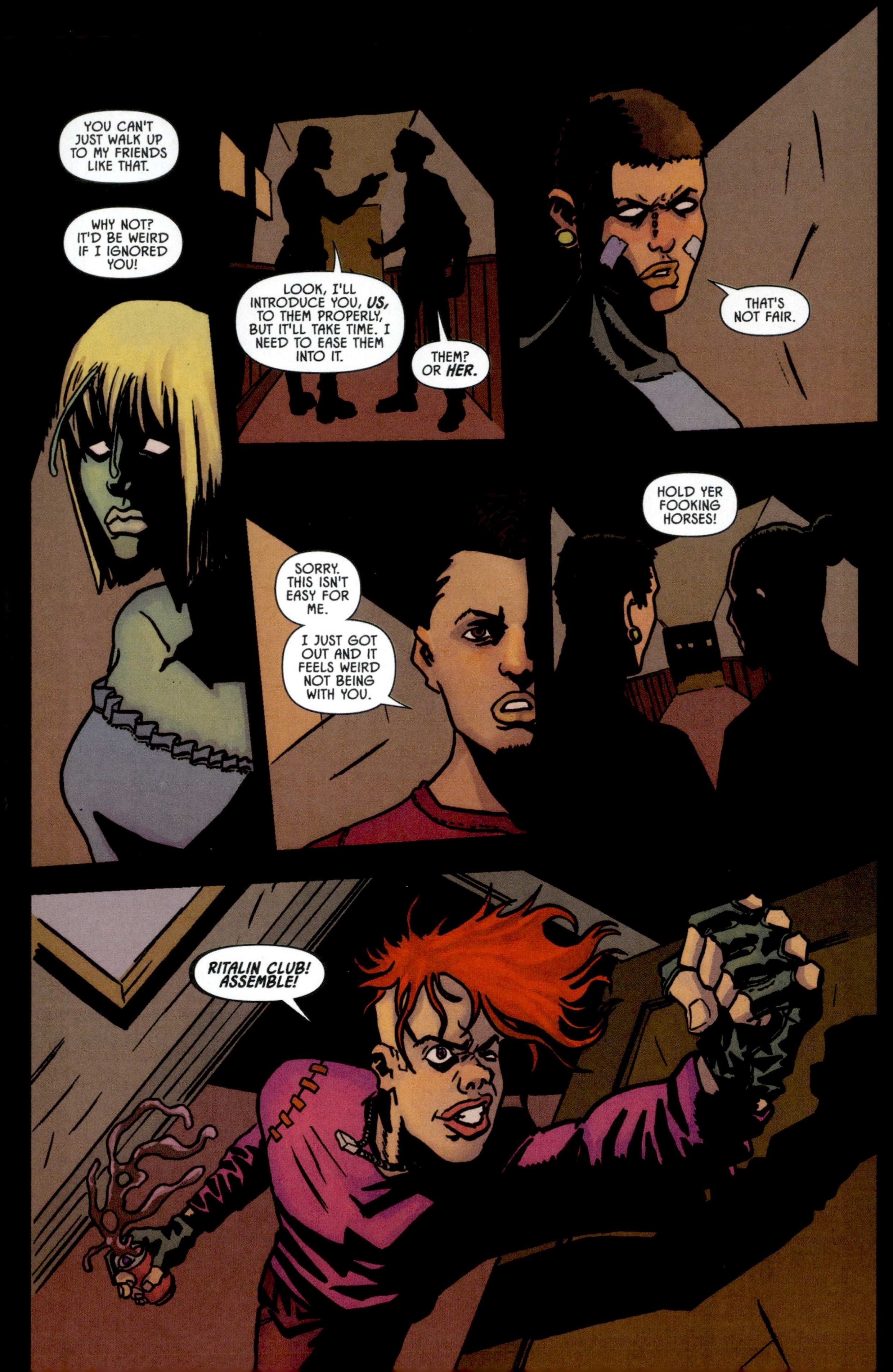
YOU CAN'T JUST WALK UP TO MY FRIENDS LIKE THAT.
WHY NOT? IT'D BE WEIRD IF I IGNORED YOU!
LOOK, I'LL INTRODUCE YOU, US, TO THEM PROPERLY, BUT IT'LL TAKE TIME. I NEED TO EASE THEM INTO IT.
THEM? OR HER.
THAT'S NOT FAIR.
SORRY. THIS ISN'T EASY FOR ME.
I JUST GOT OUT AND IT FEELS WEIRD NOT BEING WITH YOU.
HOLD YER FOOKING HORSES!
RITALIN CLUB! ASSEMBLE!

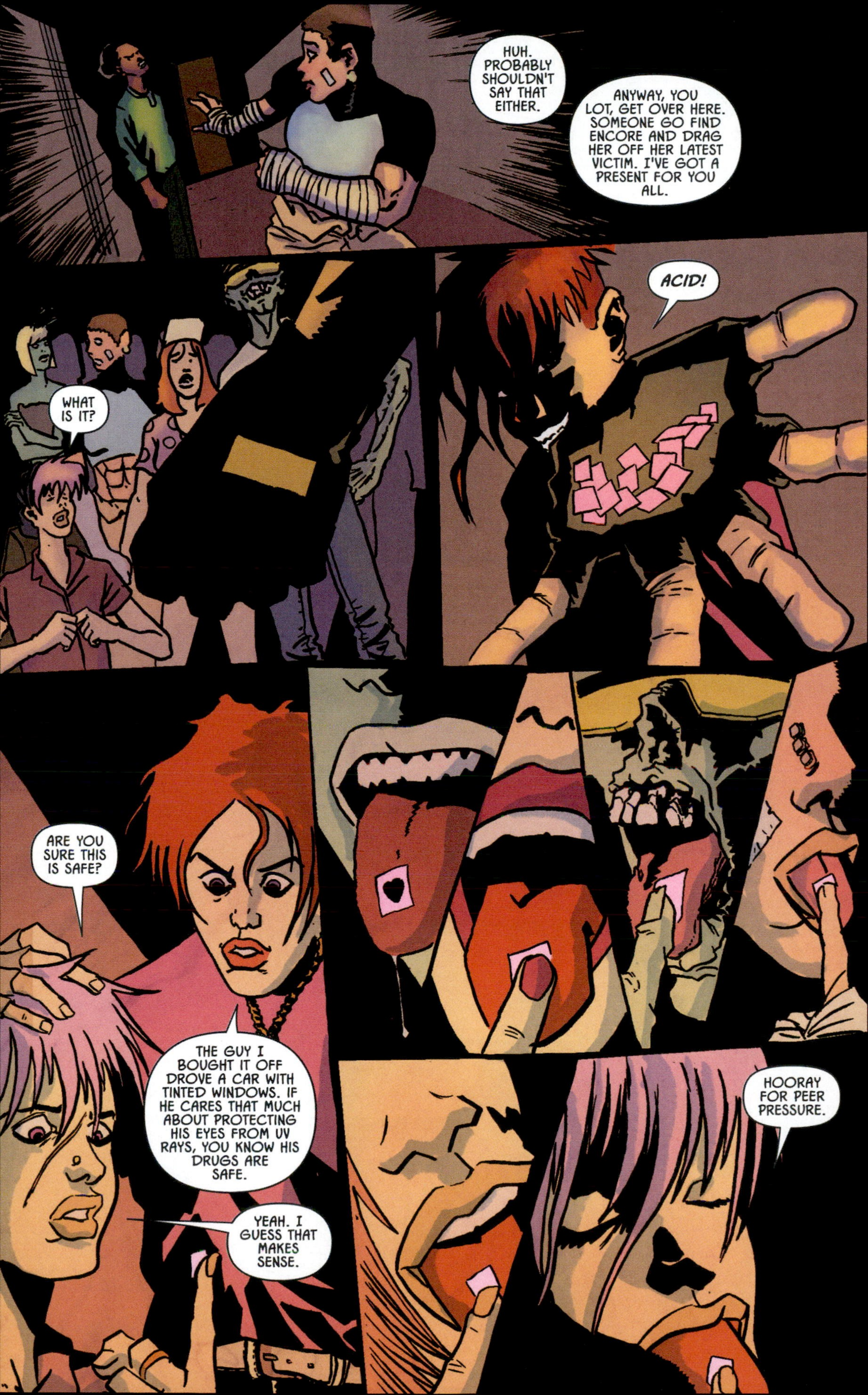
HUH. PROBABLY SHOULDN'T SAY THAT EITHER.
ANYWAY, YOU LOT, GET OVER HERE. SOMEONE GO FIND ENCORE AND DRAG HER OFF HER LATEST VICTIM. I'VE GOT A PRESENT FOR YOU ALL.
WHAT IS IT?
ACID!
ARE YOU SURE THIS IS SAFE?
THE GUY I BOUGHT IT OFF DROVE A CAR WITH TINTED WINDOWS. IF HE CARES THAT MUCH ABOUT PROTECTING HIS EYES FROM UV RAYS, YOU KNOW HIS DRUGS ARE SAFE.
YEAH. I GUESS THAT MAKES SENSE.
HOORAY FOR PEER PRESSURE.

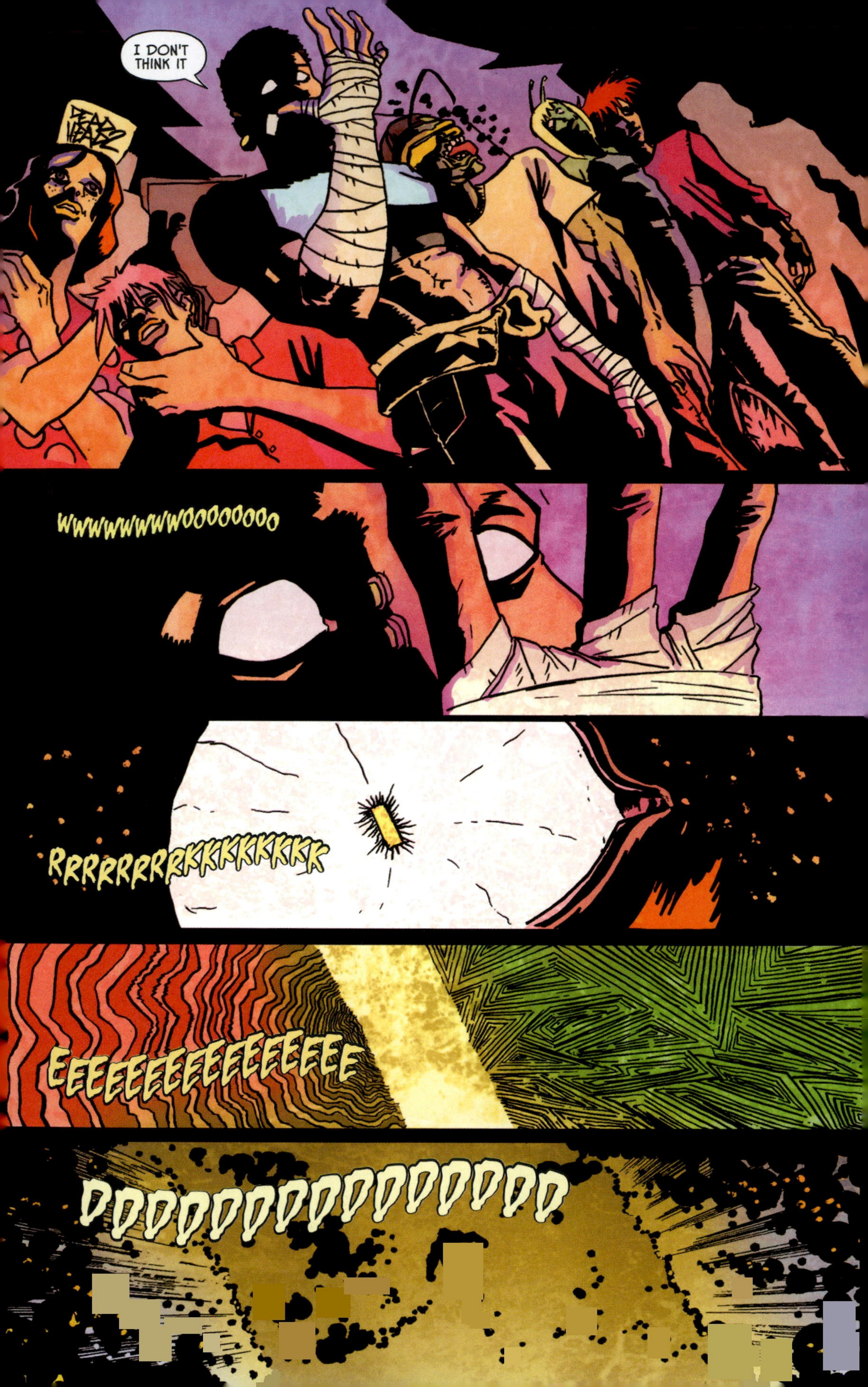

I DON'T THINK IT
WWWWWWWWOOOOOOOO
RRRRRRRRKKKKKKKK
EEEEEEEEEEEEEEEE
DDDDDDDDDDDDDDDDD

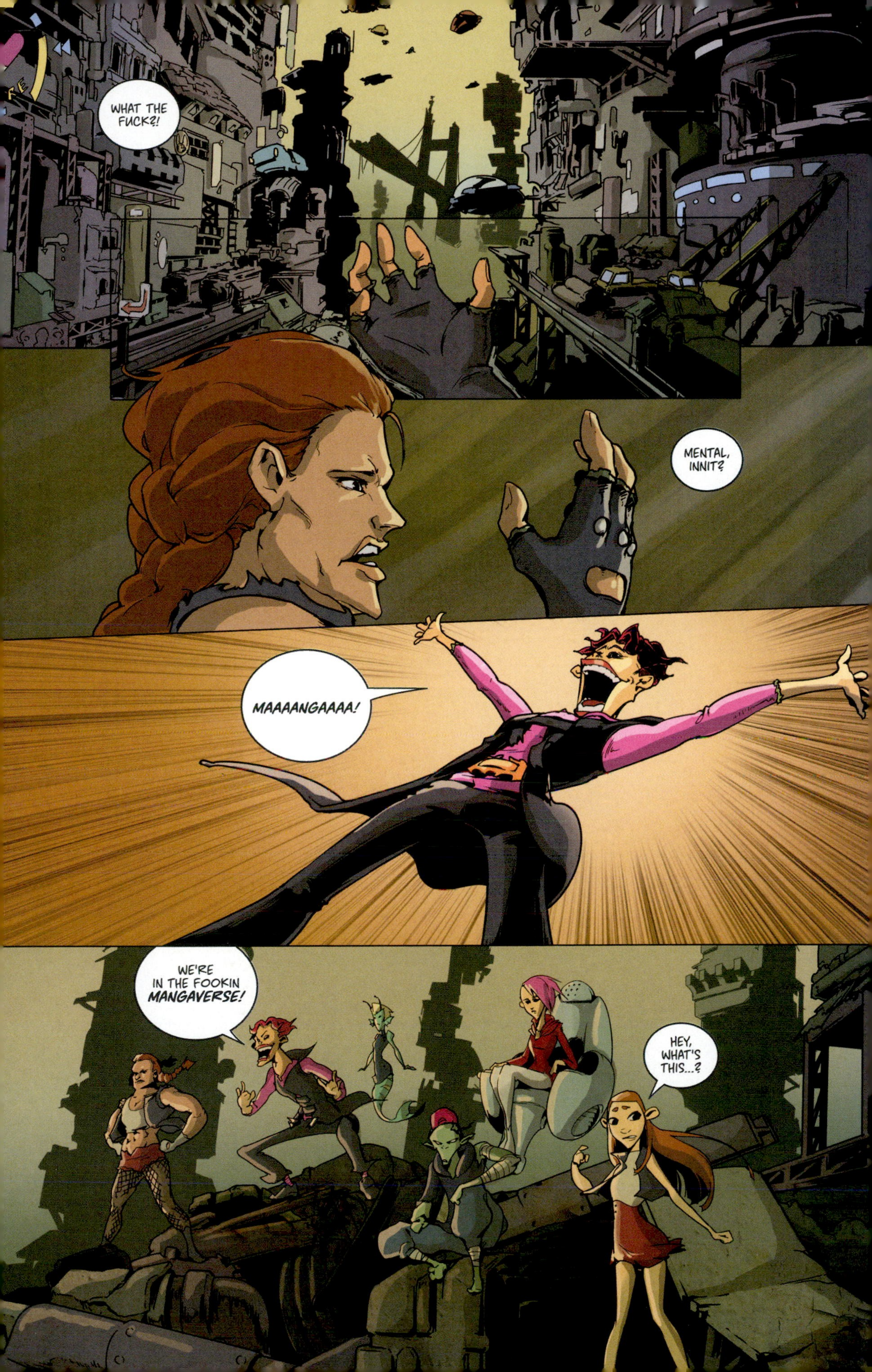
WHAT THE FUCK?!
MENTAL, INNIT?
MAAAANGAAAA!
WE'RE IN THE FOOKIN MANGAVERSE!
HEY, WHAT'S THIS...?

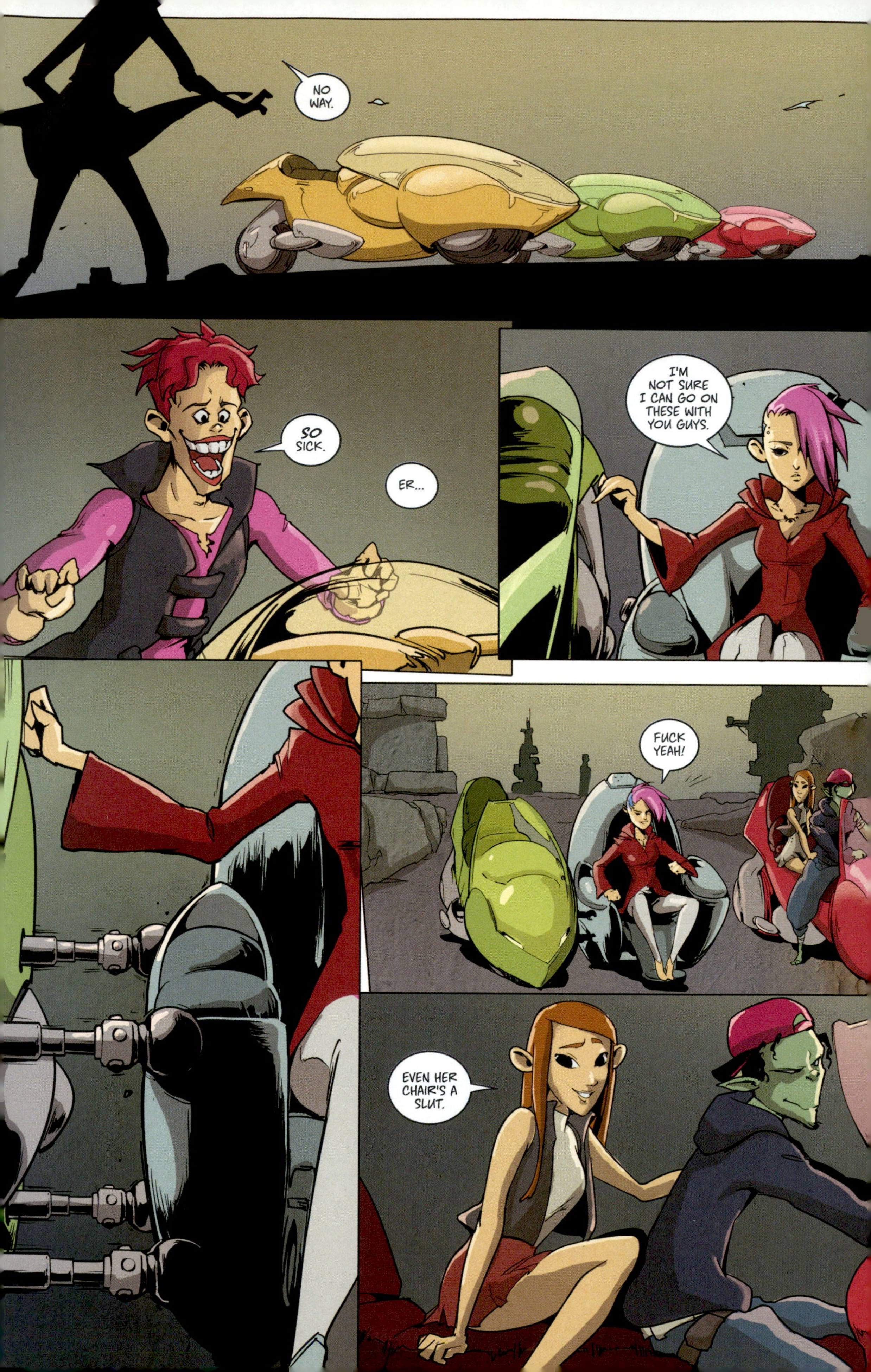
NO WAY.
SO SICK.
ER...
I'M NOT SURE I CAN GO ON THESE WITH YOU GUYS.
FUCK YEAH!
EVEN HER CHAIR'S A SLUT.

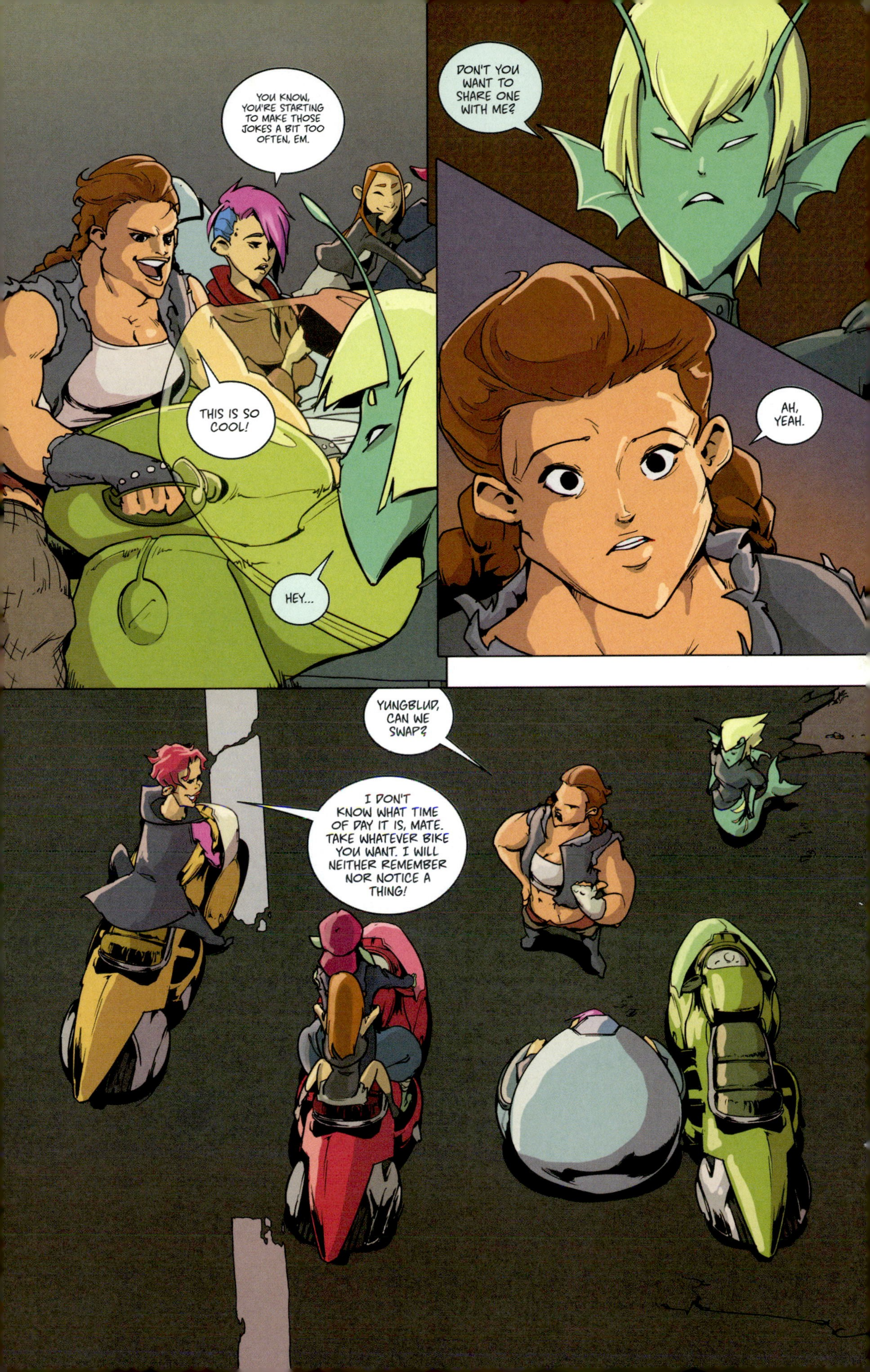
YOU KNOW, YOU'RE STARTING TO MAKE THOSE JOKES A BIT TOO OFTEN, EM.
THIS IS SO COOL!
HEY...
DON'T YOU WANT TO SHARE ONE WITH ME?
AH, YEAH.
YUNGBLUD, CAN WE SWAP?
I DON'T KNOW WHAT TIME OF DAY IT IS, MATE. TAKE WHATEVER BIKE YOU WANT. I WILL NEITHER REMEMBER NOR NOTICE A THING!

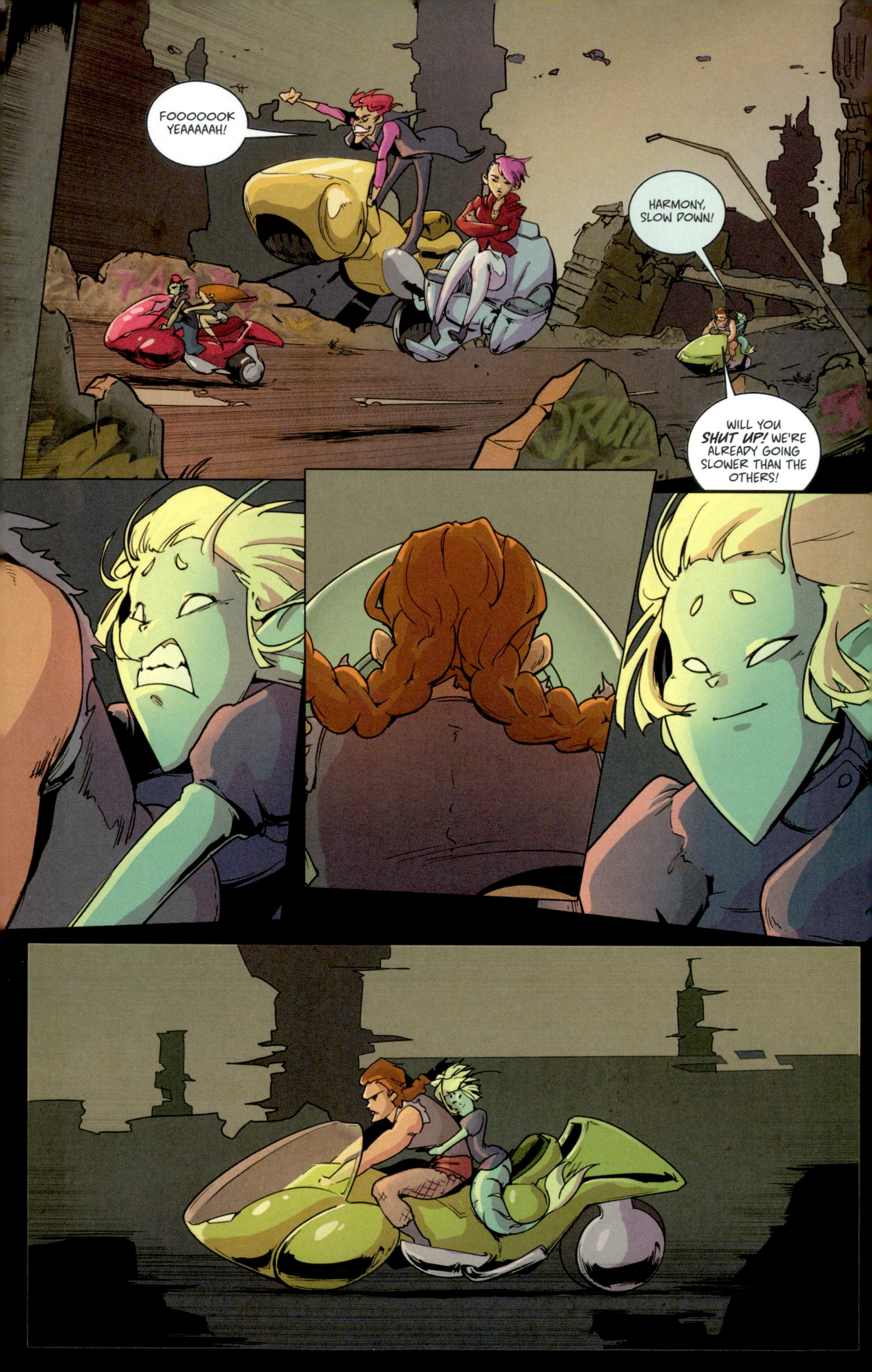
FOOOOOOK YEAAAAAH!
HARMONY, SLOW DOWN!
WILL YOU SHUT UP! WE'RE ALREADY GOING SLOWER THAN THE OTHERS!

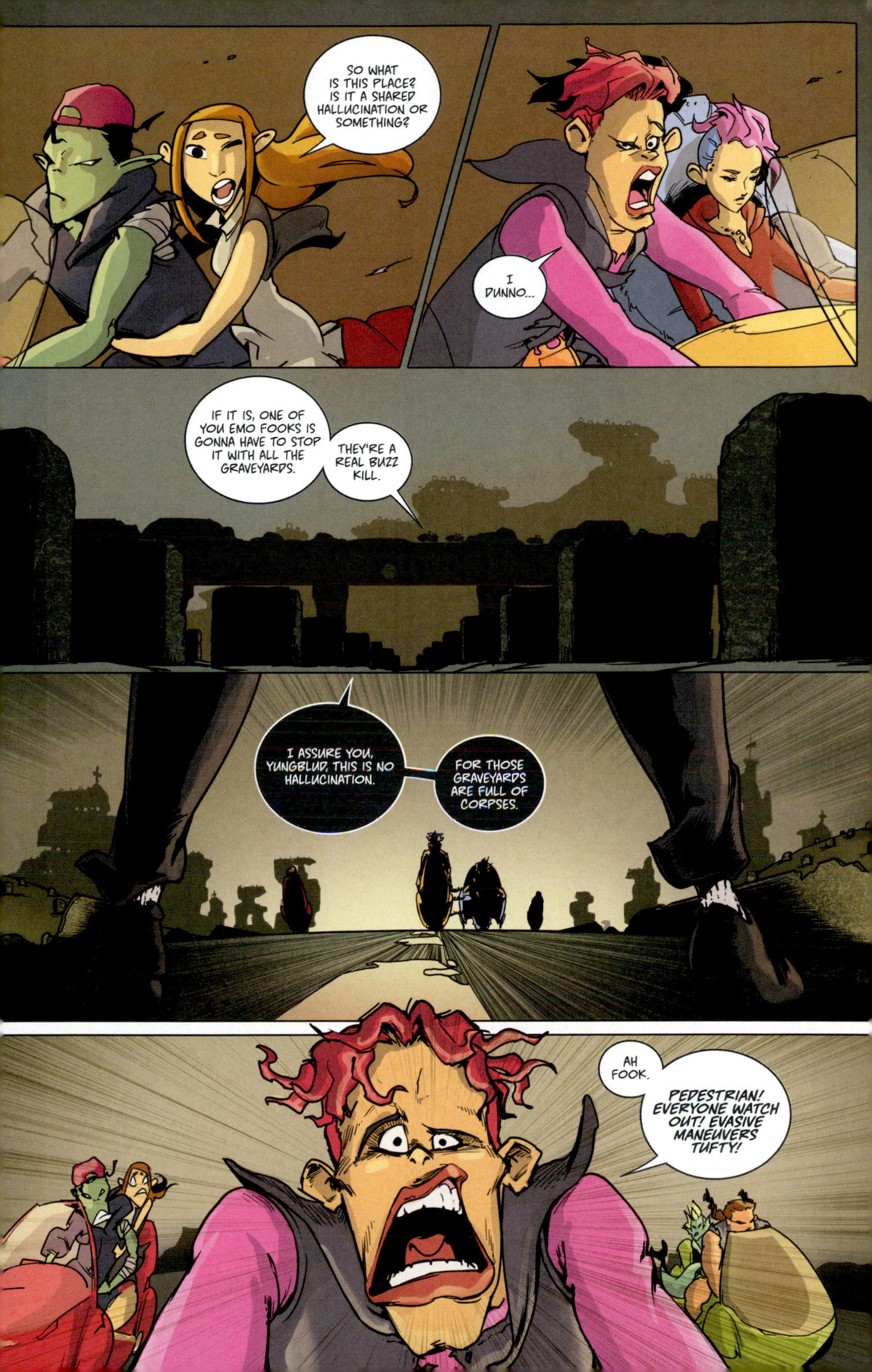
SO WHAT IS THIS PLACE? IS IT A SHARED HALLUCINATION OR SOMETHING?
I DUNNO...
IF IT IS, ONE OF YOU EMO FOOKS IS GONNA HAVE TO STOP IT WITH ALL THE GRAVEYARDS.
THEY'RE A REAL BUZZ KILL.
I ASSURE YOU, YUNGBLUD, THIS IS NO HALLUCINATION.
FOR THOSE GRAVEYARDS ARE FULL OF CORPSES.
AH FOOK.
PEDESTRIAN! EVERYONE WATCH OUT! EVASIVE MANEUVERS TUFTY!

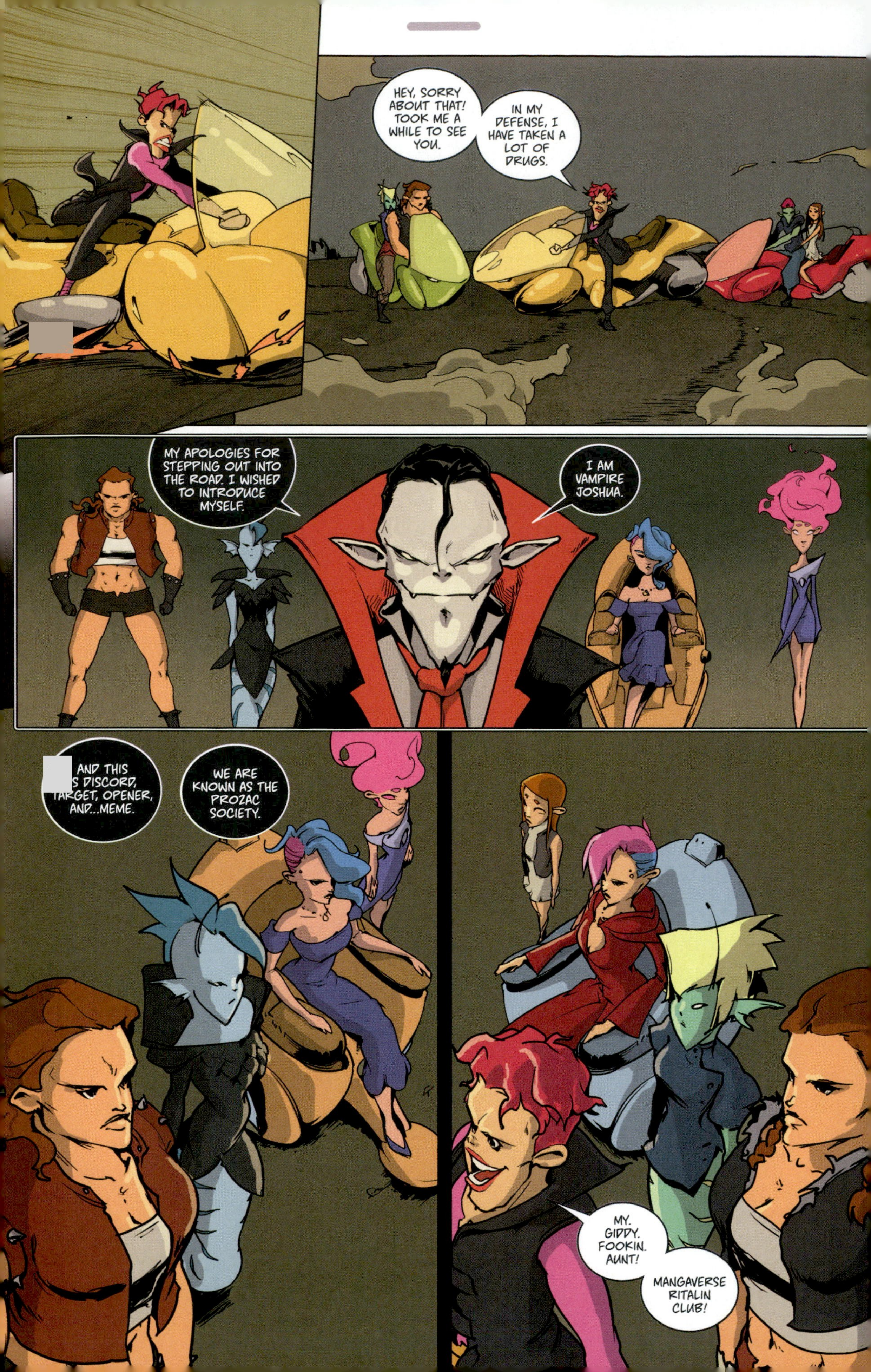
HEY, SORRY ABOUT THAT! TOOK ME A WHILE TO SEE YOU.
IN MY DEFENSE, I HAVE TAKEN A LOT OF DRUGS.
MY APOLOGIES FOR STEPPING OUT INTO THE ROAD. I WISHED TO INTRODUCE MYSELF.
I AM VAMPIRE JOSHUA.
AND THIS S DISCORD, ARGET, OPENER, AND...MEME.
WE ARE KNOWN AS THE PROZAC SOCIETY.
MY. GIDDY. FOOKIN. AUNT!
MANGAVERSE RITALIN CLUB!

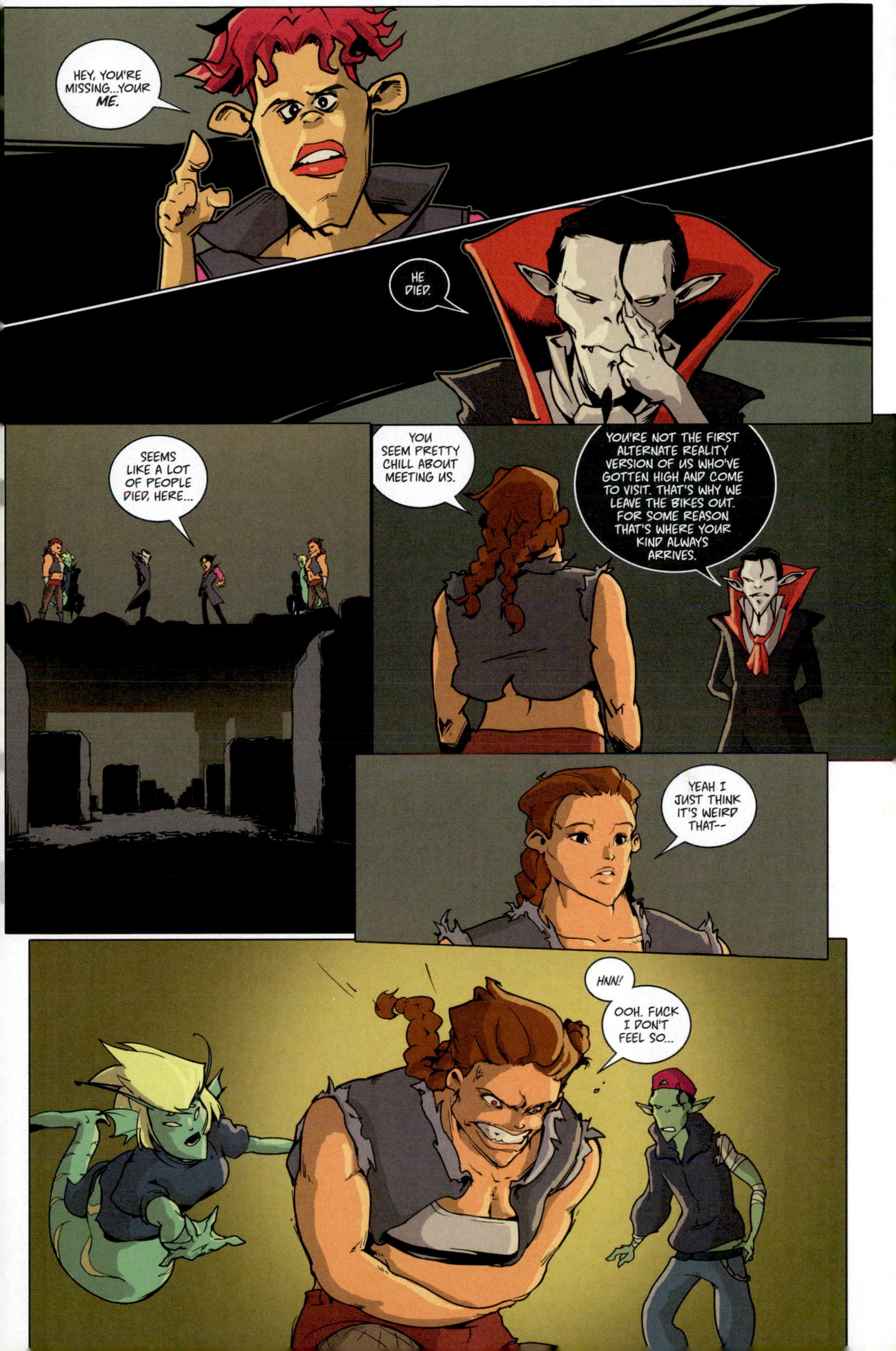
HEY, YOU'RE MISSING...YOUR ME.
HE DIED.
SEEMS LIKE A LOT OF PEOPLE DIED, HERE...
YOU SEEM PRETTY CHILL ABOUT MEETING US.
YOU'RE NOT THE FIRST ALTERNATE REALITY VERSION OF US WHO'VE GOTTEN HIGH AND COME TO VISIT. THAT'S WHY WE LEAVE THE BIKES OUT. FOR SOME REASON THAT'S WHERE YOUR KIND ALWAYS ARRIVES.
YEAH I JUST THINK IT'S WEIRD THAT--
HNN!
OOH. FUCK I DON'T FEEL SO...

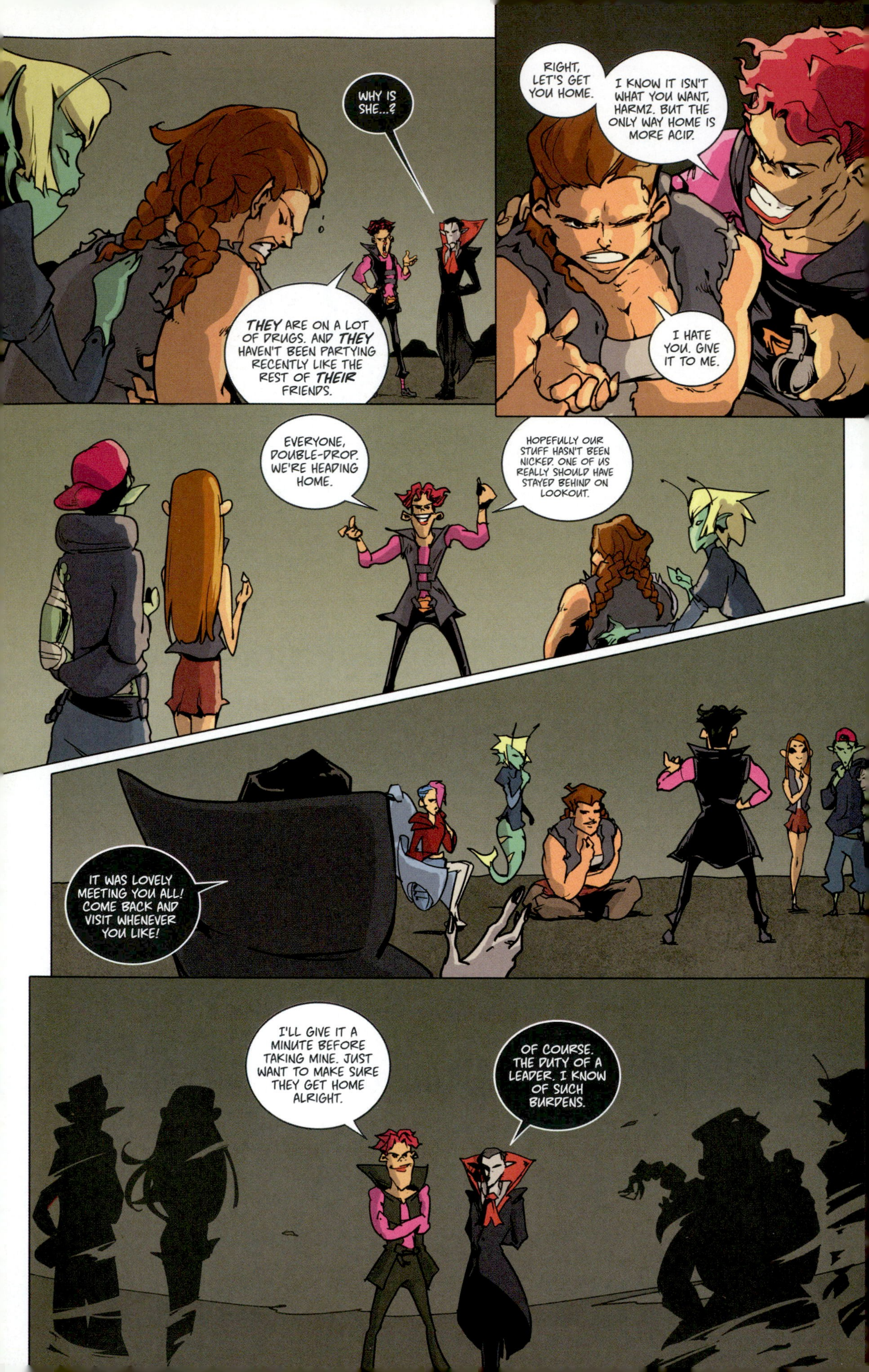
WHY IS SHE...?
THEY ARE ON A LOT OF DRUGS. AND THEY HAVEN'T BEEN PARTYING RECENTLY LIKE THE REST OF THEIR FRIENDS.
RIGHT, LET'S GET YOU HOME.
I KNOW IT ISN'T WHAT YOU WANT, HARMZ. BUT THE ONLY WAY HOME IS MORE ACID.
I HATE YOU. GIVE IT TO ME.
EVERYONE, DOUBLE-DROP. WE'RE HEADING HOME.
HOPEFULLY OUR STUFF HASN'T BEEN NICKED. ONE OF US REALLY SHOULD HAVE STAYED BEHIND ON LOOKOUT.
IT WAS LOVELY MEETING YOU ALL! COME BACK AND VISIT WHENEVER YOU LIKE!
I'LL GIVE IT A MINUTE BEFORE TAKING MINE. JUST WANT TO MAKE SURE THEY GET HOME ALRIGHT.
OF COURSE. THE DUTY OF A LEADER. I KNOW OF SUCH BURDENS.

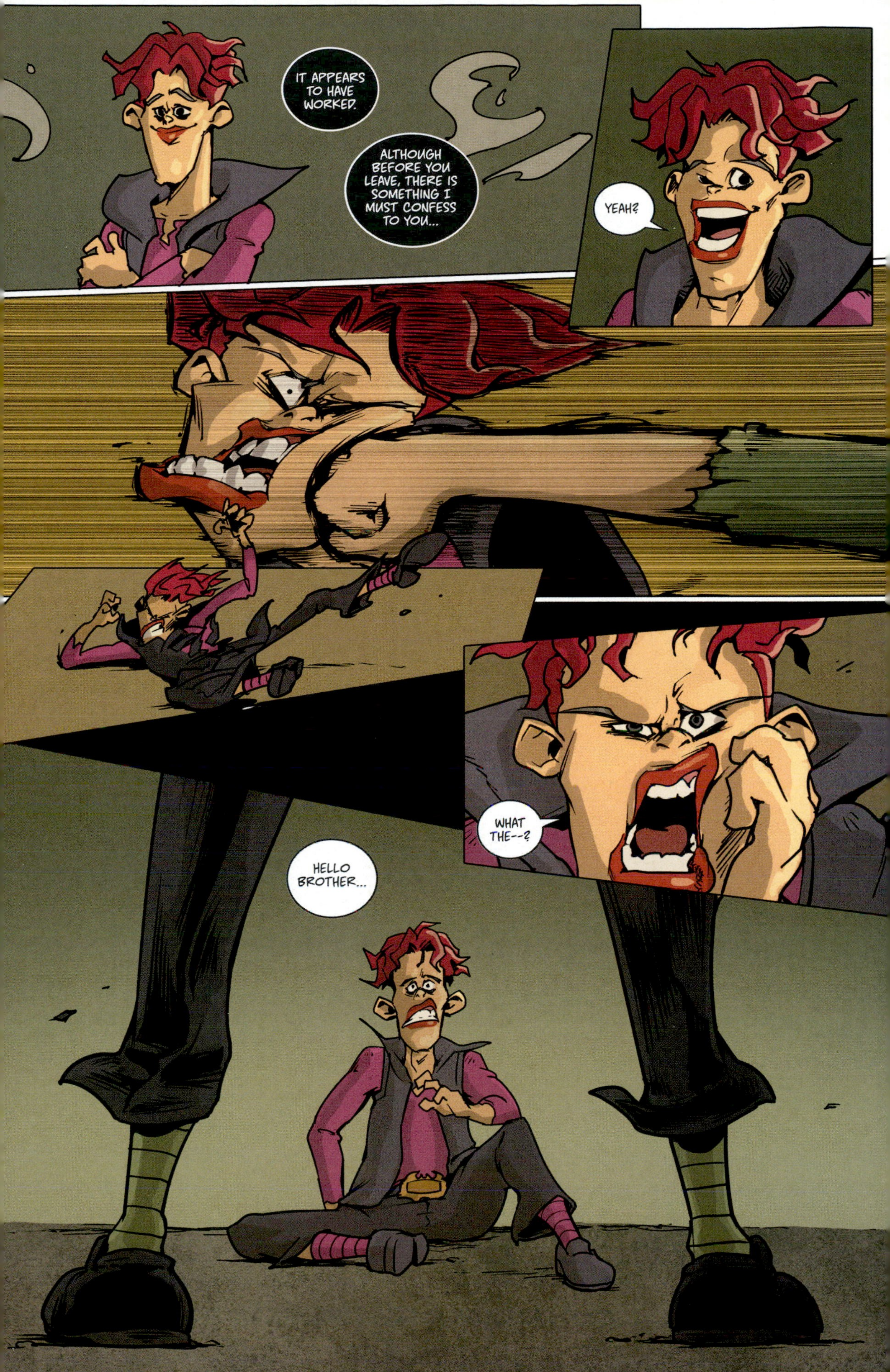
IT APPEARS TO HAVE WORKED.
ALTHOUGH BEFORE YOU LEAVE, THERE IS SOMETHING I MUST CONFESS TO YOU...
YEAH?
WHAT THE--?
HELLO BROTHER...

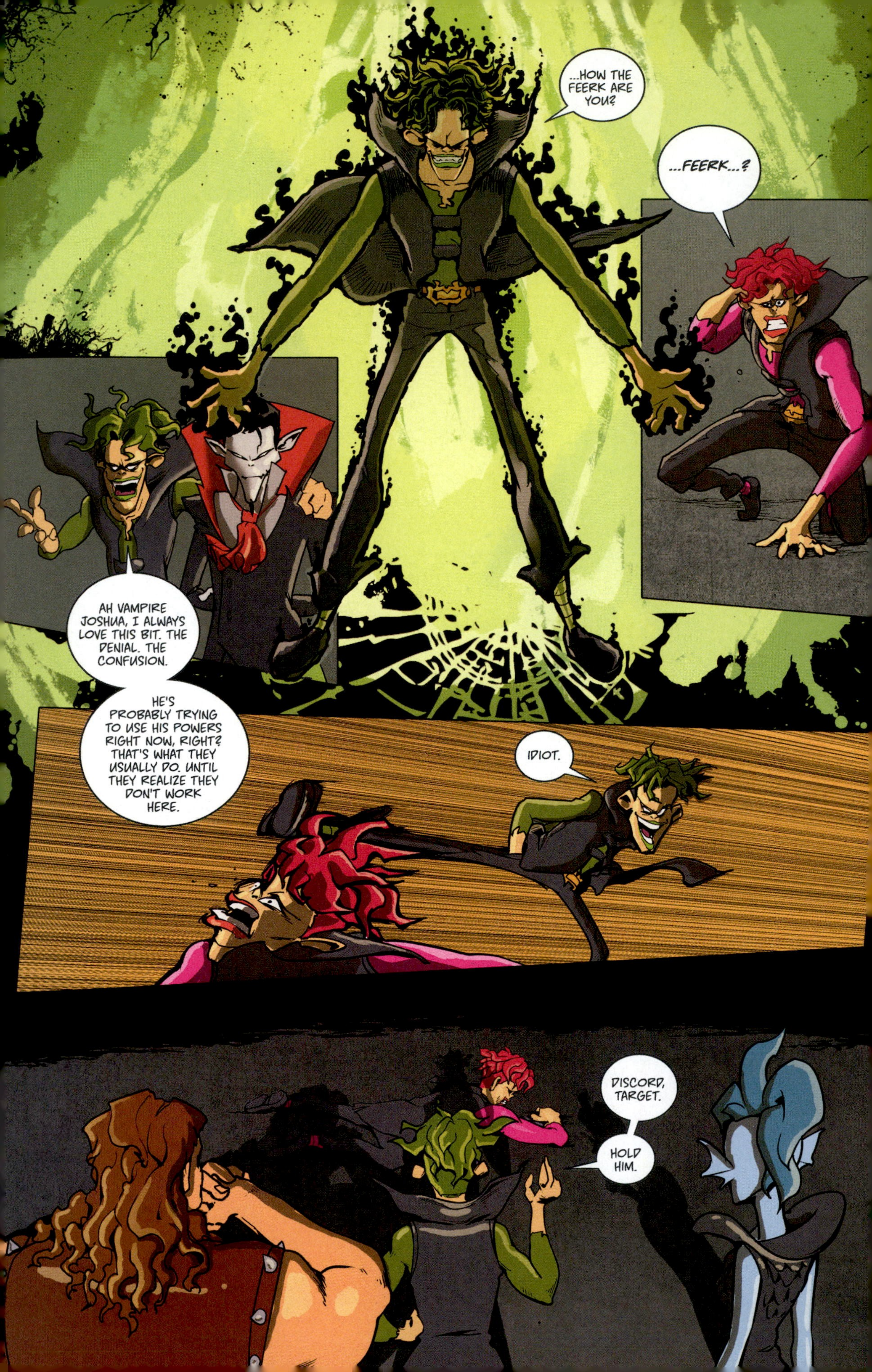

...HOW THE FEERK ARE YOU?
...FEERK...?
AH VAMPIRE JOSHUA, I ALWAYS LOVE THIS BIT. THE DENIAL. THE CONFUSION.
HE'S PROBABLY TRYING TO USE HIS POWERS RIGHT NOW, RIGHT? THAT'S WHAT THEY USUALLY DO. UNTIL THEY REALIZE THEY DON'T WORK HERE.
IDIOT.
DISCORD, TARGET.
HOLD HIM.

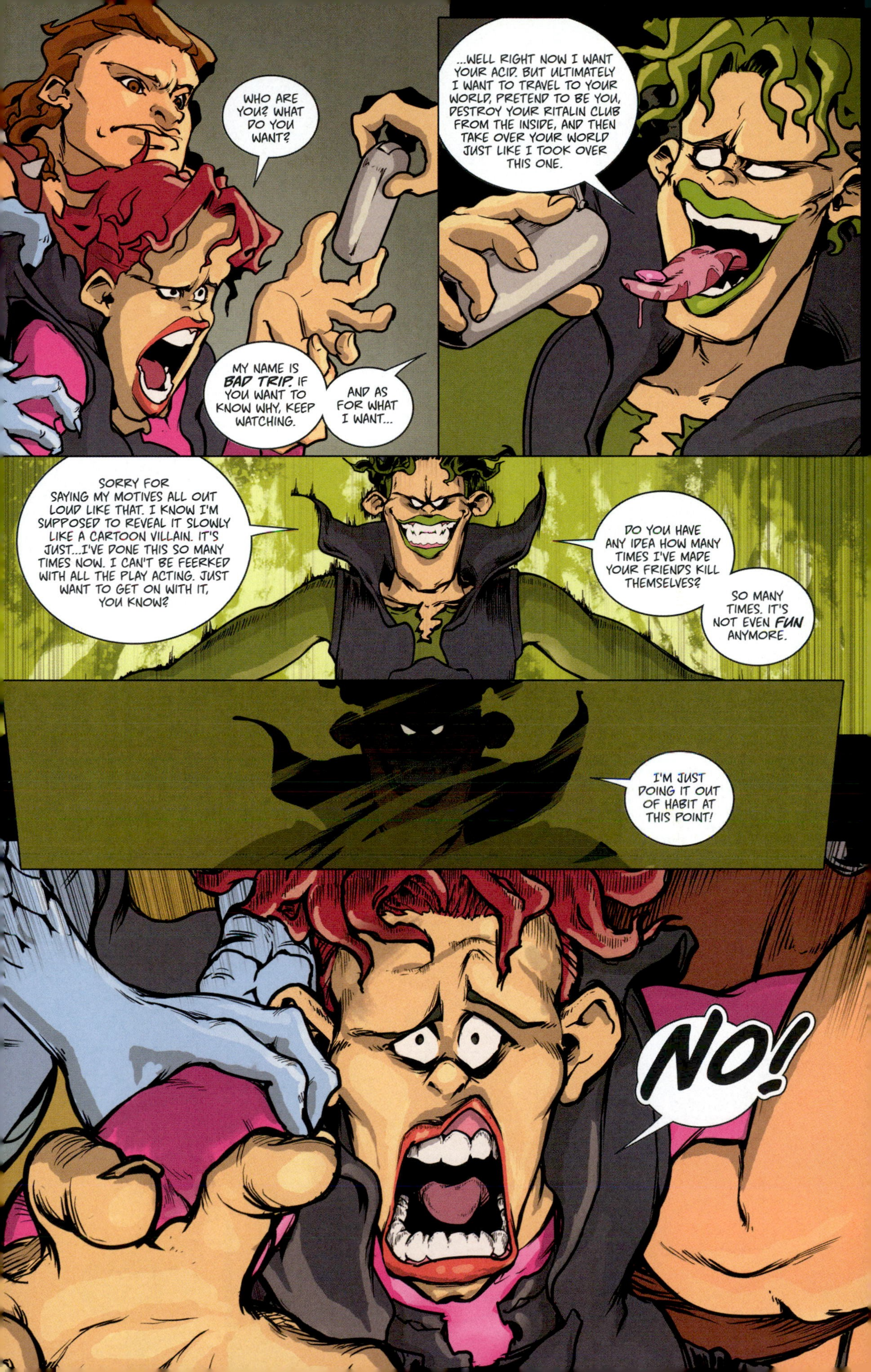
WHO ARE YOU? WHAT DO YOU WANT?
MY NAME IS **BAD TRIP.** IF YOU WANT TO KNOW WHY, KEEP WATCHING.
AND AS FOR WHAT I WANT...
...WELL RIGHT NOW I WANT YOUR ACID. BUT ULTIMATELY I WANT TO TRAVEL TO YOUR WORLD, PRETEND TO BE YOU, DESTROY YOUR RITALIN CLUB FROM THE INSIDE, AND THEN TAKE OVER YOUR WORLD JUST LIKE I TOOK OVER THIS ONE.
SORRY FOR SAYING MY MOTIVES ALL OUT LOUD LIKE THAT. I KNOW I'M SUPPOSED TO REVEAL IT SLOWLY LIKE A CARTOON VILLAIN. IT'S JUST...I'VE DONE THIS SO MANY TIMES NOW. I CAN'T BE FEERKED WITH ALL THE PLAY ACTING. JUST WANT TO GET ON WITH IT, YOU KNOW?
DO YOU HAVE ANY IDEA HOW MANY TIMES I'VE MADE YOUR FRIENDS KILL THEMSELVES?
SO MANY TIMES. IT'S NOT EVEN *FUN* ANYMORE.
I'M JUST DOING IT OUT OF HABIT AT THIS POINT!
NO!

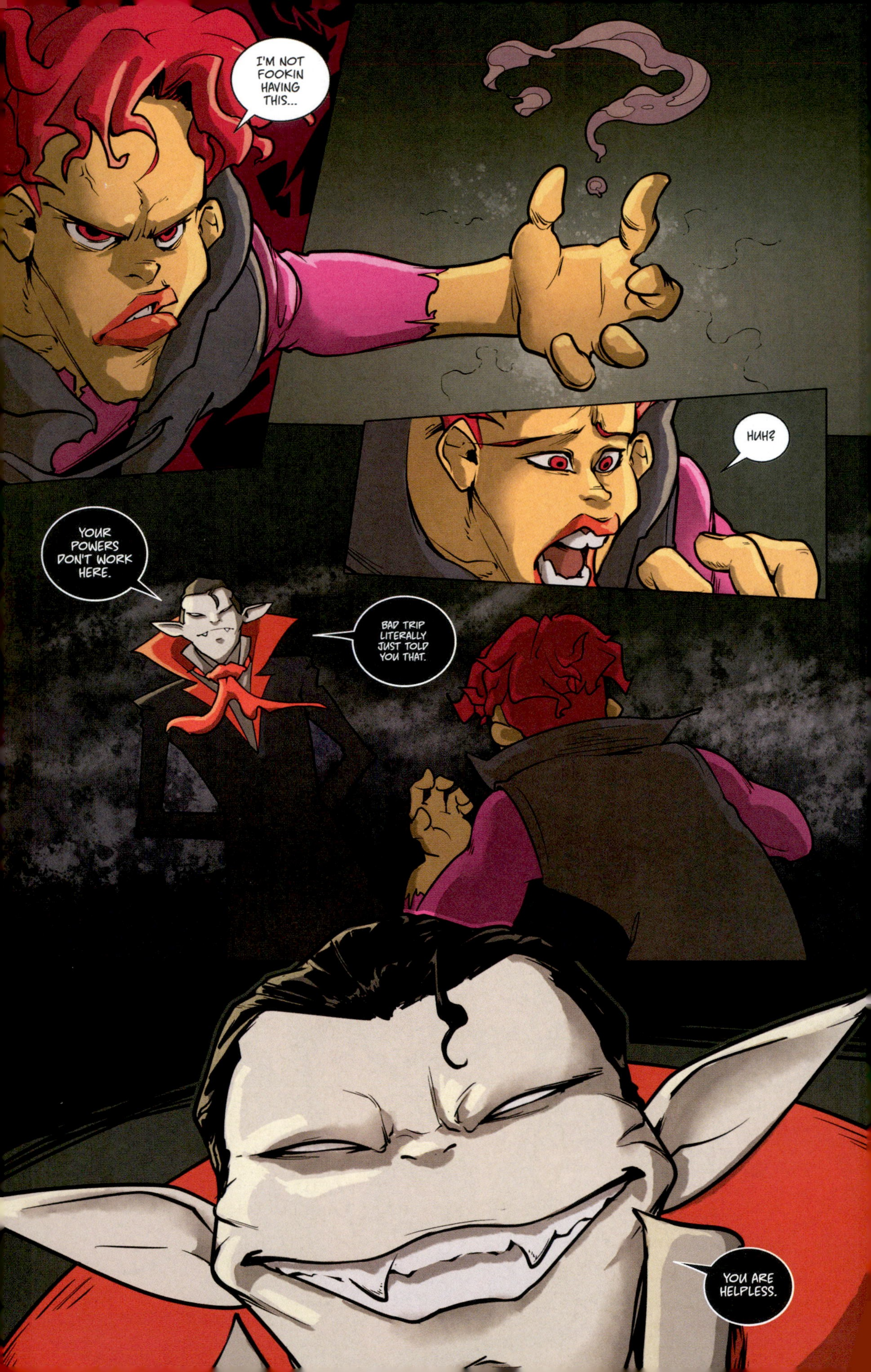
I'M NOT FOOKIN HAVING THIS...
HUH?
YOUR POWERS DON'T WORK HERE.
BAD TRIP LITERALLY JUST TOLD YOU THAT.
YOU ARE HELPLESS.

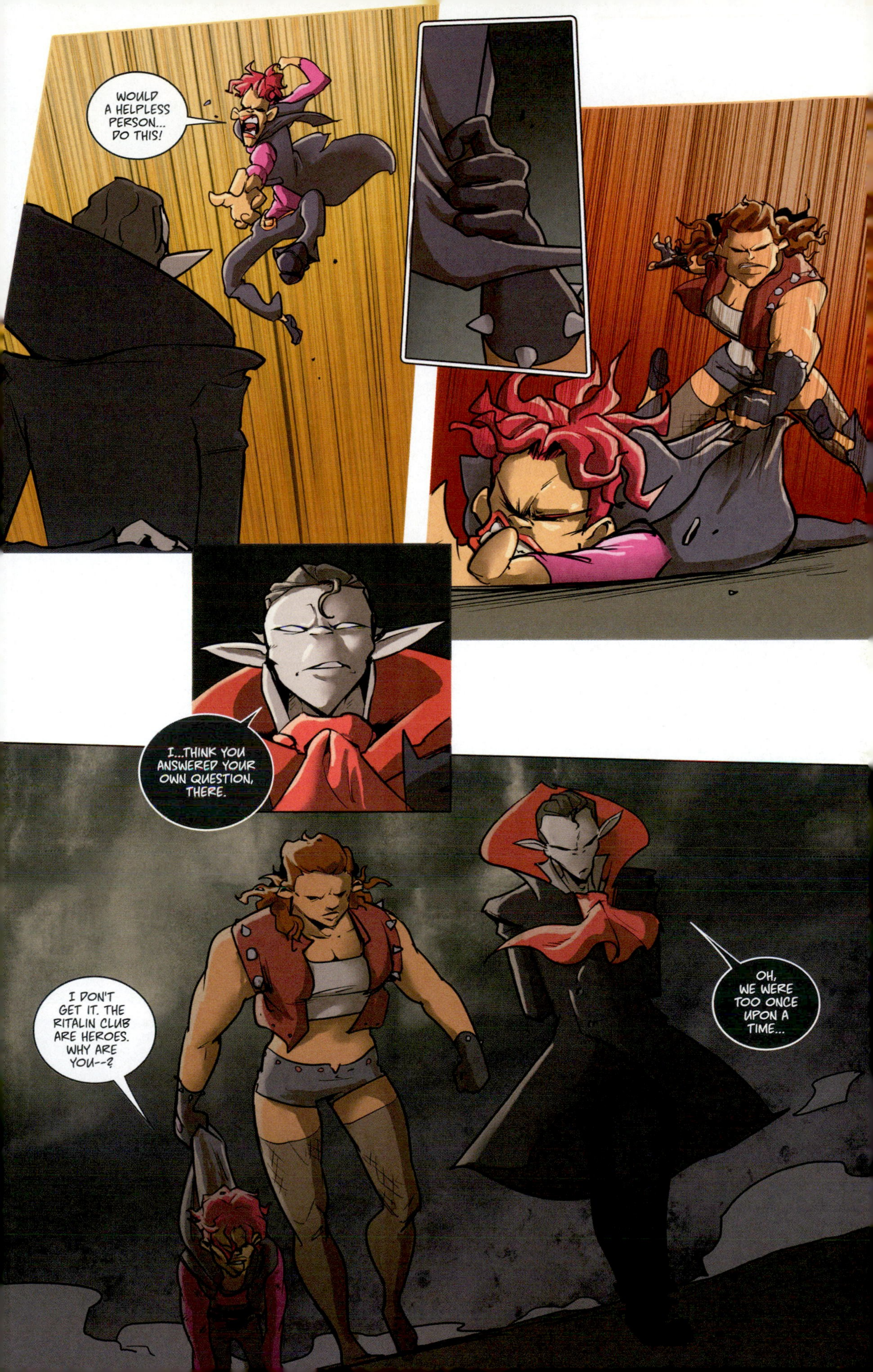
WOULD A HELPLESS PERSON... DO THIS!
I...THINK YOU ANSWERED YOUR OWN QUESTION, THERE.
I DON'T GET IT. THE RITALIN CLUB ARE HEROES. WHY ARE YOU--?
OH, WE WERE TOO ONCE UPON A TIME...

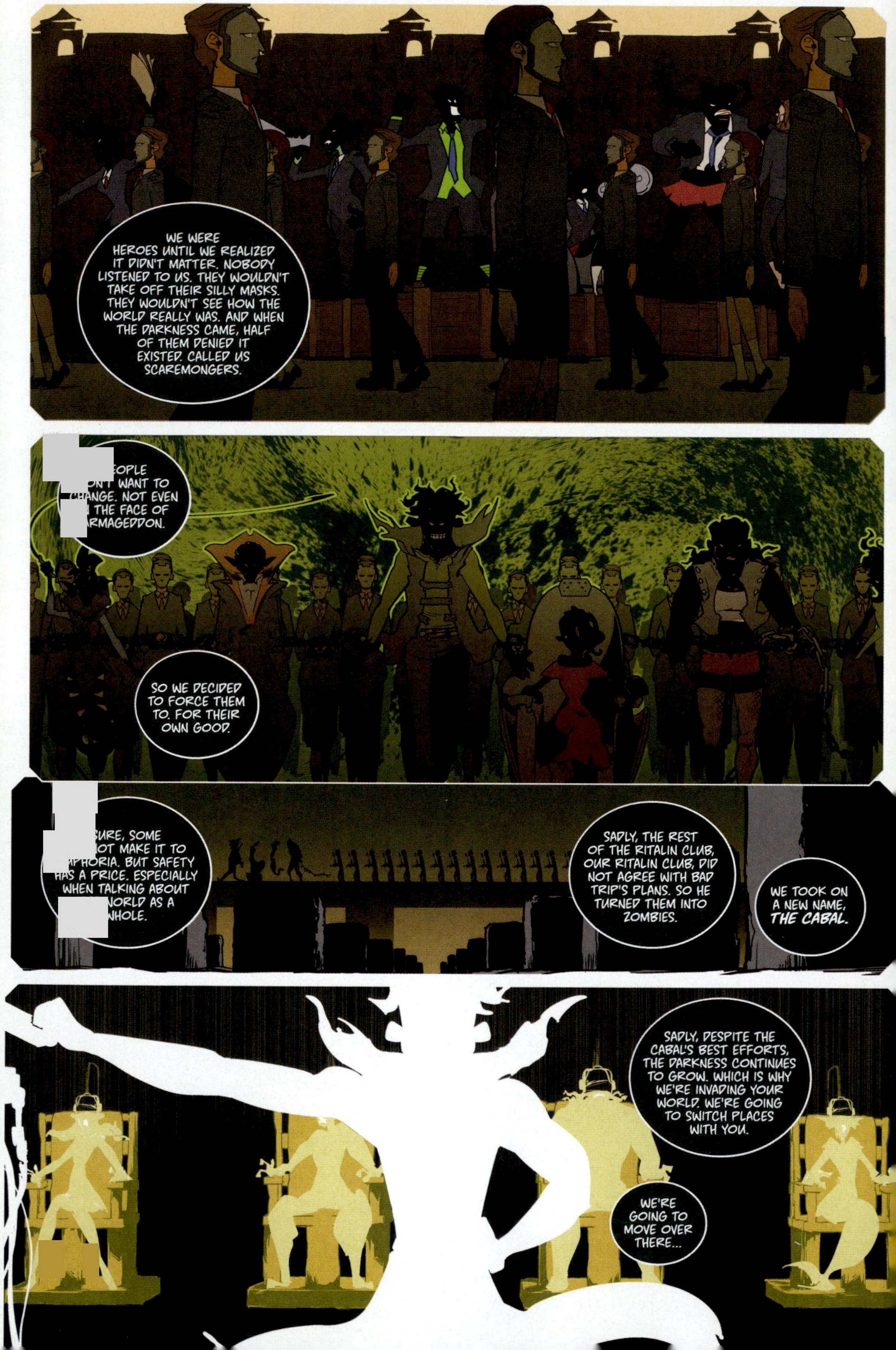
WE WERE HEROES UNTIL WE REALIZED IT DIDN'T MATTER. NOBODY LISTENED TO US. THEY WOULDN'T TAKE OFF THEIR SILLY MASKS. THEY WOULDN'T SEE HOW THE WORLD REALLY WAS. AND WHEN THE DARKNESS CAME, HALF OF THEM DENIED IT EXISTED. CALLED US SCAREMONGERS.
EOPLE ON'T WANT TO CHANGE. NOT EVEN N THE FACE OF ARMAGEDDON.
SO WE DECIDED TO FORCE THEM TO. FOR THEIR OWN GOOD.
SURE, SOME OT MAKE IT TO PHORIA. BUT SAFETY HAS A PRICE. ESPECIALLY WHEN TALKING ABOUT WORLD AS A WHOLE.
SADLY, THE REST OF THE RITALIN CLUB, OUR RITALIN CLUB, DID NOT AGREE WITH BAD TRIP'S PLANS. SO HE TURNED THEM INTO ZOMBIES.
WE TOOK ON A NEW NAME, ***THE CABAL.***
SADLY, DESPITE THE CABAL'S BEST EFFORTS, THE DARKNESS CONTINUES TO GROW. WHICH IS WHY WE'RE INVADING YOUR WORLD. WE'RE GOING TO SWITCH PLACES WITH YOU.
WE'RE GOING TO MOVE OVER THERE...

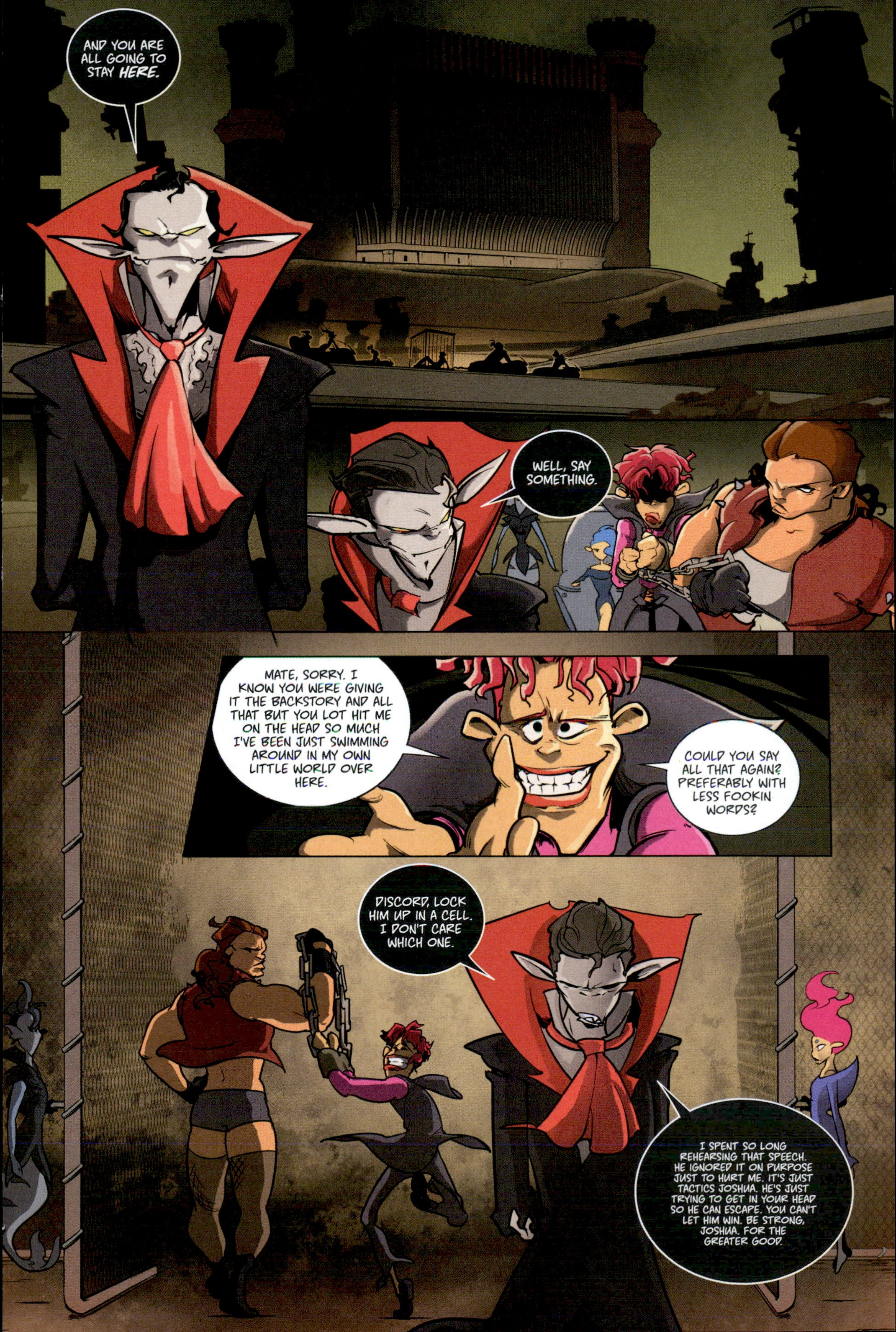
AND YOU ARE ALL GOING TO STAY HERE.
WELL, SAY SOMETHING.
MATE, SORRY. I KNOW YOU WERE GIVING IT THE BACKSTORY AND ALL THAT BUT YOU LOT HIT ME ON THE HEAD SO MUCH I'VE BEEN JUST SWIMMING AROUND IN MY OWN LITTLE WORLD OVER HERE.
COULD YOU SAY ALL THAT AGAIN? PREFERABLY WITH LESS FOOKIN WORDS?
DISCORD, LOCK HIM UP IN A CELL. I DON'T CARE WHICH ONE.
I SPENT SO LONG REHEARSING THAT SPEECH. HE IGNORED IT ON PURPOSE JUST TO HURT ME. IT'S JUST TACTICS JOSHUA. HE'S JUST TRYING TO GET IN YOUR HEAD SO HE CAN ESCAPE. YOU CAN'T LET HIM WIN. BE STRONG, JOSHUA. FOR THE GREATER GOOD.

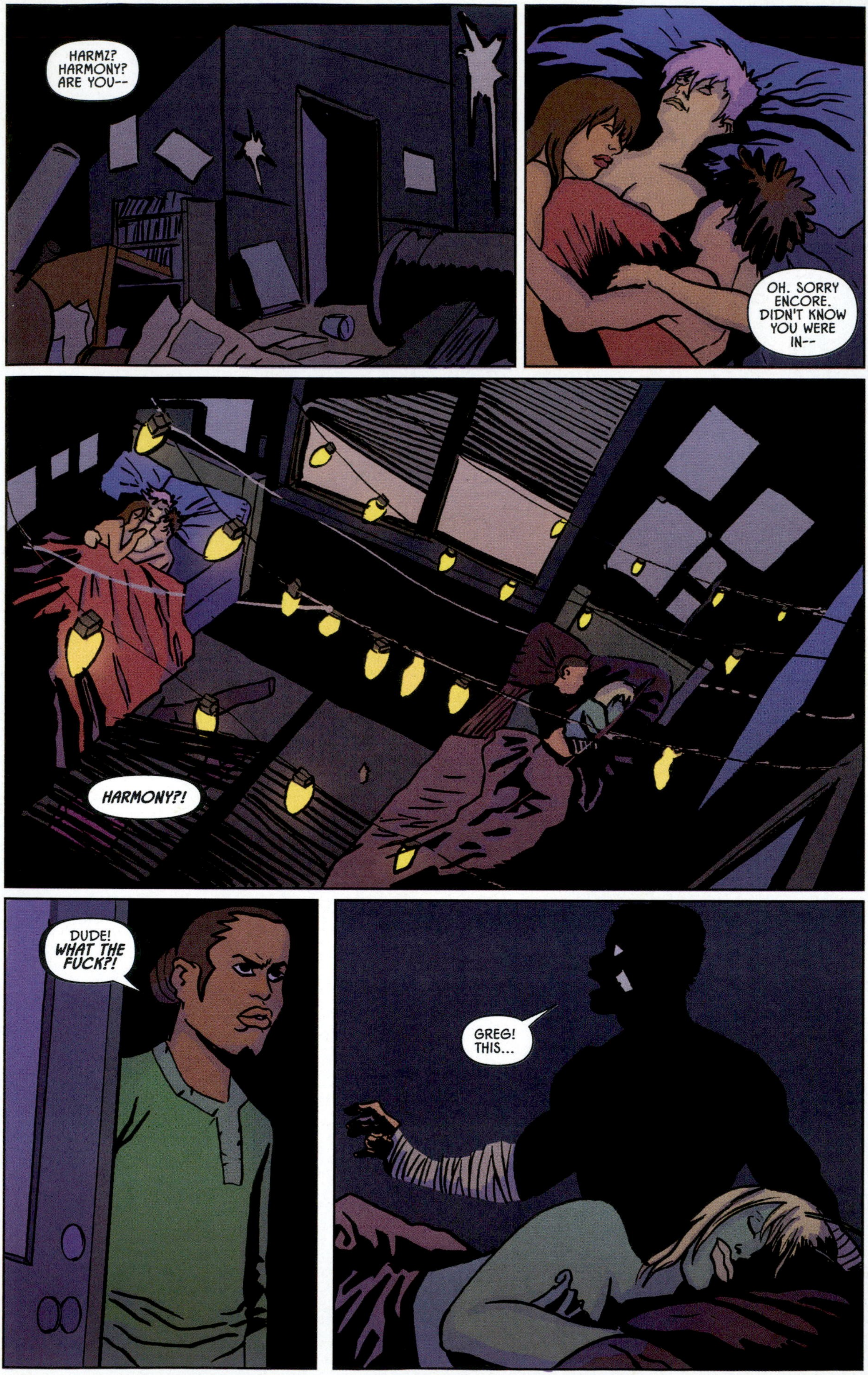
HARMZ? HARMONY? ARE YOU--
OH. SORRY ENCORE. DIDN'T KNOW YOU WERE IN--
HARMONY?!
DUDE! WHAT THE FUCK?!
GREG! THIS...

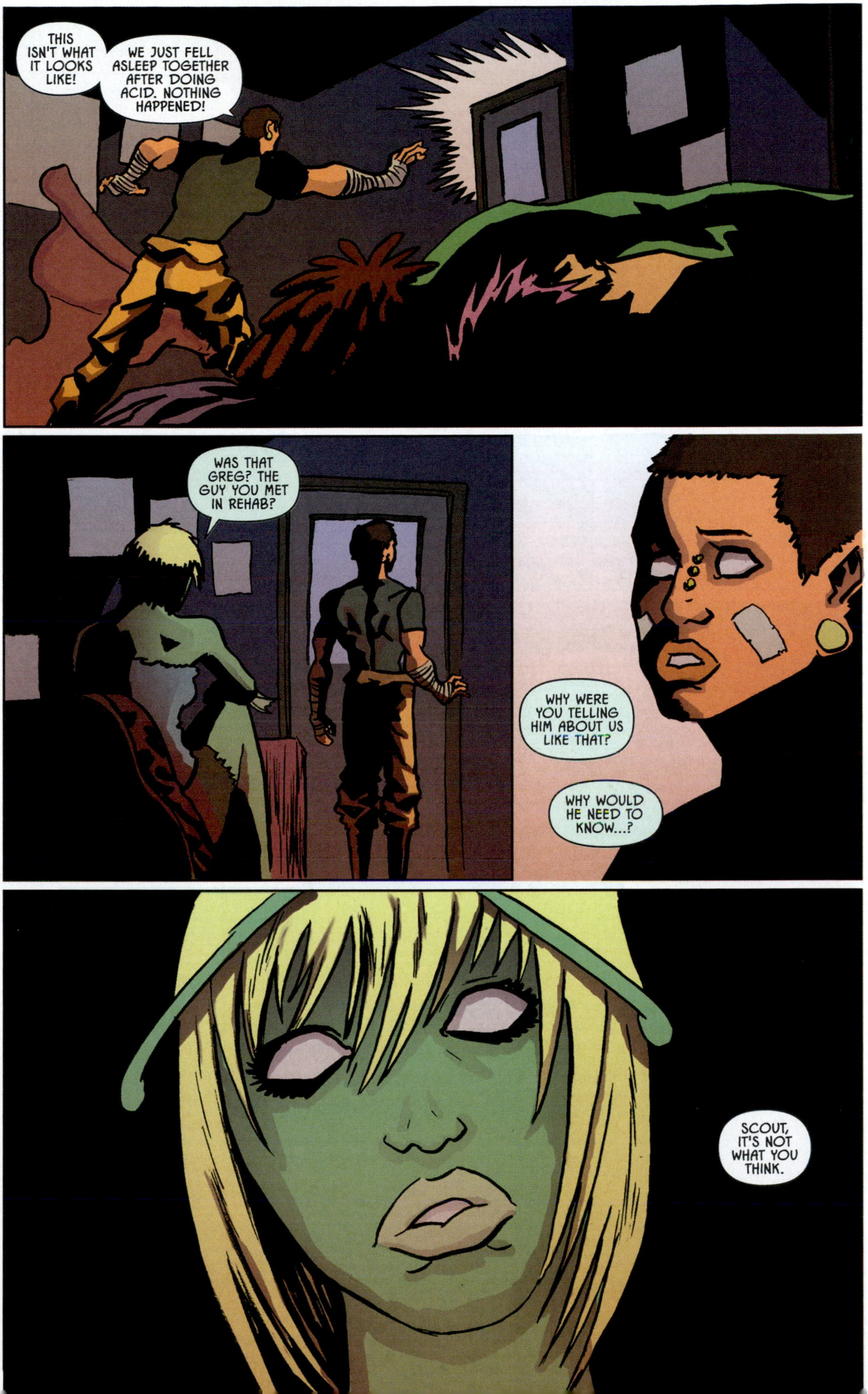
THIS ISN'T WHAT IT LOOKS LIKE!
WE JUST FELL ASLEEP TOGETHER AFTER DOING ACID. NOTHING HAPPENED!
WAS THAT GREG? THE GUY YOU MET IN REHAB?
WHY WERE YOU TELLING HIM ABOUT US LIKE THAT?
WHY WOULD HE NEED TO KNOW...?
SCOUT, IT'S NOT WHAT YOU THINK.

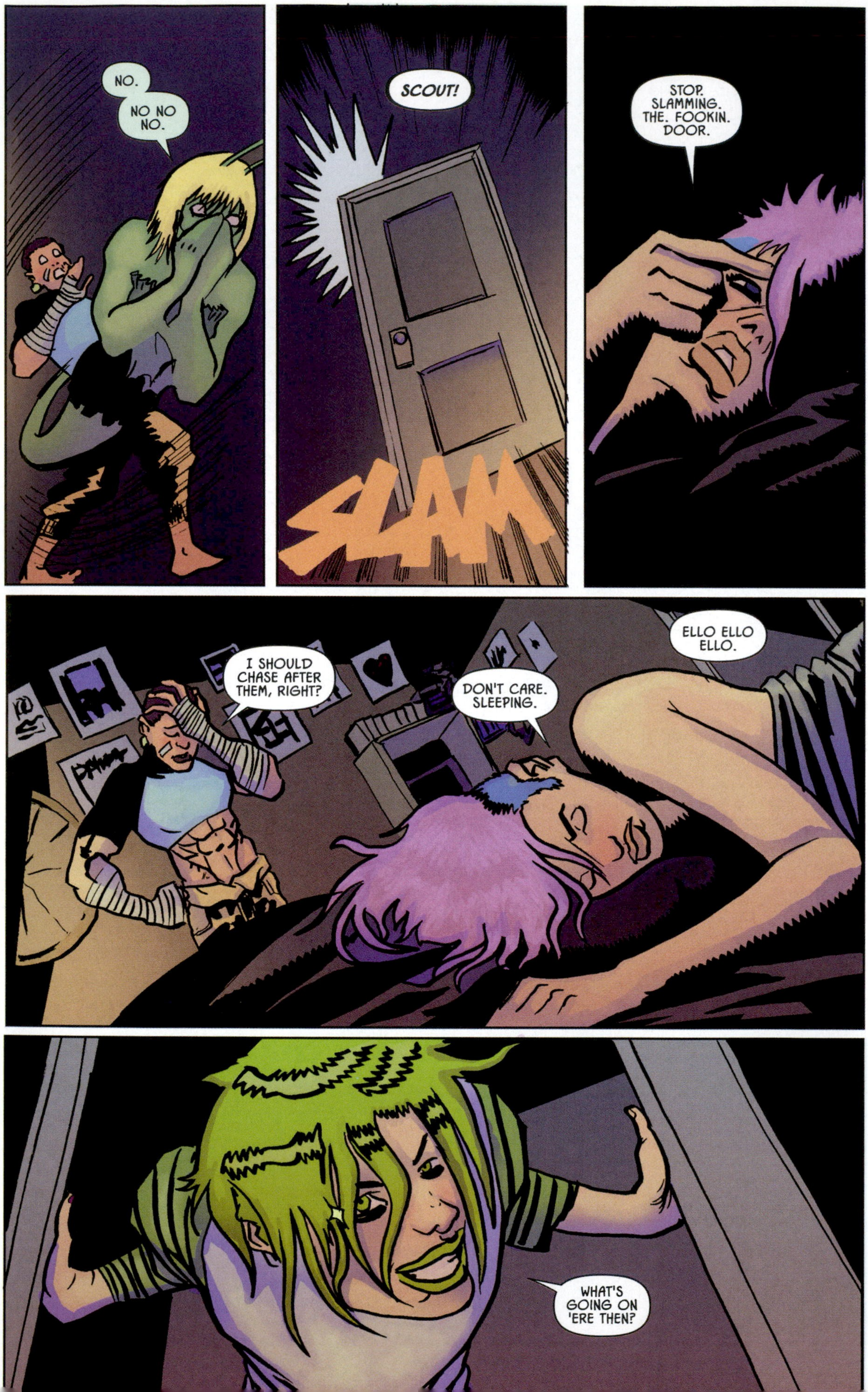
NO.
NO NO NO.
SCOUT!
SLAM
STOP. SLAMMING. THE. FOOKIN. DOOR.
I SHOULD CHASE AFTER THEM, RIGHT?
DON'T CARE. SLEEPING.
ELLO ELLO ELLO.
WHAT'S GOING ON 'ERE THEN?

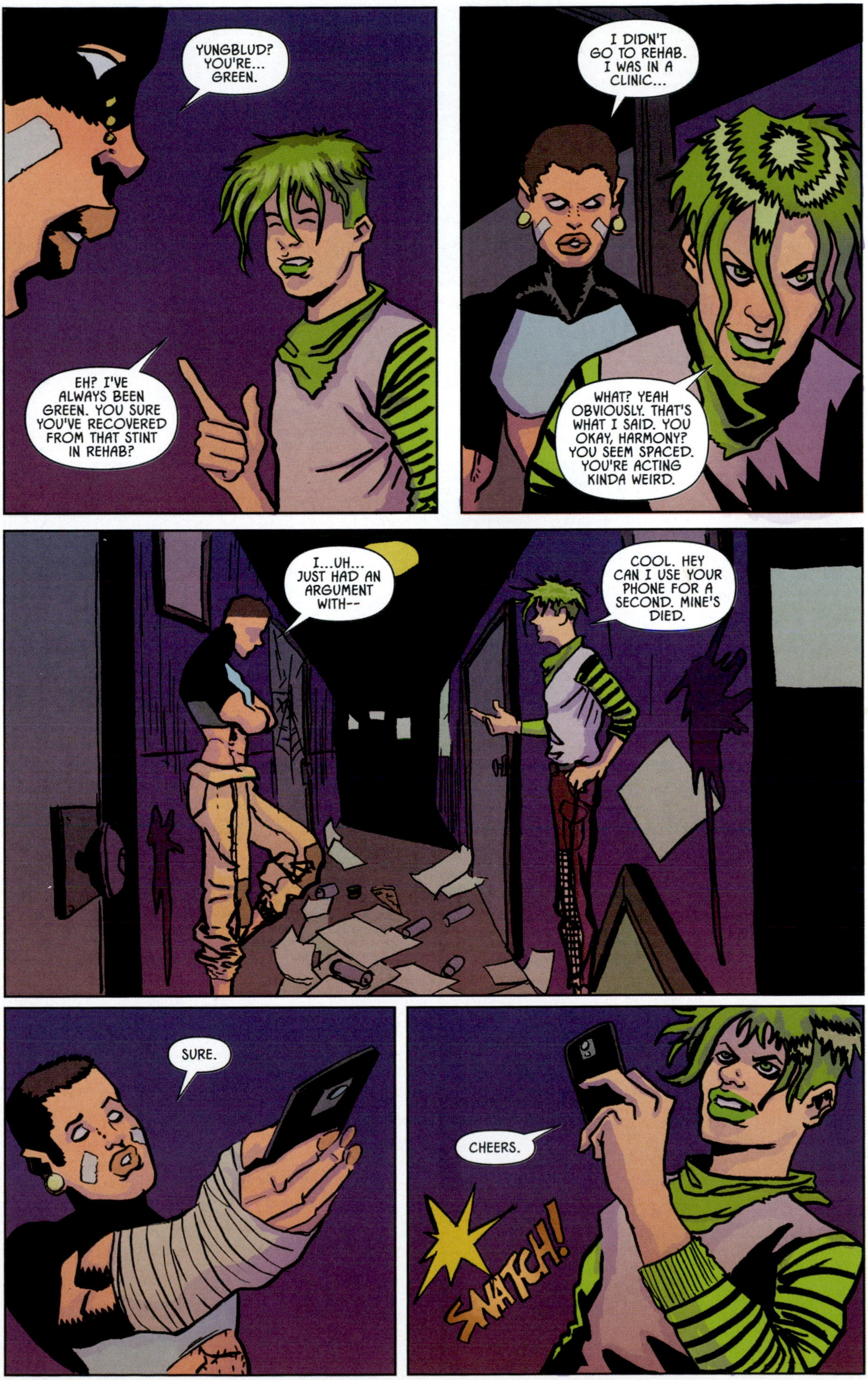
YUNGBLUD? YOU'RE... GREEN.
EH? I'VE ALWAYS BEEN GREEN. YOU SURE YOU'VE RECOVERED FROM THAT STINT IN REHAB?
I DIDN'T GO TO REHAB. I WAS IN A CLINIC...
WHAT? YEAH OBVIOUSLY. THAT'S WHAT I SAID. YOU OKAY, HARMONY? YOU SEEM SPACED. YOU'RE ACTING KINDA WEIRD.
I...UH... JUST HAD AN ARGUMENT WITH--
COOL. HEY CAN I USE YOUR PHONE FOR A SECOND. MINE'S DIED.
SURE.
CHEERS.
SNATCH!

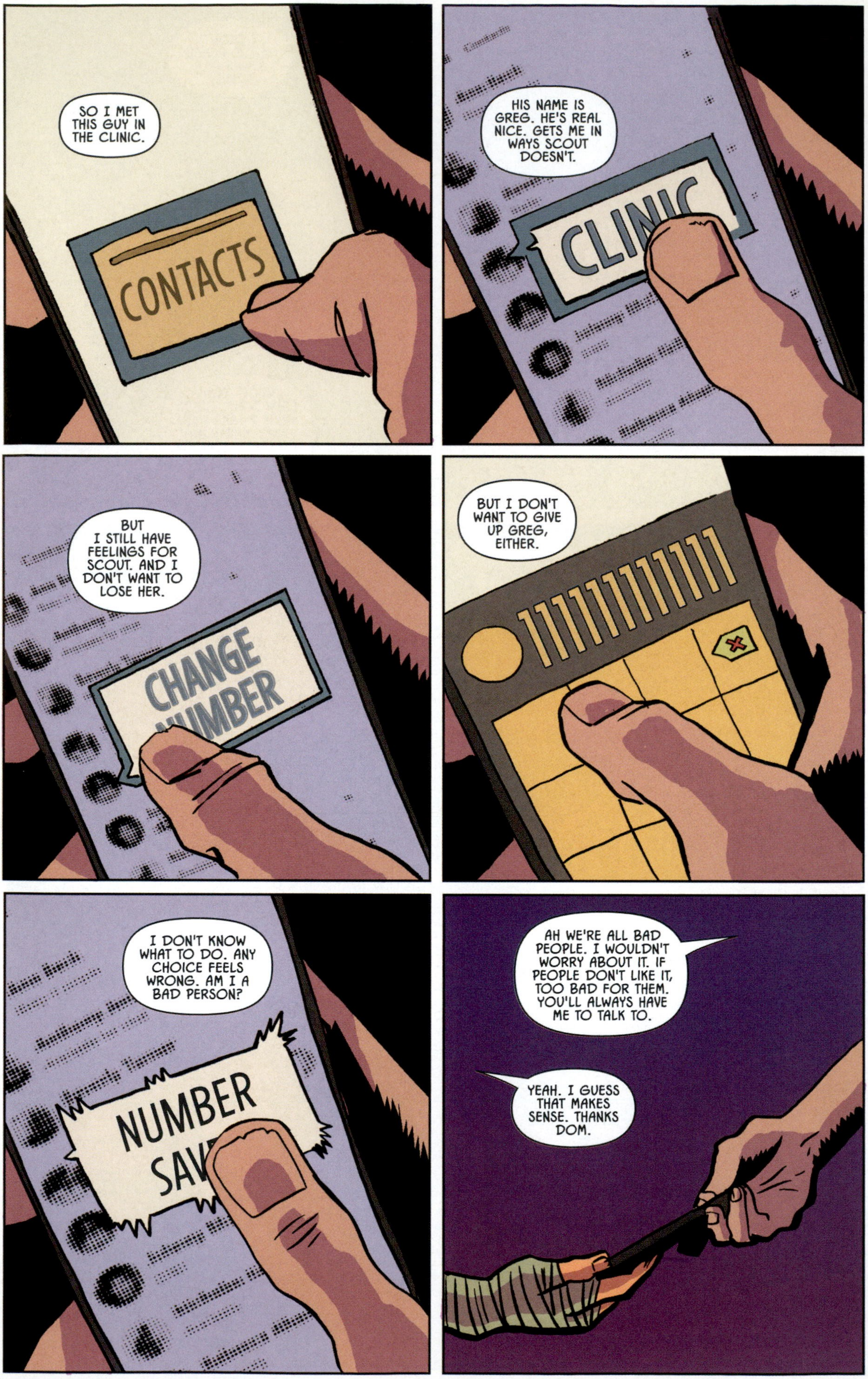
SO I MET THIS GUY IN THE CLINIC.
CONTACTS
HIS NAME IS GREG. HE'S REAL NICE. GETS ME IN WAYS SCOUT DOESN'T.
BUT I STILL HAVE FEELINGS FOR SCOUT. AND I DON'T WANT TO LOSE HER.
CHANGE
BUT I DON'T WANT TO GIVE UP GREG, EITHER.
I DON'T KNOW WHAT TO DO. ANY CHOICE FEELS WRONG. AM I A BAD PERSON?
NUMBER
AH WE'RE ALL BAD PEOPLE. I WOULDN'T WORRY ABOUT IT. IF PEOPLE DON'T LIKE IT, TOO BAD FOR THEM. YOU'LL ALWAYS HAVE ME TO TALK TO.
YEAH. I GUESS THAT MAKES SENSE. THANKS DOM.

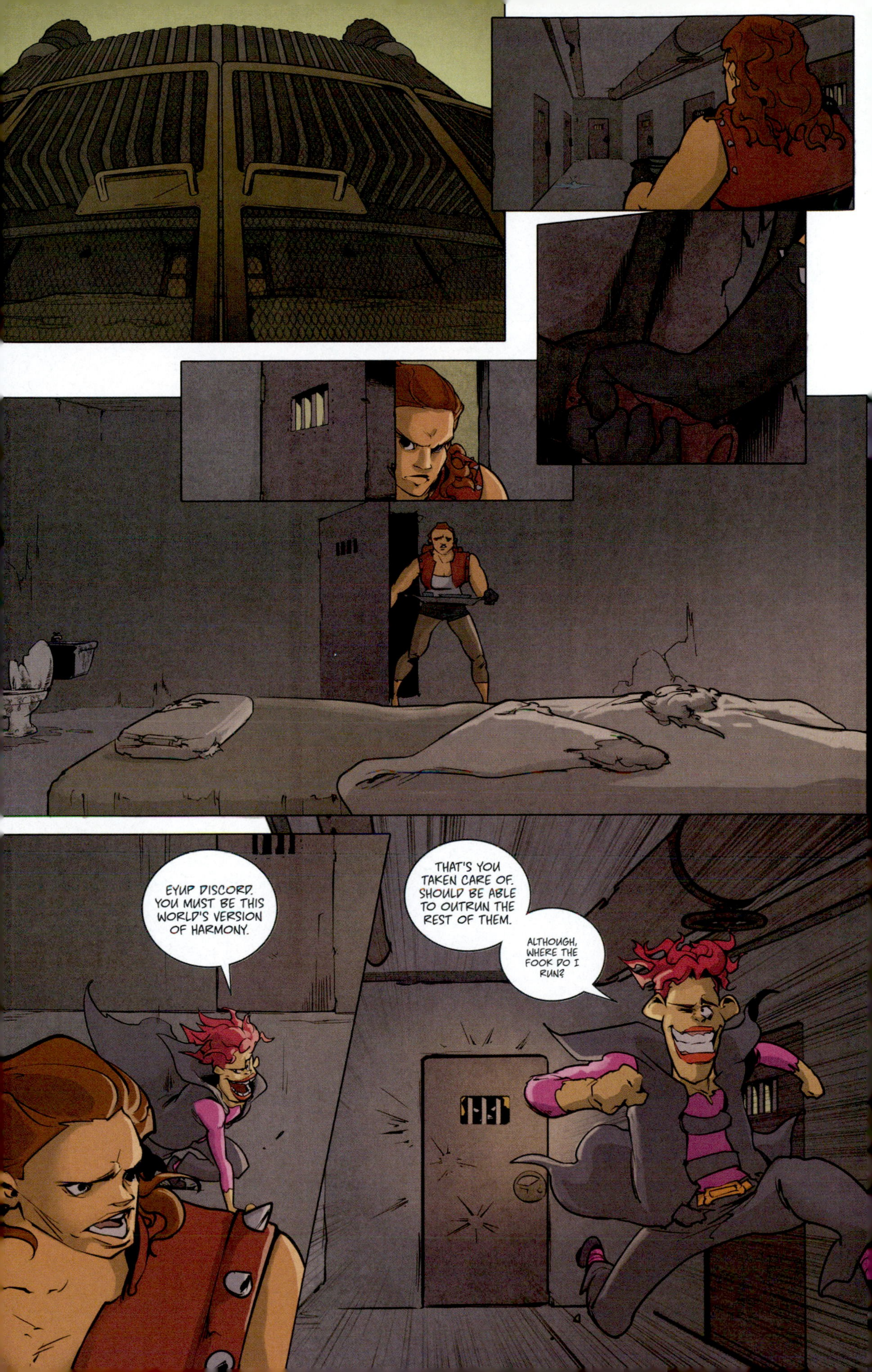
EYUP DISCORD. YOU MUST BE THIS WORLD'S VERSION OF HARMONY.
THAT'S YOU TAKEN CARE OF. SHOULD BE ABLE TO OUTRUN THE REST OF THEM.
ALTHOUGH, WHERE THE FOOK DO I RUN?

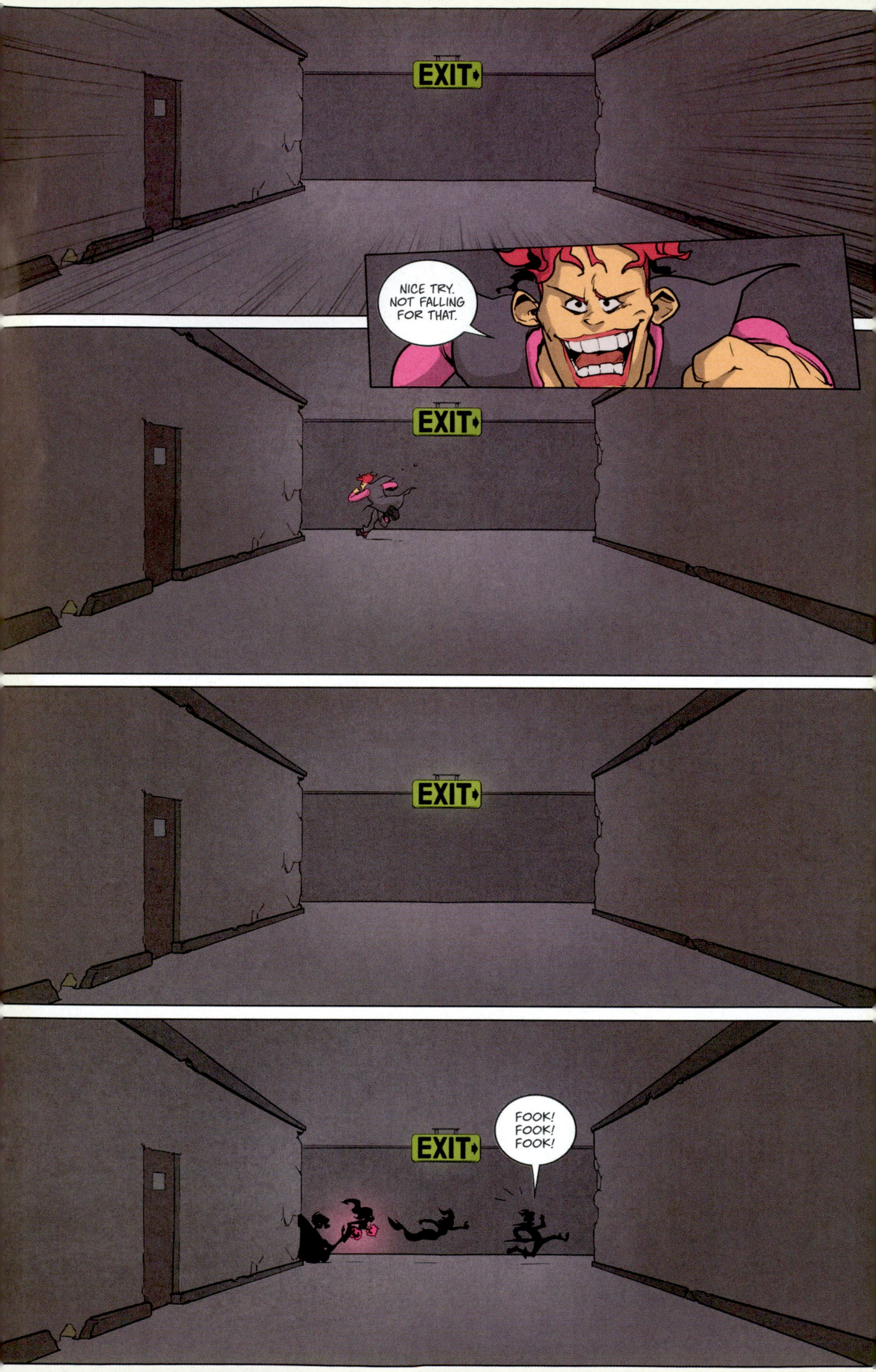
EXIT
NICE TRY. NOT FALLING FOR THAT.
EXIT
EXIT
EXIT
FOOK! FOOK! FOOK!

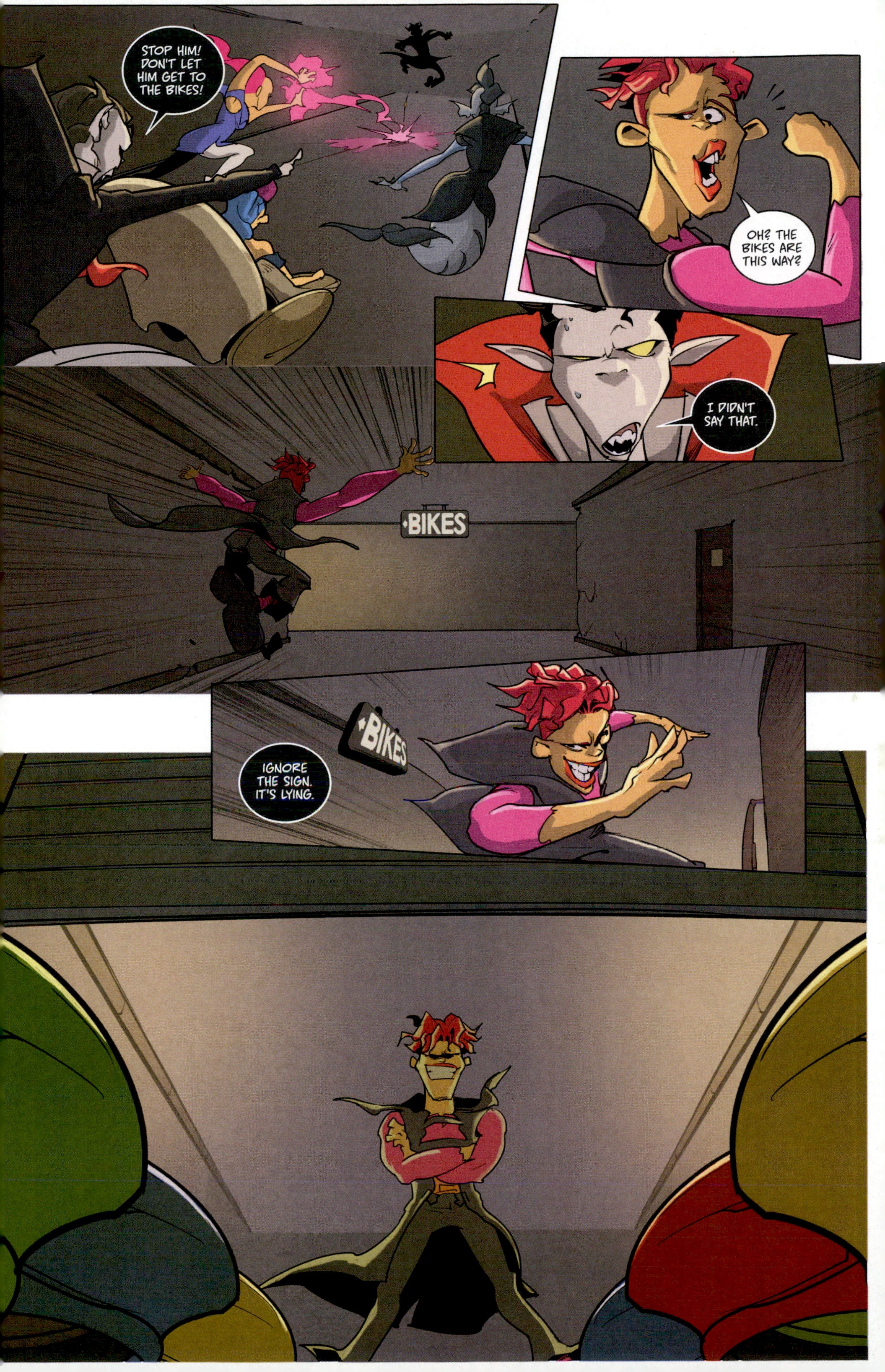
STOP HIM! DON'T LET HIM GET TO THE BIKES!
OH? THE BIKES ARE THIS WAY?
I DIDN'T SAY THAT.
BIKES
BIKES
IGNORE THE SIGN. IT'S LYING.

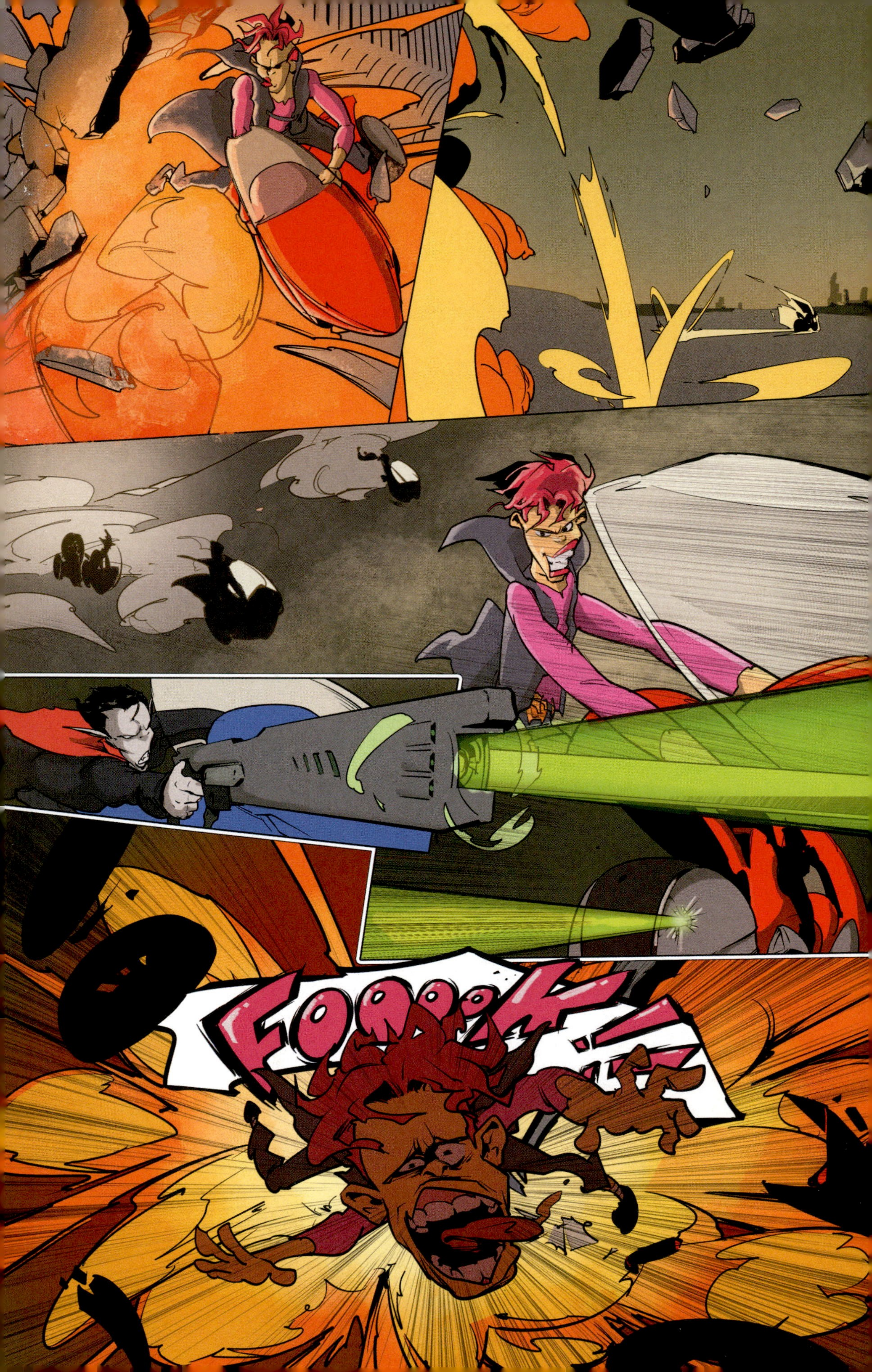
FOOOOK!!

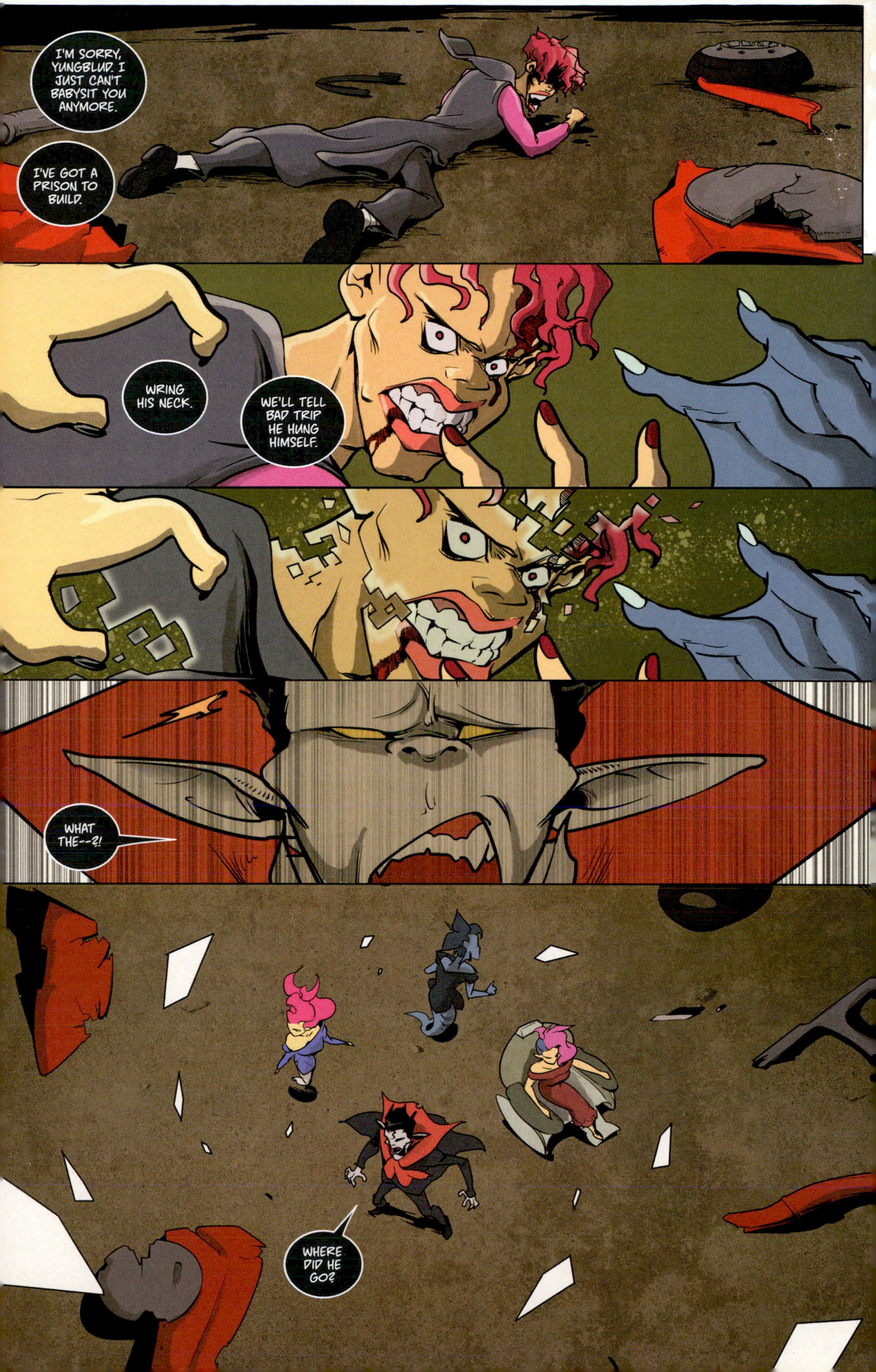
I'M SORRY, YUNGBLUD. I JUST CAN'T BABYSIT YOU ANYMORE.
I'VE GOT A PRISON TO BUILD.
WRING HIS NECK.
WE'LL TELL BAD TRIP HE HUNG HIMSELF.
WHAT THE--?!
WHERE DID HE GO?

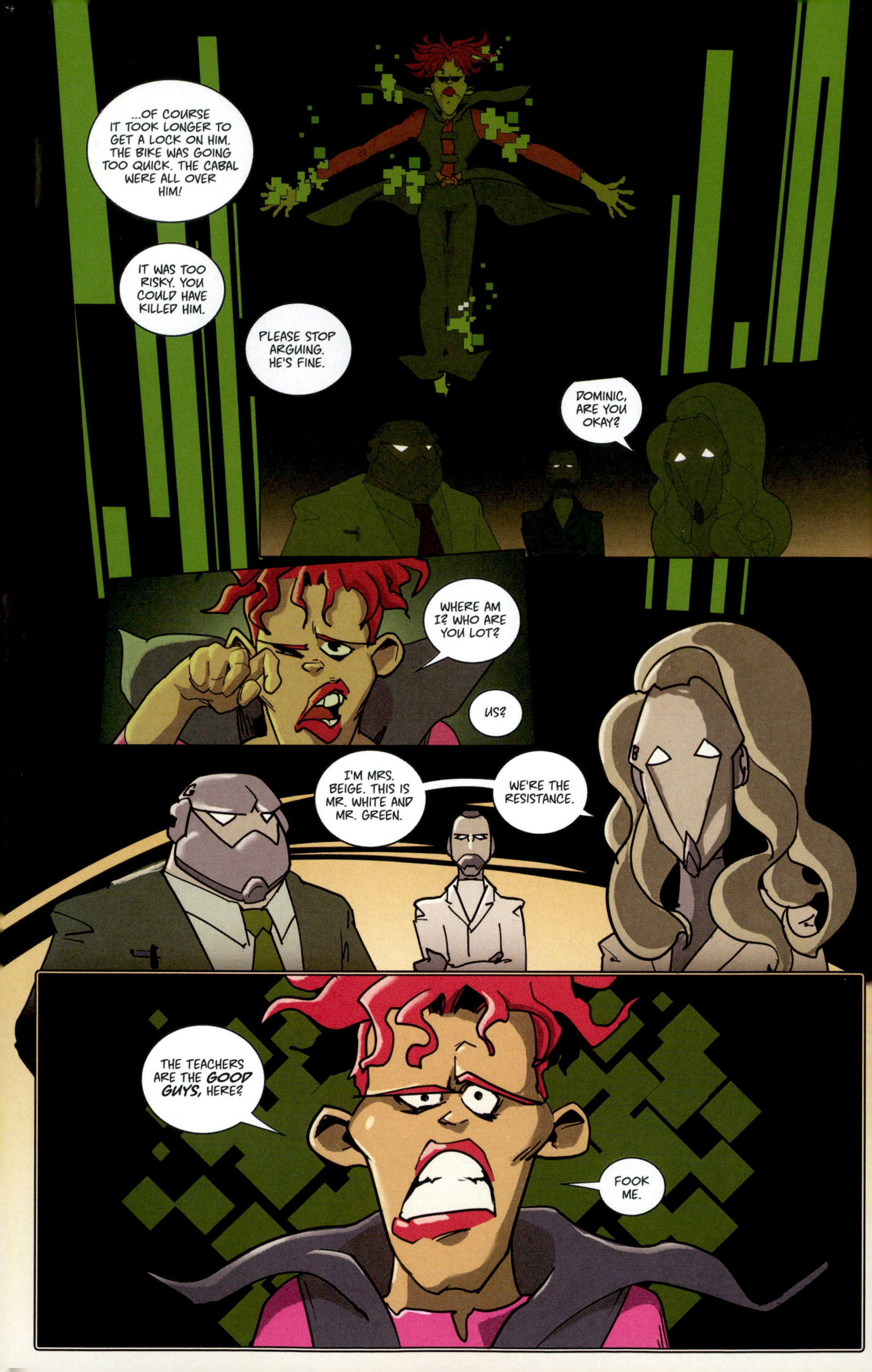
...OF COURSE IT TOOK LONGER TO GET A LOCK ON HIM. THE BIKE WAS GOING TOO QUICK. THE CABAL WERE ALL OVER HIM!
IT WAS TOO RISKY. YOU COULD HAVE KILLED HIM.
PLEASE STOP ARGUING. HE'S FINE.
DOMINIC, ARE YOU OKAY?
WHERE AM I? WHO ARE YOU LOT?
US?
I'M MRS. BEIGE. THIS IS MR. WHITE AND MR. GREEN.
WE'RE THE RESISTANCE.
THE TEACHERS ARE THE *GOOD GUYS*, HERE?
FOOK ME.

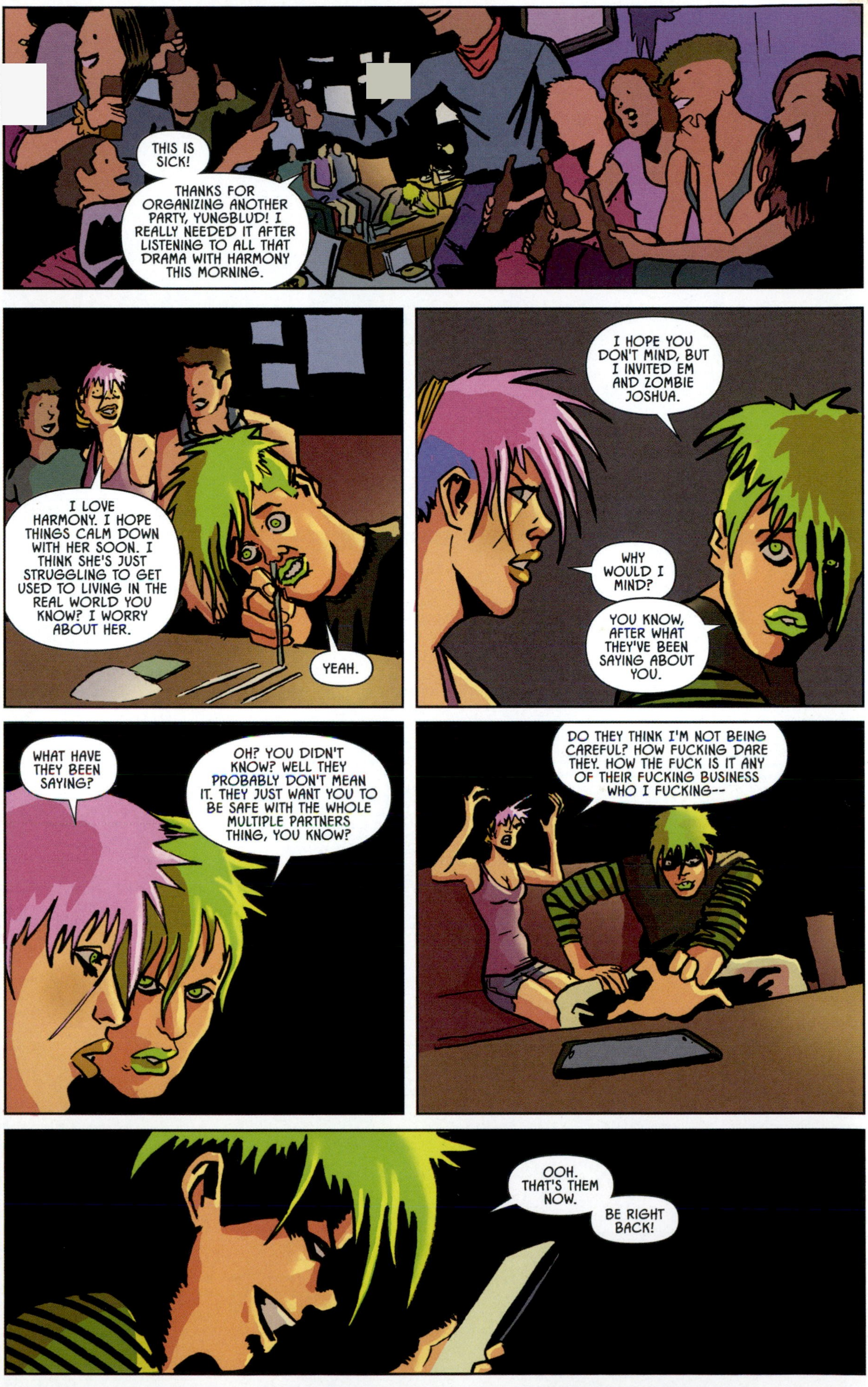
THIS IS SICK!
THANKS FOR ORGANIZING ANOTHER PARTY, YUNGBLUD! I REALLY NEEDED IT AFTER LISTENING TO ALL THAT DRAMA WITH HARMONY THIS MORNING.
I LOVE HARMONY. I HOPE THINGS CALM DOWN WITH HER SOON. I THINK SHE'S JUST STRUGGLING TO GET USED TO LIVING IN THE REAL WORLD YOU KNOW? I WORRY ABOUT HER.
YEAH.
I HOPE YOU DON'T MIND, BUT I INVITED EM AND ZOMBIE JOSHUA.
WHY WOULD I MIND?
YOU KNOW, AFTER WHAT THEY'VE BEEN SAYING ABOUT YOU.
WHAT HAVE THEY BEEN SAYING?
OH? YOU DIDN'T KNOW? WELL THEY PROBABLY DON'T MEAN IT. THEY JUST WANT YOU TO BE SAFE WITH THE WHOLE MULTIPLE PARTNERS THING, YOU KNOW?
DO THEY THINK I'M NOT BEING CAREFUL? HOW FUCKING DARE THEY. HOW THE FUCK IS IT ANY OF THEIR FUCKING BUSINESS WHO I FUCKING--
OOH. THAT'S THEM NOW.
BE RIGHT BACK!

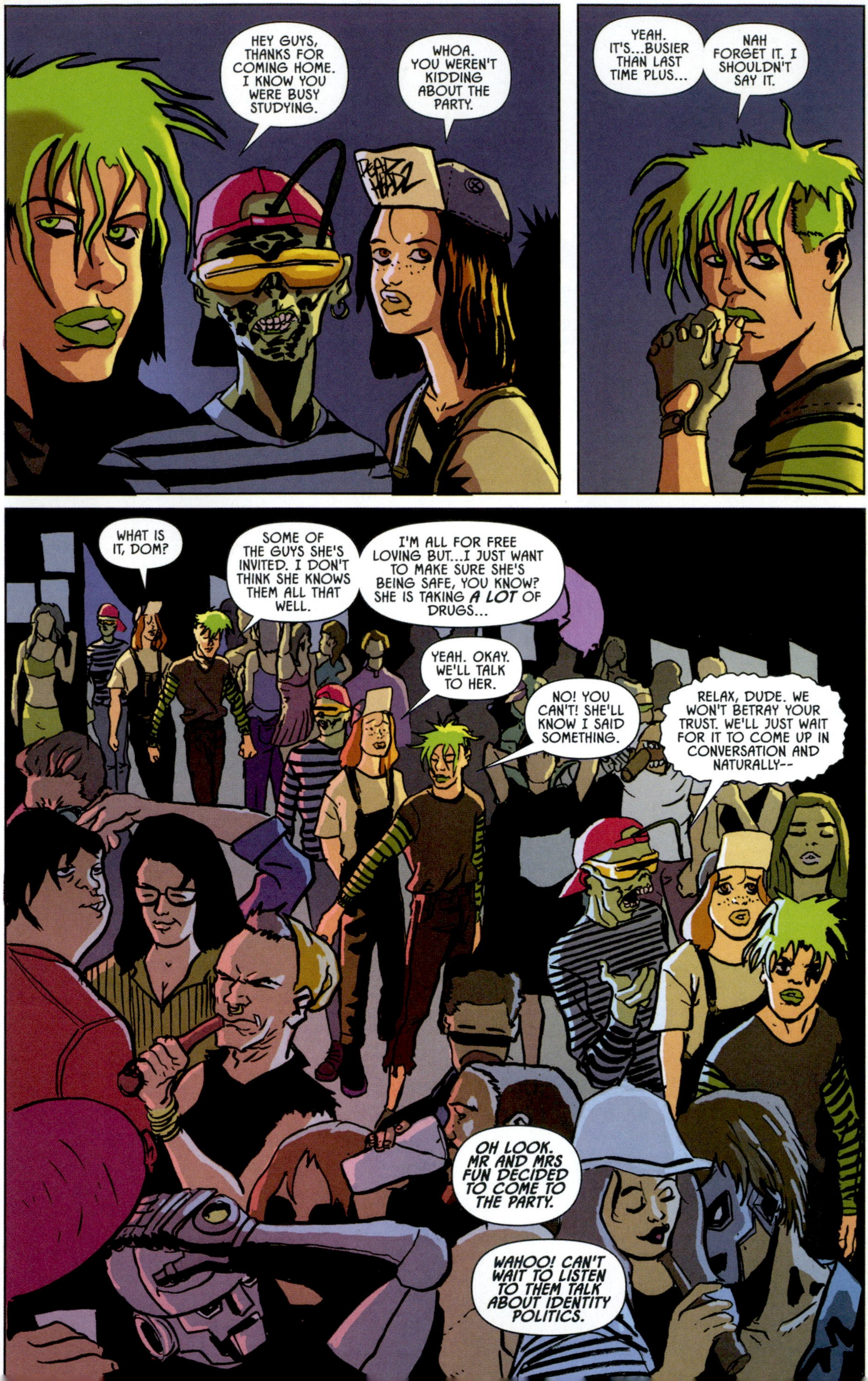

HEY GUYS, THANKS FOR COMING HOME. I KNOW YOU WERE BUSY STUDYING.
WHOA. YOU WEREN'T KIDDING ABOUT THE PARTY.
YEAH. IT'S...BUSIER THAN LAST TIME PLUS...
NAH FORGET IT. I SHOULDN'T SAY IT.
WHAT IS IT, DOM?
SOME OF THE GUYS SHE'S INVITED. I DON'T THINK SHE KNOWS THEM ALL THAT WELL.
I'M ALL FOR FREE LOVING BUT...I JUST WANT TO MAKE SURE SHE'S BEING SAFE, YOU KNOW? SHE IS TAKING **A LOT** OF DRUGS...
YEAH. OKAY. WE'LL TALK TO HER.
NO! YOU CAN'T! SHE'LL KNOW I SAID SOMETHING.
RELAX, DUDE. WE WON'T BETRAY YOUR TRUST. WE'LL JUST WAIT FOR IT TO COME UP IN CONVERSATION AND NATURALLY--
OH LOOK. MR AND MRS FUN DECIDED TO COME TO THE PARTY.
WAHOO! CAN'T WAIT TO LISTEN TO THEM TALK ABOUT IDENTITY POLITICS.

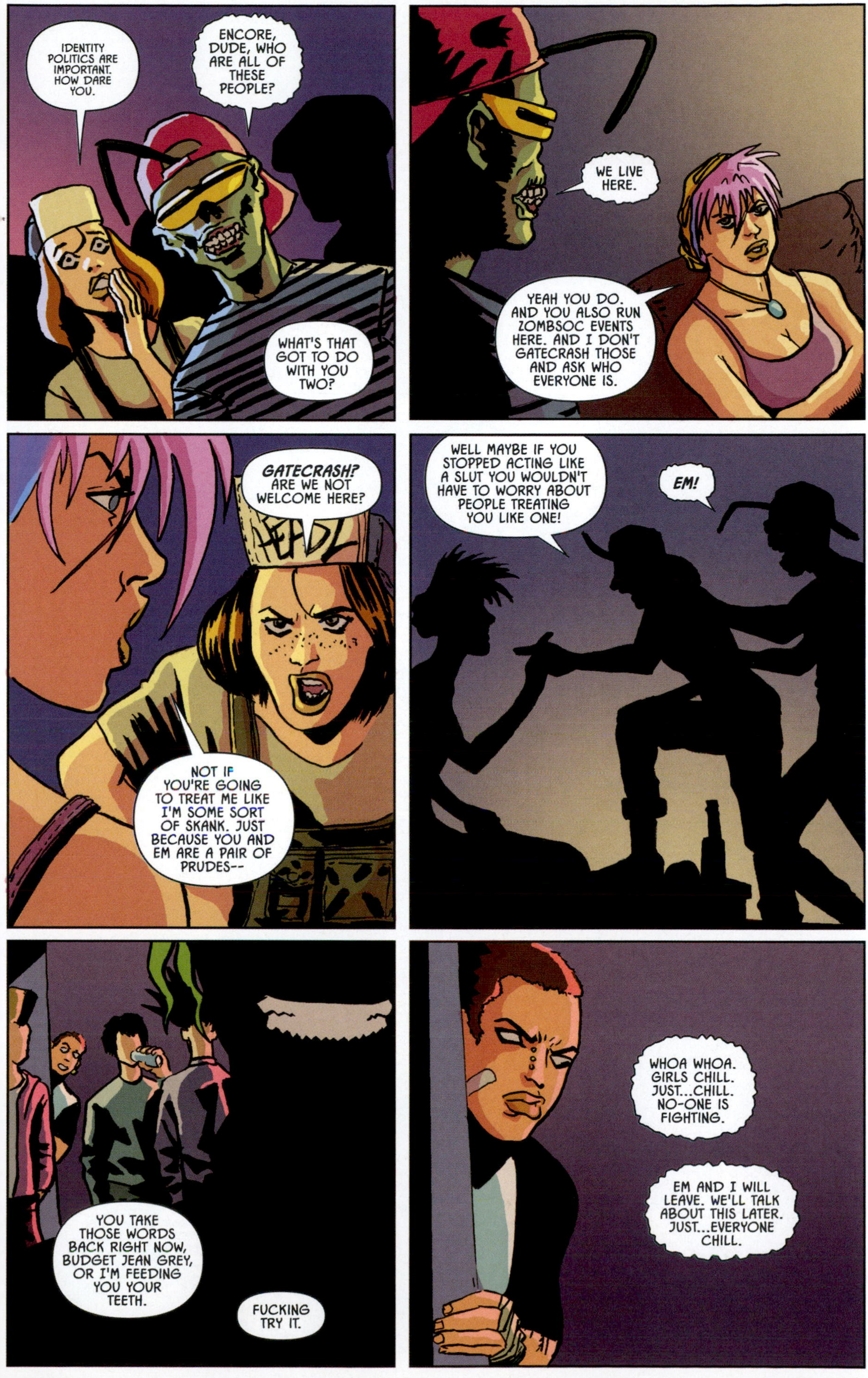
IDENTITY POLITICS ARE IMPORTANT. HOW DARE YOU.
ENCORE, DUDE, WHO ARE ALL OF THESE PEOPLE?
WHAT'S THAT GOT TO DO WITH YOU TWO?
WE LIVE HERE.
YEAH YOU DO. AND YOU ALSO RUN ZOMBSOC EVENTS HERE. AND I DON'T GATECRASH THOSE AND ASK WHO EVERYONE IS.
GATECRASH? ARE WE NOT WELCOME HERE?
NOT IF YOU'RE GOING TO TREAT ME LIKE I'M SOME SORT OF SKANK. JUST BECAUSE YOU AND EM ARE A PAIR OF PRUDES--
WELL MAYBE IF YOU STOPPED ACTING LIKE A SLUT YOU WOULDN'T HAVE TO WORRY ABOUT PEOPLE TREATING YOU LIKE ONE!
EM!
YOU TAKE THOSE WORDS BACK RIGHT NOW, BUDGET JEAN GREY, OR I'M FEEDING YOU YOUR TEETH.
FUCKING TRY IT.
WHOA WHOA. GIRLS CHILL. JUST...CHILL. NO-ONE IS FIGHTING.
EM AND I WILL LEAVE. WE'LL TALK ABOUT THIS LATER. JUST...EVERYONE CHILL.

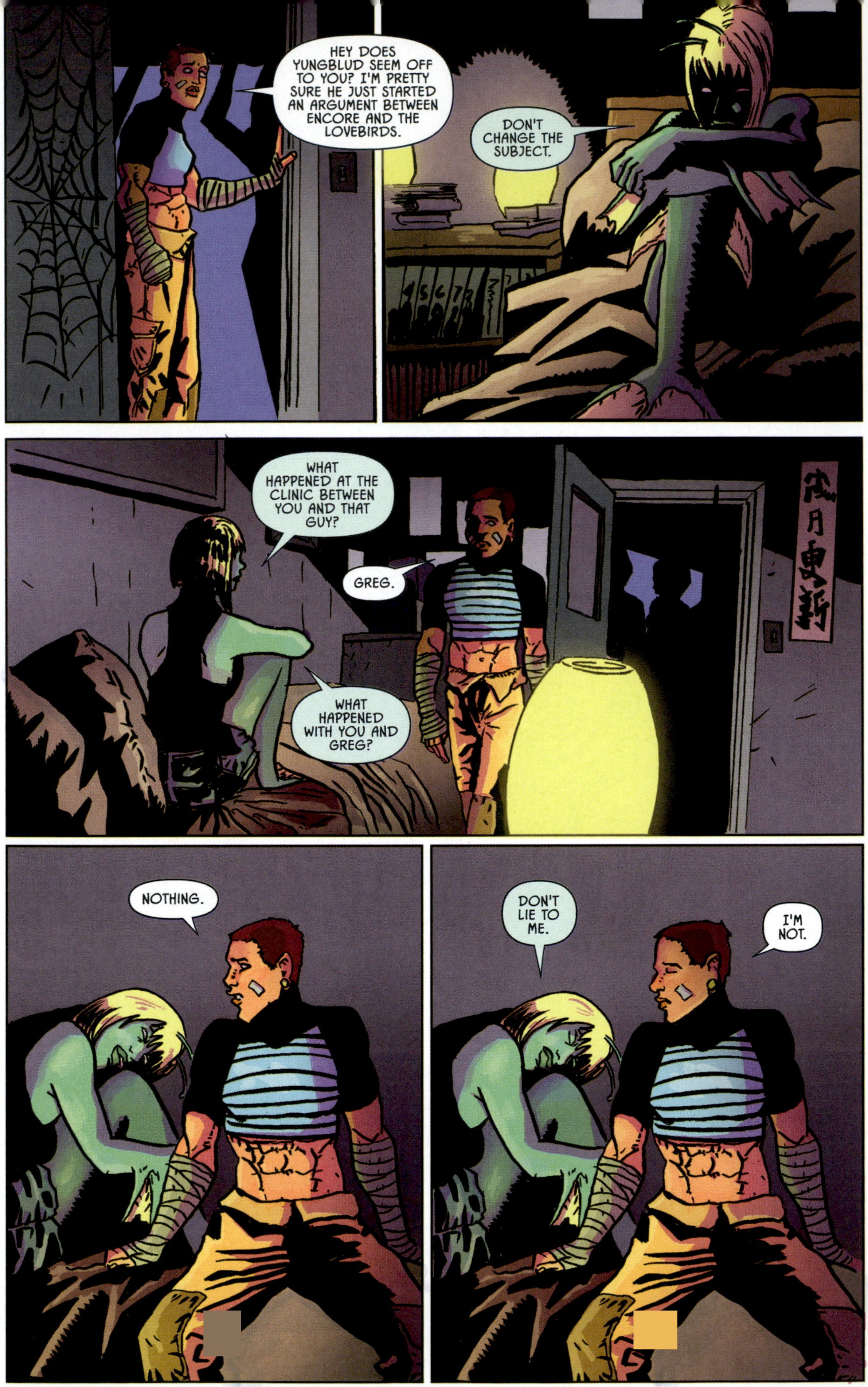
HEY DOES YUNGBLUD SEEM OFF TO YOU? I'M PRETTY SURE HE JUST STARTED AN ARGUMENT BETWEEN ENCORE AND THE LOVEBIRDS.
DON'T CHANGE THE SUBJECT.
WHAT HAPPENED AT THE CLINIC BETWEEN YOU AND THAT GUY?
GREG.
WHAT HAPPENED WITH YOU AND GREG?
NOTHING.
DON'T LIE TO ME.
I'M NOT.

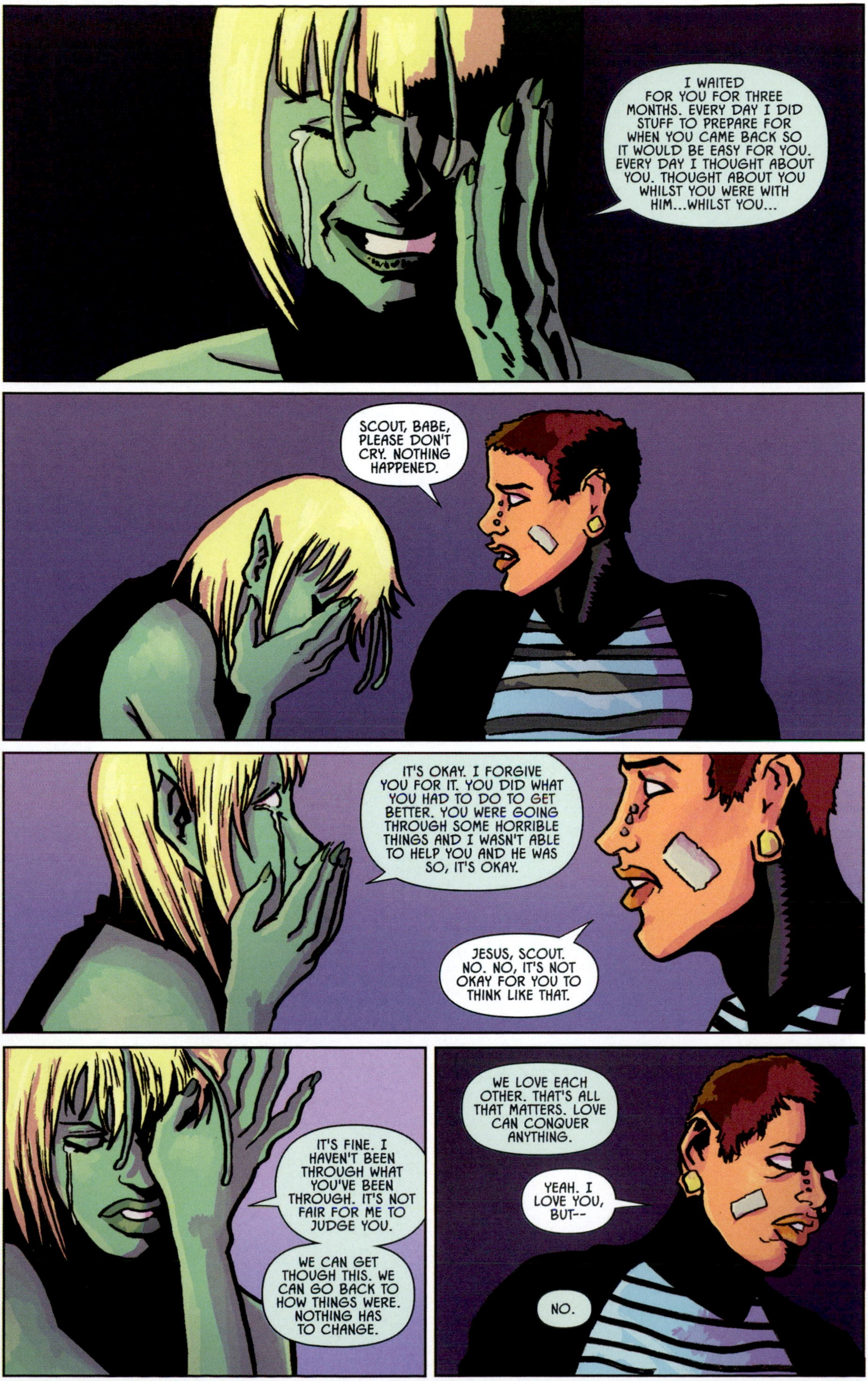
I WAITED FOR YOU FOR THREE MONTHS. EVERY DAY I DID STUFF TO PREPARE FOR WHEN YOU CAME BACK SO IT WOULD BE EASY FOR YOU. EVERY DAY I THOUGHT ABOUT YOU. THOUGHT ABOUT YOU WHILST YOU WERE WITH HIM...WHILST YOU...
SCOUT, BABE, PLEASE DON'T CRY. NOTHING HAPPENED.
IT'S OKAY. I FORGIVE YOU FOR IT. YOU DID WHAT YOU HAD TO DO TO GET BETTER. YOU WERE GOING THROUGH SOME HORRIBLE THINGS AND I WASN'T ABLE TO HELP YOU AND HE WAS SO, IT'S OKAY.
JESUS, SCOUT. NO. NO, IT'S NOT OKAY FOR YOU TO THINK LIKE THAT.
IT'S FINE. I HAVEN'T BEEN THROUGH WHAT YOU'VE BEEN THROUGH. IT'S NOT FAIR FOR ME TO JUDGE YOU.
WE CAN GET THOUGH THIS. WE CAN GO BACK TO HOW THINGS WERE. NOTHING HAS TO CHANGE.
WE LOVE EACH OTHER. THAT'S ALL THAT MATTERS. LOVE CAN CONQUER ANYTHING.
YEAH. I LOVE YOU, BUT--
NO.

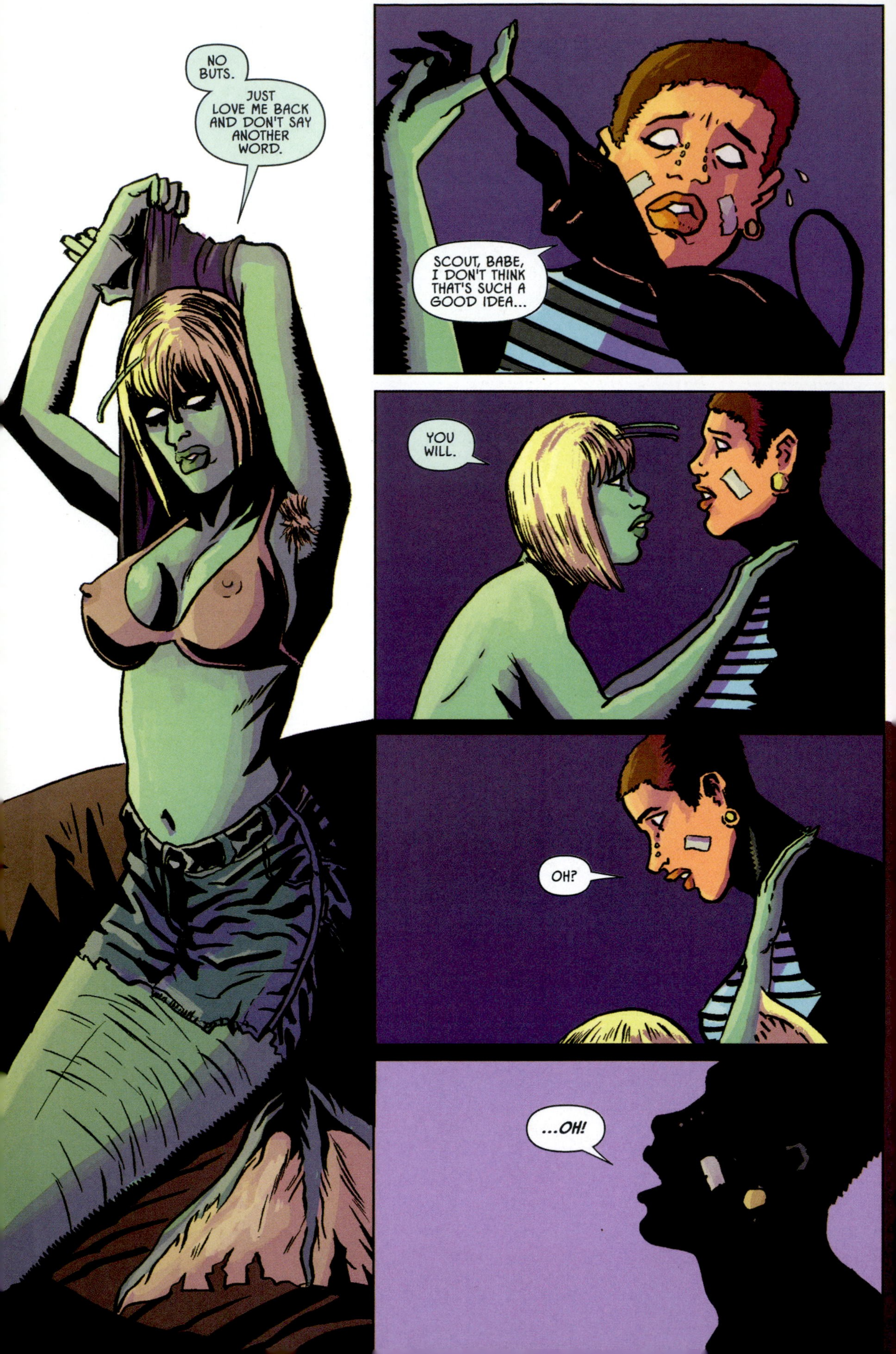
NO BUTS.
JUST LOVE ME BACK AND DON'T SAY ANOTHER WORD.
SCOUT, BABE, I DON'T THINK THAT'S SUCH A GOOD IDEA...
YOU WILL.
OH?
...OH!

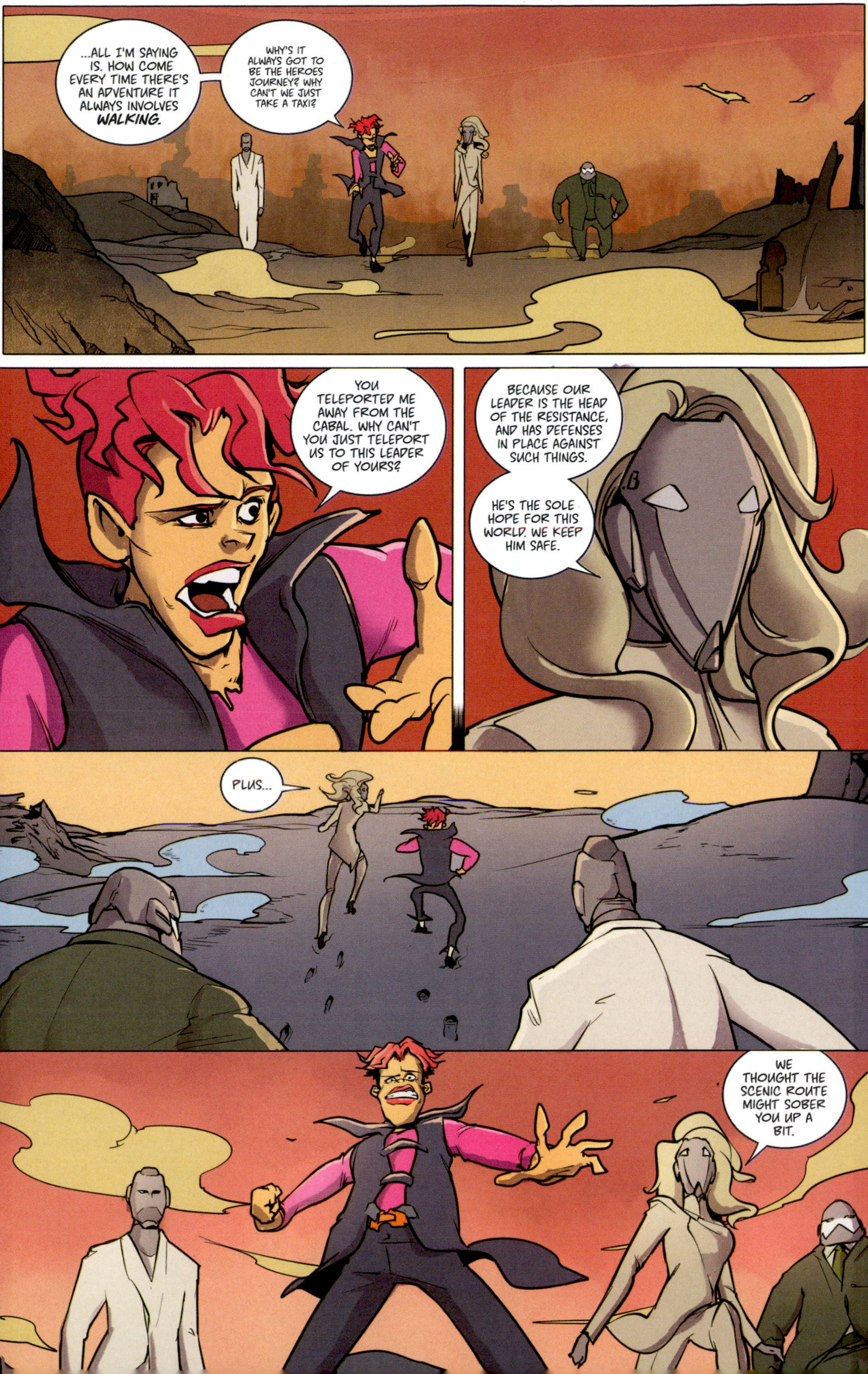
...ALL I'M SAYING IS. HOW COME EVERY TIME THERE'S AN ADVENTURE IT ALWAYS INVOLVES **WALKING.**
WHY'S IT ALWAYS GOT TO BE THE HEROES JOURNEY? WHY CAN'T WE JUST TAKE A TAXI?
YOU TELEPORTED ME AWAY FROM THE CABAL. WHY CAN'T YOU JUST TELEPORT US TO THIS LEADER OF YOURS?
BECAUSE OUR LEADER IS THE HEAD OF THE RESISTANCE, AND HAS DEFENSES IN PLACE AGAINST SUCH THINGS.
HE'S THE SOLE HOPE FOR THIS WORLD. WE KEEP HIM SAFE.
PLUS...
WE THOUGHT THE SCENIC ROUTE MIGHT SOBER YOU UP A BIT.

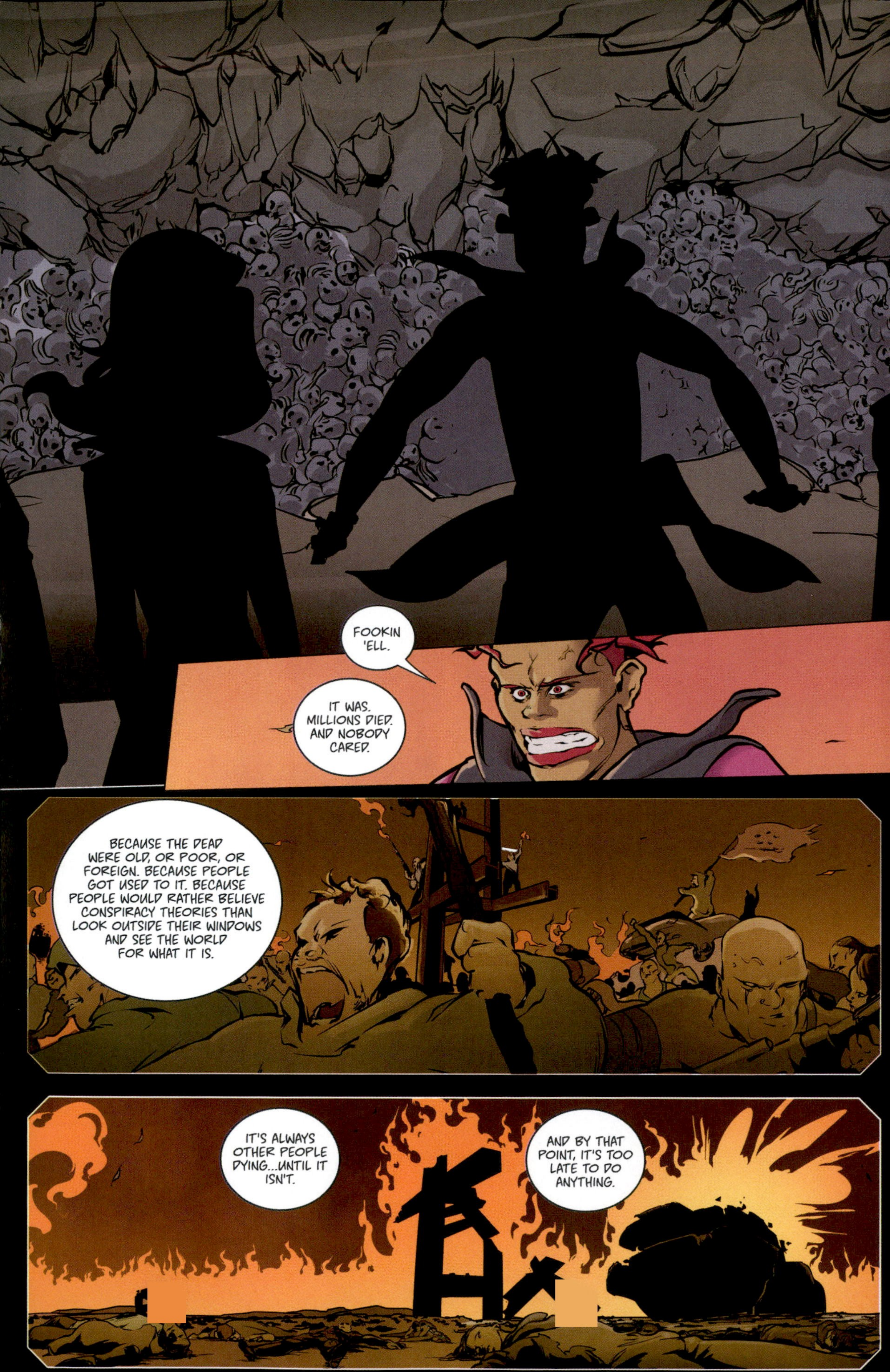
FOOKIN 'ELL.
IT WAS. MILLIONS DIED. AND NOBODY CARED.
BECAUSE THE DEAD WERE OLD, OR POOR, OR FOREIGN. BECAUSE PEOPLE GOT USED TO IT. BECAUSE PEOPLE WOULD RATHER BELIEVE CONSPIRACY THEORIES THAN LOOK OUTSIDE THEIR WINDOWS AND SEE THE WORLD FOR WHAT IT IS.
IT'S ALWAYS OTHER PEOPLE DYING...UNTIL IT ISN'T.
AND BY THAT POINT, IT'S TOO LATE TO DO ANYTHING.

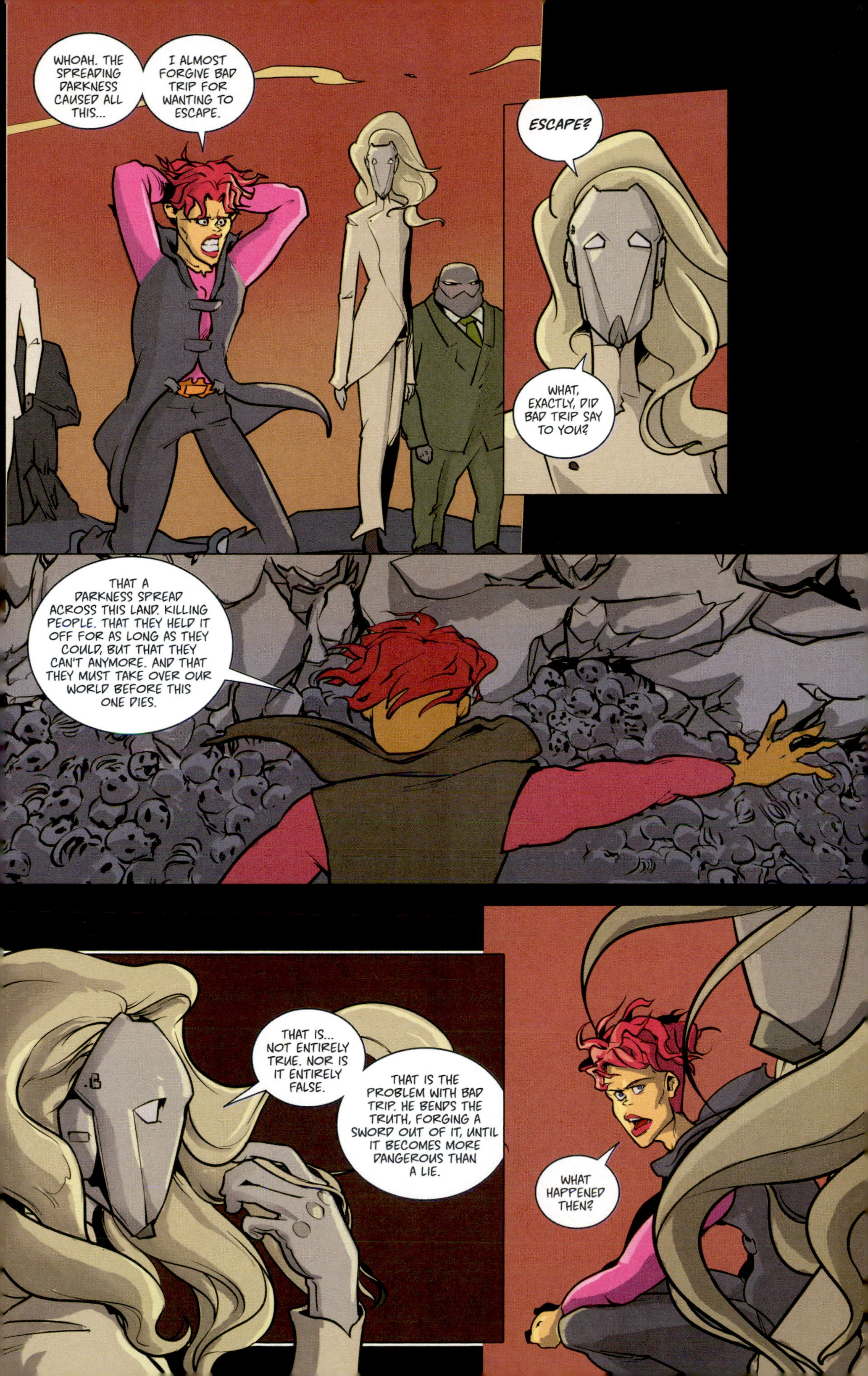
WHOAH. THE SPREADING DARKNESS CAUSED ALL THIS...
I ALMOST FORGIVE BAD TRIP FOR WANTING TO ESCAPE.
ESCAPE?
WHAT, EXACTLY, DID BAD TRIP SAY TO YOU?
THAT A DARKNESS SPREAD ACROSS THIS LAND, KILLING PEOPLE. THAT THEY HELD IT OFF FOR AS LONG AS THEY COULD, BUT THAT THEY CAN'T ANYMORE. AND THAT THEY MUST TAKE OVER OUR WORLD BEFORE THIS ONE DIES.
THAT IS... NOT ENTIRELY TRUE. NOR IS IT ENTIRELY FALSE.
THAT IS THE PROBLEM WITH BAD TRIP. HE BENDS THE TRUTH, FORGING A SWORD OUT OF IT, UNTIL IT BECOMES MORE DANGEROUS THAN A LIE.
WHAT HAPPENED THEN?

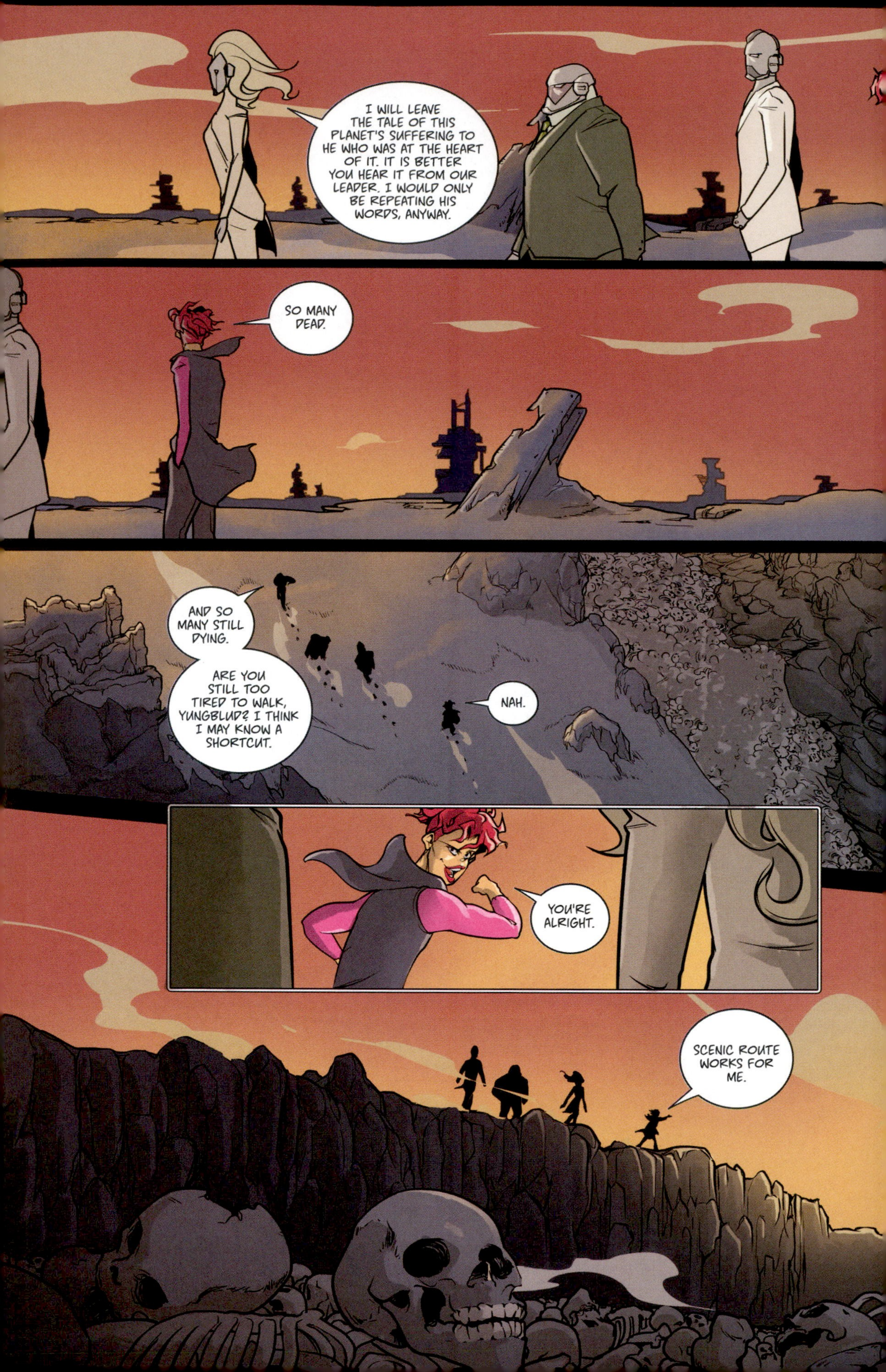
I WILL LEAVE THE TALE OF THIS PLANET'S SUFFERING TO HE WHO WAS AT THE HEART OF IT. IT IS BETTER YOU HEAR IT FROM OUR LEADER. I WOULD ONLY BE REPEATING HIS WORDS, ANYWAY.
SO MANY DEAD.
AND SO MANY STILL DYING.
ARE YOU STILL TOO TIRED TO WALK, YUNGBLUD? I THINK I MAY KNOW A SHORTCUT.
NAH.
YOU'RE ALRIGHT.
SCENIC ROUTE WORKS FOR ME.

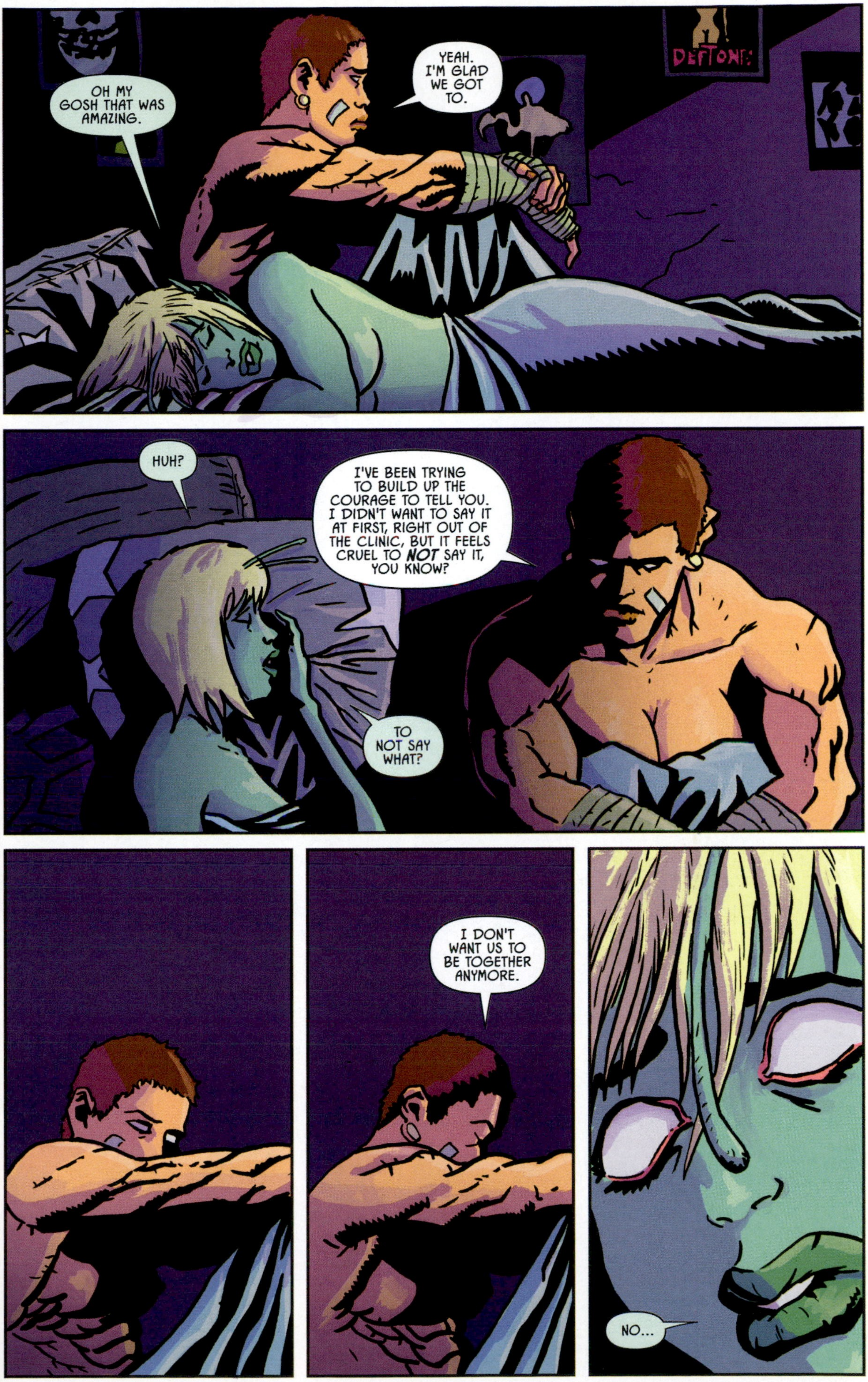
OH MY GOSH THAT WAS AMAZING.
YEAH. I'M GLAD WE GOT TO.
DEFTONES
HUH?
I'VE BEEN TRYING TO BUILD UP THE COURAGE TO TELL YOU. I DIDN'T WANT TO SAY IT AT FIRST, RIGHT OUT OF THE CLINIC, BUT IT FEELS CRUEL TO NOT SAY IT, YOU KNOW?
TO NOT SAY WHAT?
I DON'T WANT US TO BE TOGETHER ANYMORE.
NO...

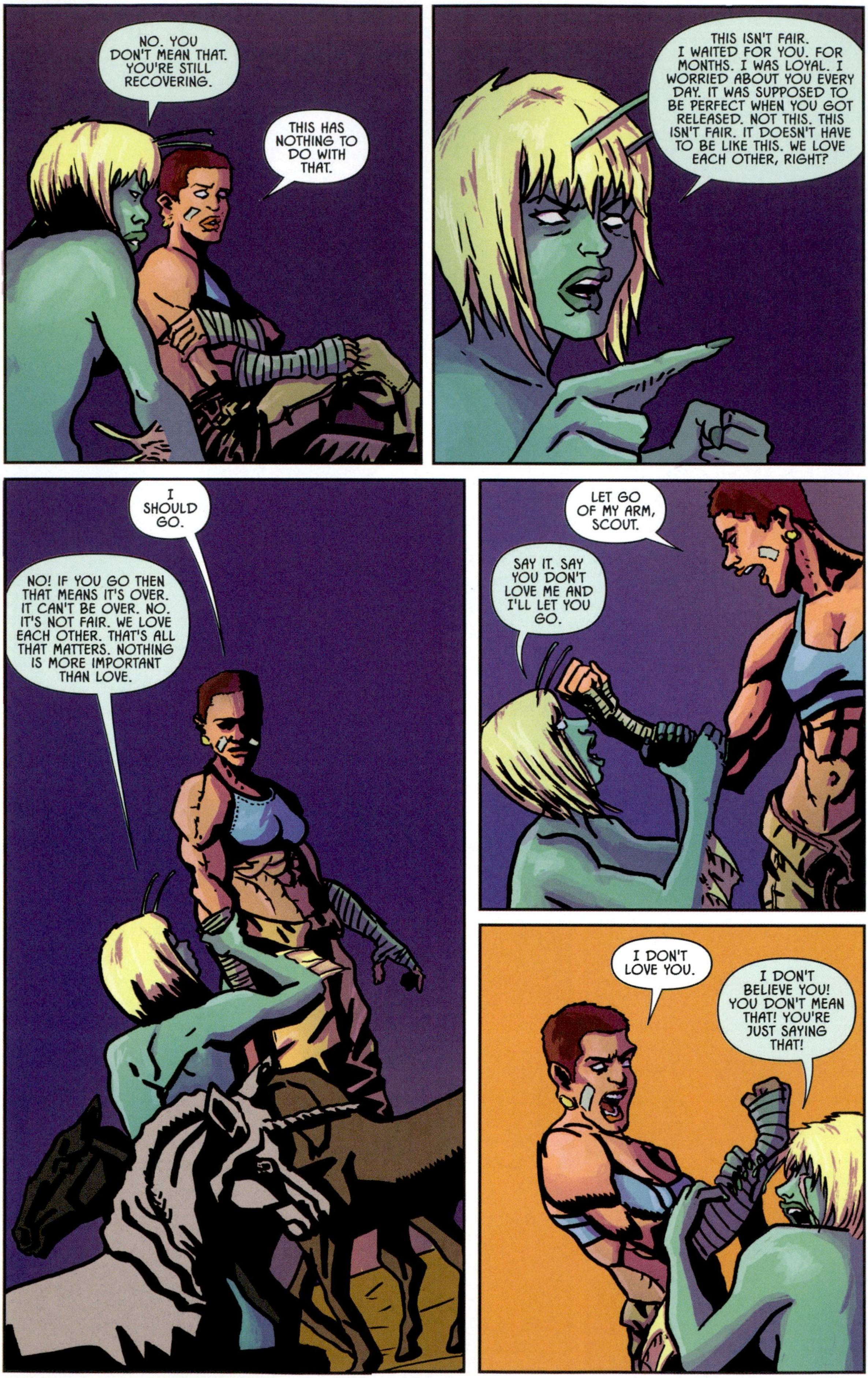
NO. YOU DON'T MEAN THAT. YOU'RE STILL RECOVERING.
THIS HAS NOTHING TO DO WITH THAT.
THIS ISN'T FAIR. I WAITED FOR YOU. FOR MONTHS. I WAS LOYAL. I WORRIED ABOUT YOU EVERY DAY. IT WAS SUPPOSED TO BE PERFECT WHEN YOU GOT RELEASED. NOT THIS. THIS ISN'T FAIR. IT DOESN'T HAVE TO BE LIKE THIS. WE LOVE EACH OTHER, RIGHT?
I SHOULD GO.
NO! IF YOU GO THEN THAT MEANS IT'S OVER. IT CAN'T BE OVER. NO. IT'S NOT FAIR. WE LOVE EACH OTHER. THAT'S ALL THAT MATTERS. NOTHING IS MORE IMPORTANT THAN LOVE.
LET GO OF MY ARM, SCOUT.
SAY IT. SAY YOU DON'T LOVE ME AND I'LL LET YOU GO.
I DON'T LOVE YOU.
I DON'T BELIEVE YOU! YOU DON'T MEAN THAT! YOU'RE JUST SAYING THAT!

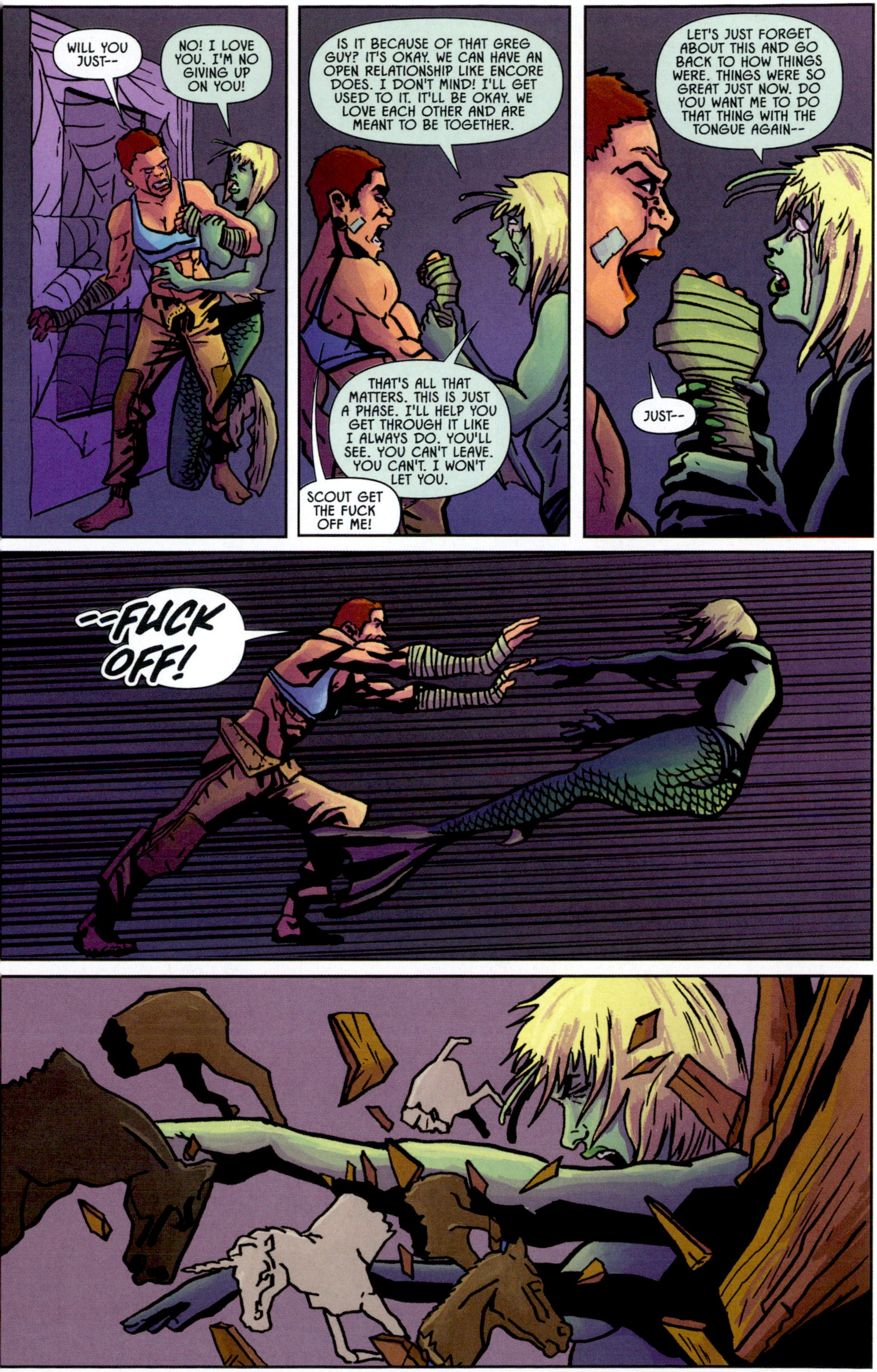
WILL YOU JUST--
NO! I LOVE YOU. I'M NO GIVING UP ON YOU!
IS IT BECAUSE OF THAT GREG GUY? IT'S OKAY. WE CAN HAVE AN OPEN RELATIONSHIP LIKE ENCORE DOES. I DON'T MIND! I'LL GET USED TO IT. IT'LL BE OKAY. WE LOVE EACH OTHER AND ARE MEANT TO BE TOGETHER.
THAT'S ALL THAT MATTERS. THIS IS JUST A PHASE. I'LL HELP YOU GET THROUGH IT LIKE I ALWAYS DO. YOU'LL SEE. YOU CAN'T LEAVE. YOU CAN'T. I WON'T LET YOU.
SCOUT GET THE FUCK OFF ME!
LET'S JUST FORGET ABOUT THIS AND GO BACK TO HOW THINGS WERE. THINGS WERE SO GREAT JUST NOW. DO YOU WANT ME TO DO THAT THING WITH THE TONGUE AGAIN--
JUST--
--FUCK OFF!

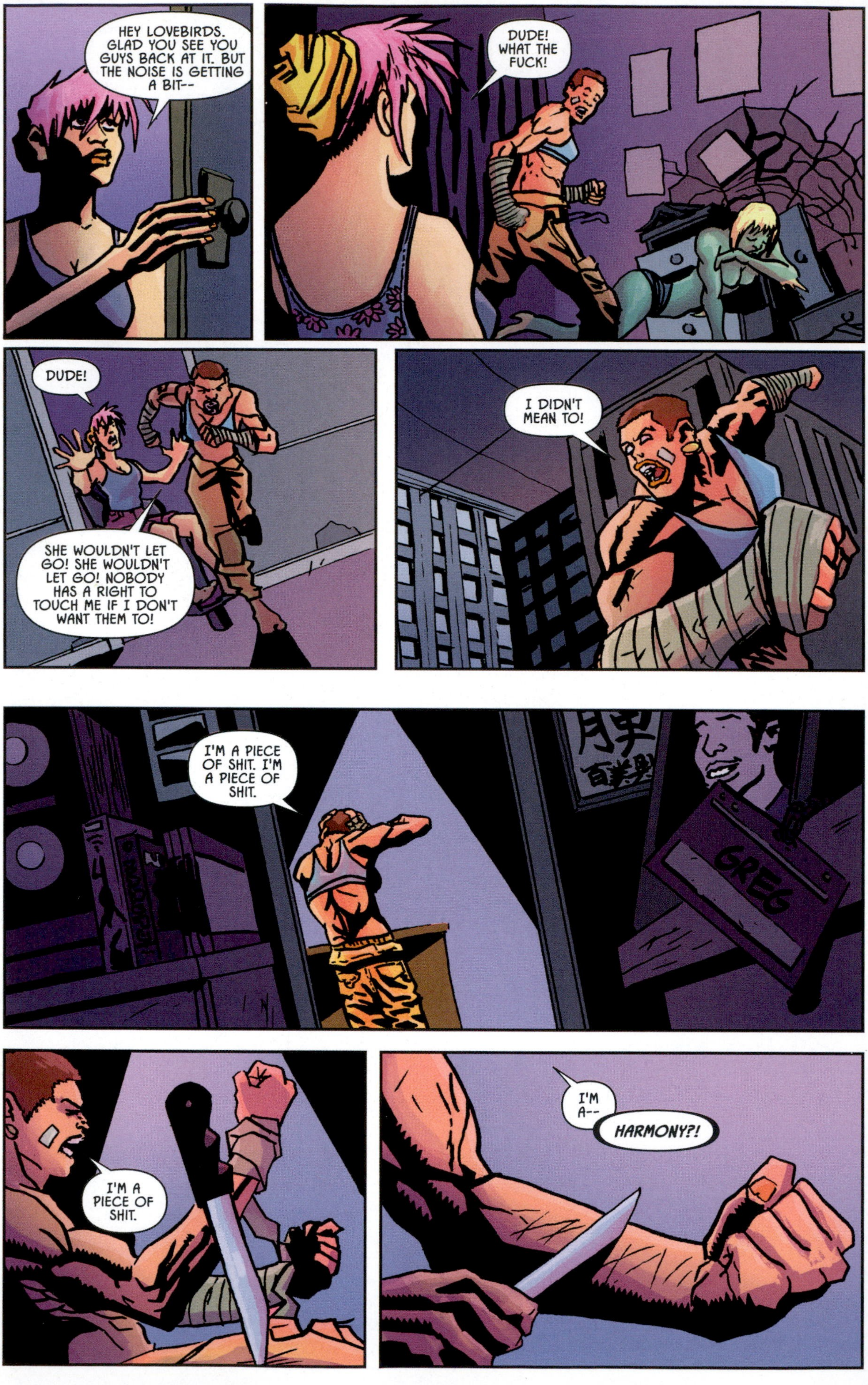
HEY LOVEBIRDS. GLAD YOU SEE YOU GUYS BACK AT IT. BUT THE NOISE IS GETTING A BIT--
DUDE! WHAT THE FUCK!
DUDE!
SHE WOULDN'T LET GO! SHE WOULDN'T LET GO! NOBODY HAS A RIGHT TO TOUCH ME IF I DON'T WANT THEM TO!
I DIDN'T MEAN TO!
I'M A PIECE OF SHIT. I'M A PIECE OF SHIT.
GREG
I'M A PIECE OF SHIT.
I'M A--
HARMONY?!

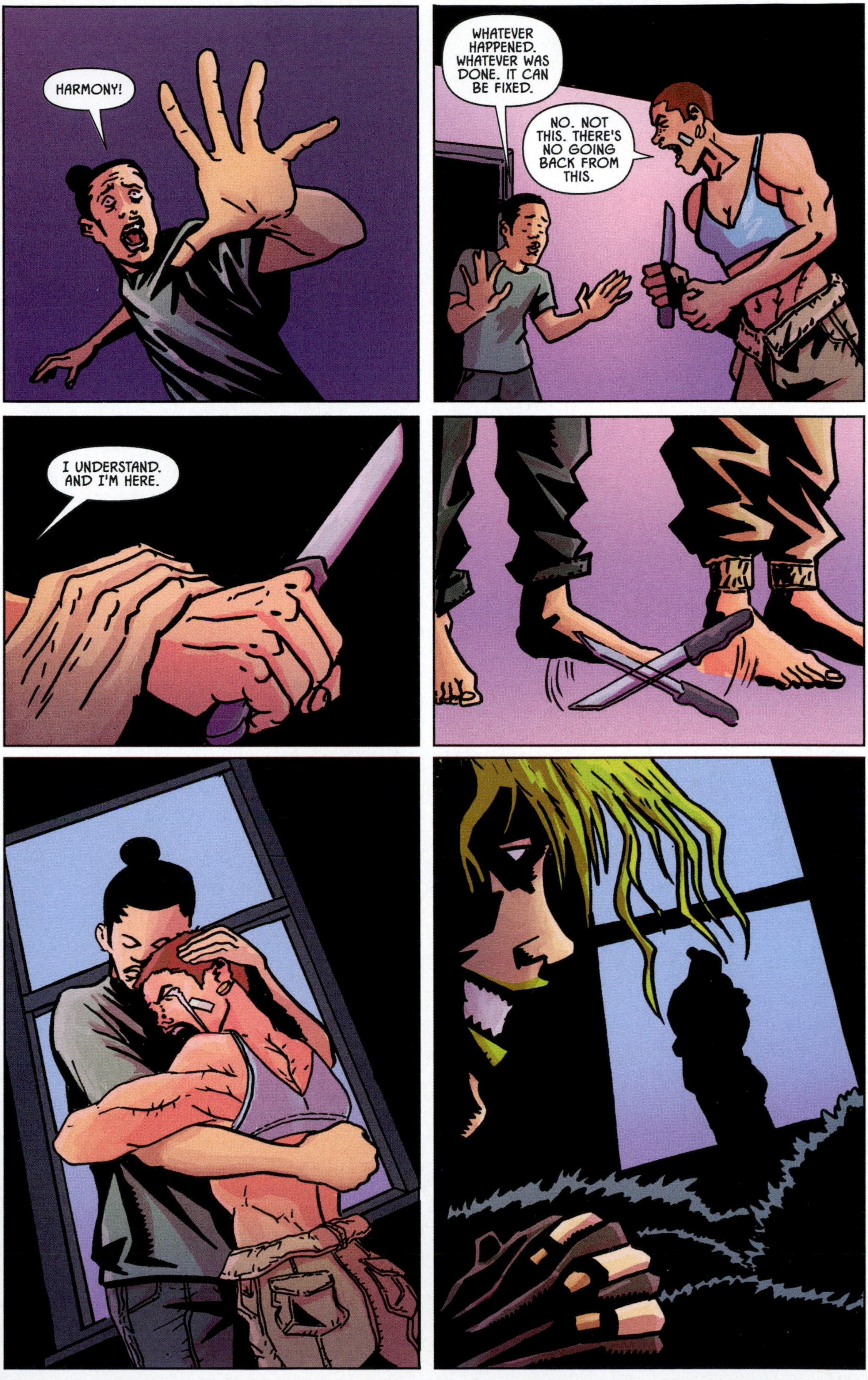
HARMONY!
WHATEVER HAPPENED. WHATEVER WAS DONE. IT CAN BE FIXED.
NO. NOT THIS. THERE'S NO GOING BACK FROM THIS.
I UNDERSTAND. AND I'M HERE.

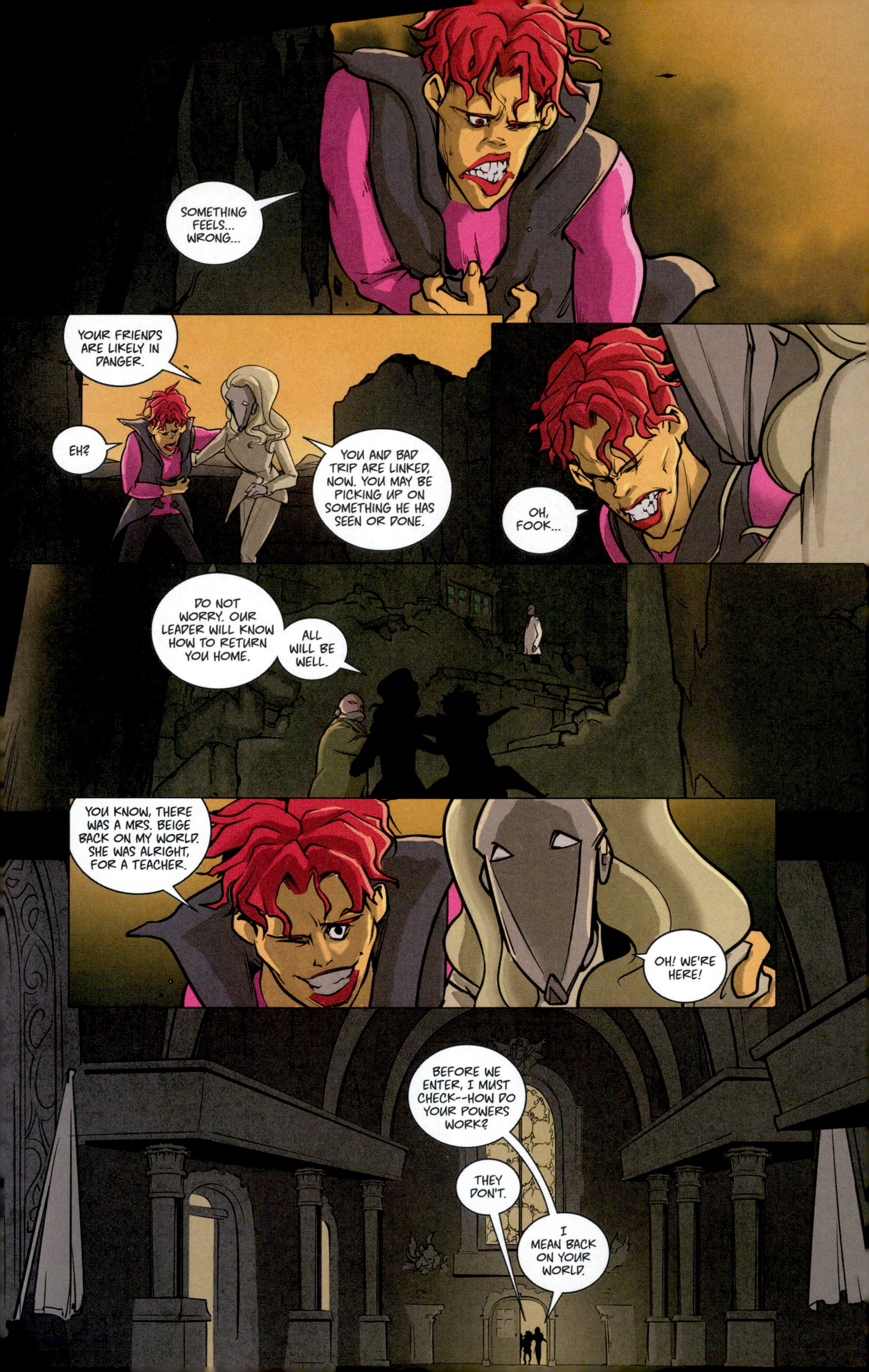

SOMETHING FEELS... WRONG...
YOUR FRIENDS ARE LIKELY IN DANGER.
EH?
YOU AND BAD TRIP ARE LINKED, NOW. YOU MAY BE PICKING UP ON SOMETHING HE HAS SEEN OR DONE.
OH, FOOK...
DO NOT WORRY. OUR LEADER WILL KNOW HOW TO RETURN YOU HOME.
ALL WILL BE WELL.
YOU KNOW, THERE WAS A MRS. BEIGE BACK ON MY WORLD. SHE WAS ALRIGHT, FOR A TEACHER.
OH! WE'RE HERE!
BEFORE WE ENTER, I MUST CHECK--HOW DO YOUR POWERS WORK?
THEY DON'T.
I MEAN BACK ON YOUR WORLD.

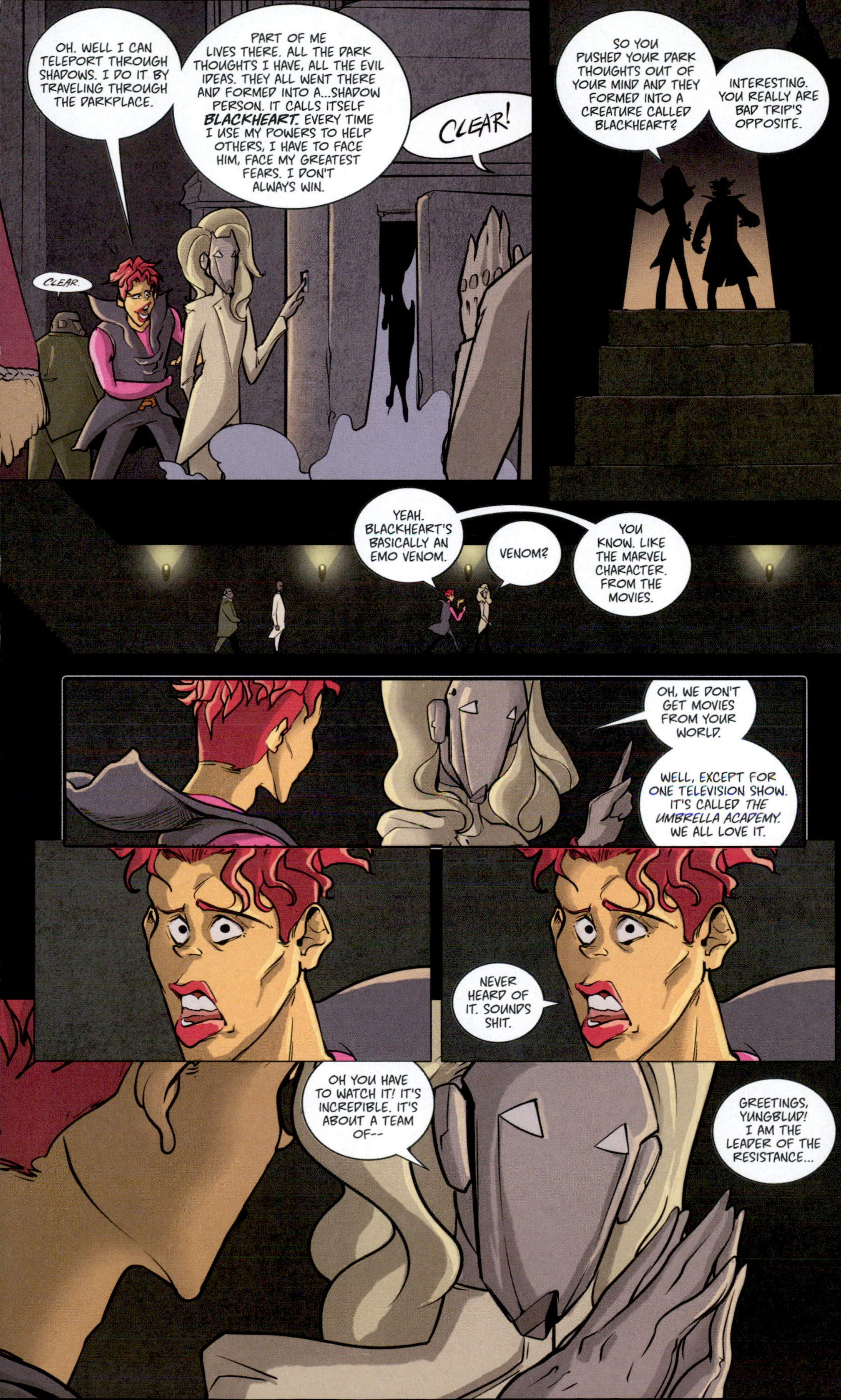
OH. WELL I CAN TELEPORT THROUGH SHADOWS. I DO IT BY TRAVELING THROUGH THE DARKPLACE.
PART OF ME LIVES THERE. ALL THE DARK THOUGHTS I HAVE, ALL THE EVIL IDEAS. THEY ALL WENT THERE AND FORMED INTO A...SHADOW PERSON. IT CALLS ITSELF BLACKHEART. EVERY TIME I USE MY POWERS TO HELP OTHERS, I HAVE TO FACE HIM, FACE MY GREATEST FEARS. I DON'T ALWAYS WIN.
CLEAR!
CLEAR.
SO YOU PUSHED YOUR DARK THOUGHTS OUT OF YOUR MIND AND THEY FORMED INTO A CREATURE CALLED BLACKHEART?
INTERESTING. YOU REALLY ARE BAD TRIP'S OPPOSITE.
YEAH. BLACKHEART'S BASICALLY AN EMO VENOM.
VENOM?
YOU KNOW. LIKE THE MARVEL CHARACTER. FROM THE MOVIES.
OH, WE DON'T GET MOVIES FROM YOUR WORLD.
WELL, EXCEPT FOR ONE TELEVISION SHOW. IT'S CALLED THE UMBRELLA ACADEMY. WE ALL LOVE IT.
NEVER HEARD OF IT. SOUNDS SHIT.
OH YOU HAVE TO WATCH IT! IT'S INCREDIBLE. IT'S ABOUT A TEAM OF--
GREETINGS, YUNGBLUD! I AM THE LEADER OF THE RESISTANCE...

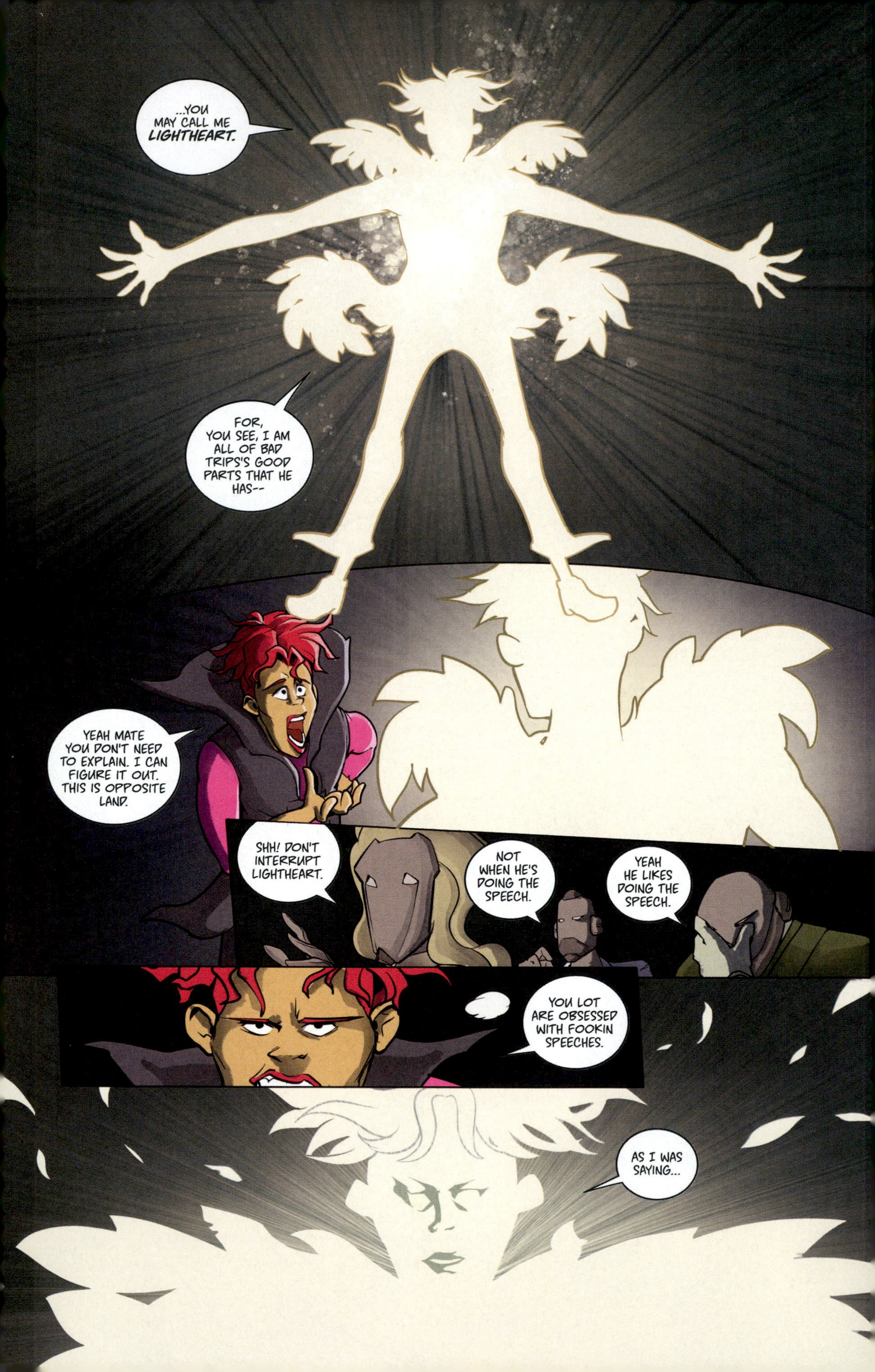
...YOU MAY CALL ME LIGHTHEART.
FOR, YOU SEE, I AM ALL OF BAD TRIPS'S GOOD PARTS THAT HE HAS--
YEAH MATE YOU DON'T NEED TO EXPLAIN. I CAN FIGURE IT OUT. THIS IS OPPOSITE LAND.
SHH! DON'T INTERRUPT LIGHTHEART.
NOT WHEN HE'S DOING THE SPEECH.
YEAH HE LIKES DOING THE SPEECH.
YOU LOT ARE OBSESSED WITH FOOKIN SPEECHES.
AS I WAS SAYING...

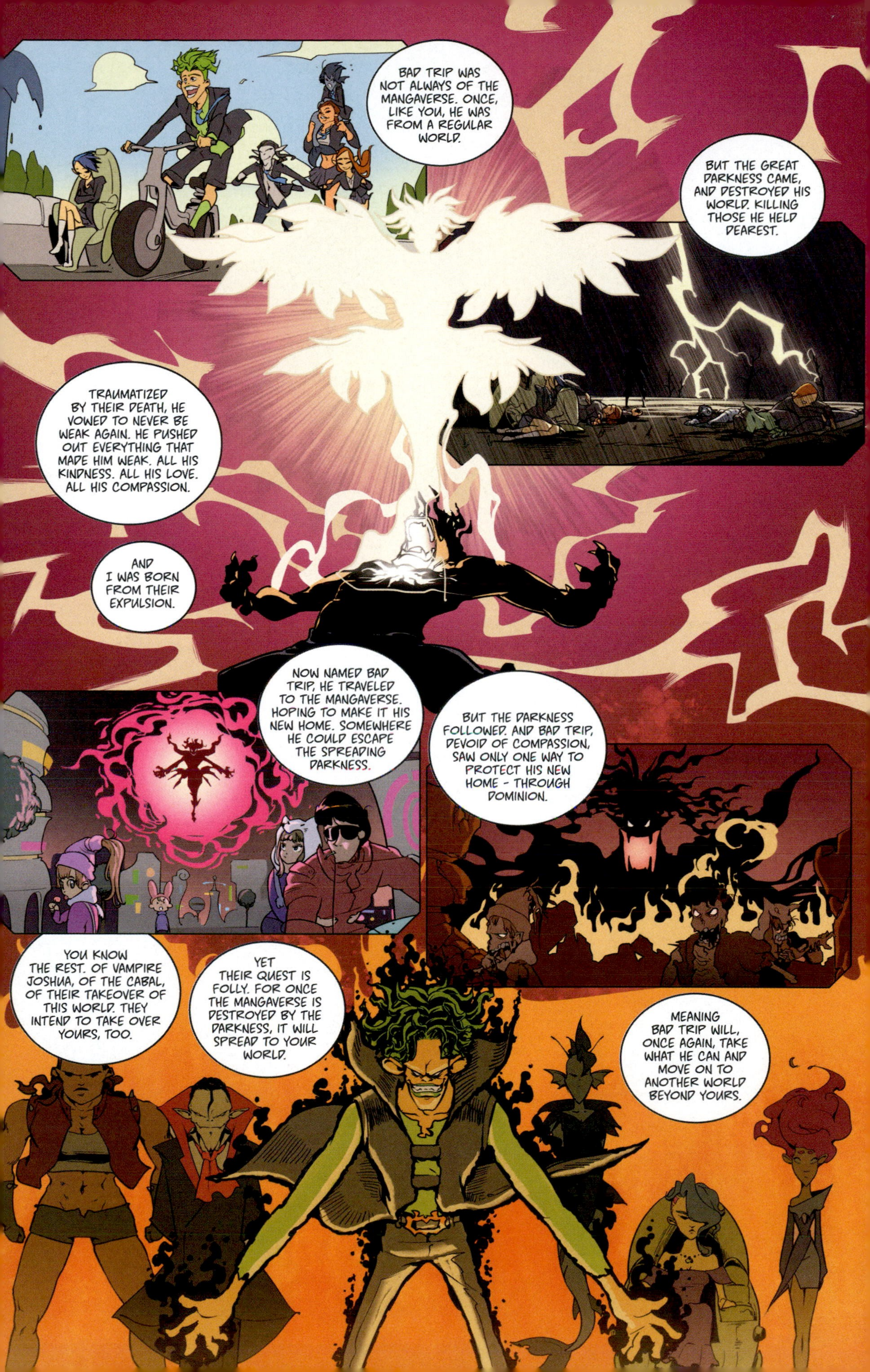
BAD TRIP WAS NOT ALWAYS OF THE MANGAVERSE. ONCE, LIKE YOU, HE WAS FROM A REGULAR WORLD.
BUT THE GREAT DARKNESS CAME, AND DESTROYED HIS WORLD. KILLING THOSE HE HELD DEAREST.
TRAUMATIZED BY THEIR DEATH, HE VOWED TO NEVER BE WEAK AGAIN. HE PUSHED OUT EVERYTHING THAT MADE HIM WEAK. ALL HIS KINDNESS. ALL HIS LOVE. ALL HIS COMPASSION.
AND I WAS BORN FROM THEIR EXPULSION.
NOW NAMED BAD TRIP, HE TRAVELED TO THE MANGAVERSE. HOPING TO MAKE IT HIS NEW HOME. SOMEWHERE HE COULD ESCAPE THE SPREADING DARKNESS.
BUT THE DARKNESS FOLLOWED. AND BAD TRIP, DEVOID OF COMPASSION, SAW ONLY ONE WAY TO PROTECT HIS NEW HOME - THROUGH DOMINION.
YOU KNOW THE REST. OF VAMPIRE JOSHUA, OF THE CABAL, OF THEIR TAKEOVER OF THIS WORLD. THEY INTEND TO TAKE OVER YOURS, TOO.
YET THEIR QUEST IS FOLLY. FOR ONCE THE MANGAVERSE IS DESTROYED BY THE DARKNESS, IT WILL SPREAD TO YOUR WORLD.
MEANING BAD TRIP WILL, ONCE AGAIN, TAKE WHAT HE CAN AND MOVE ON TO ANOTHER WORLD BEYOND YOURS.

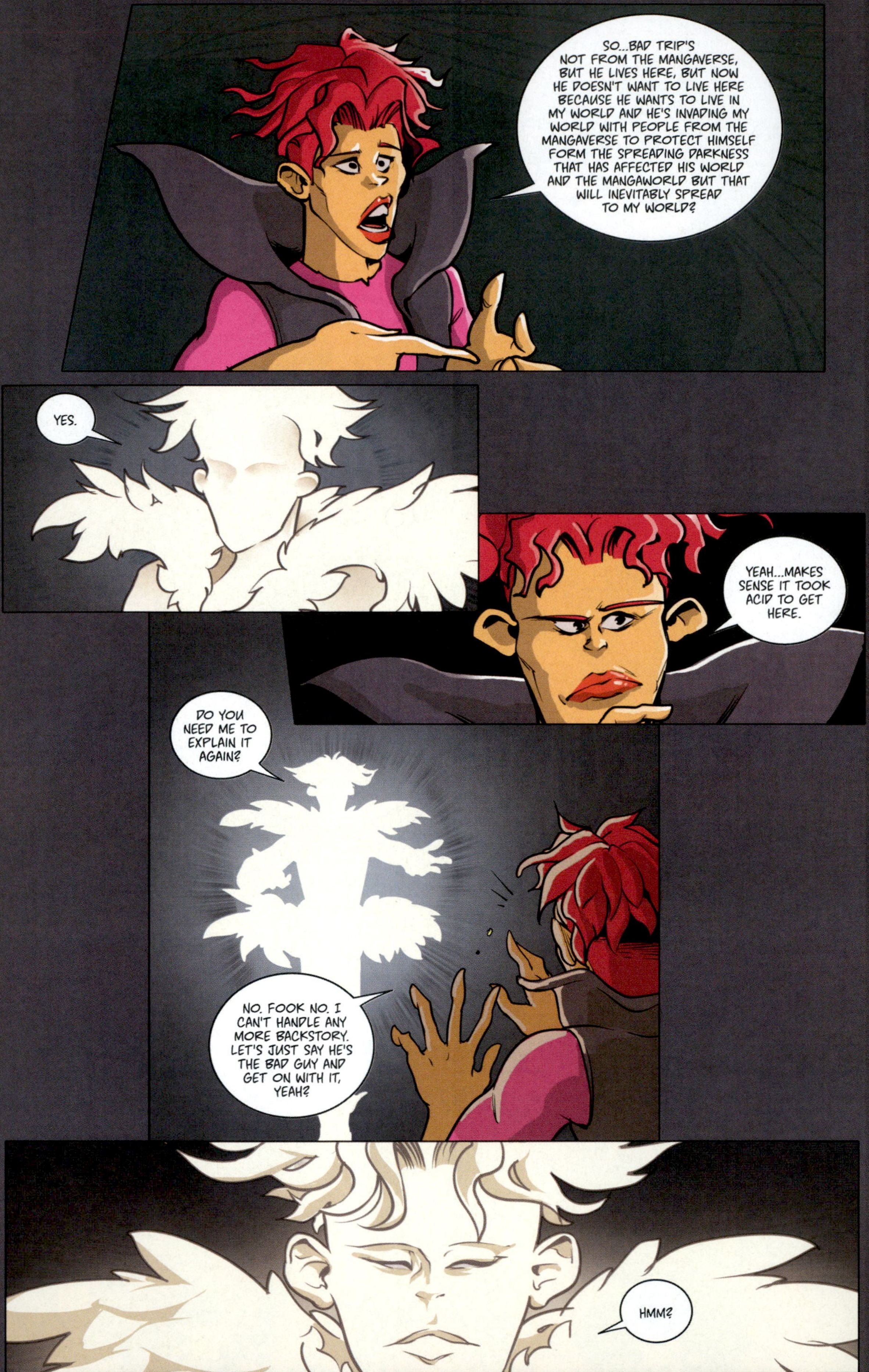
SO...BAD TRIP'S NOT FROM THE MANGAVERSE, BUT HE LIVES HERE, BUT NOW HE DOESN'T WANT TO LIVE HERE BECAUSE HE WANTS TO LIVE IN MY WORLD AND HE'S INVADING MY WORLD WITH PEOPLE FROM THE MANGAVERSE TO PROTECT HIMSELF FORM THE SPREADING DARKNESS THAT HAS AFFECTED HIS WORLD AND THE MANGAWORLD BUT THAT WILL INEVITABLY SPREAD TO MY WORLD?
YES.
YEAH...MAKES SENSE IT TOOK ACID TO GET HERE.
DO YOU NEED ME TO EXPLAIN IT AGAIN?
NO. FOOK NO. I CAN'T HANDLE ANY MORE BACKSTORY. LET'S JUST SAY HE'S THE BAD GUY AND GET ON WITH IT, YEAH?
HMM?

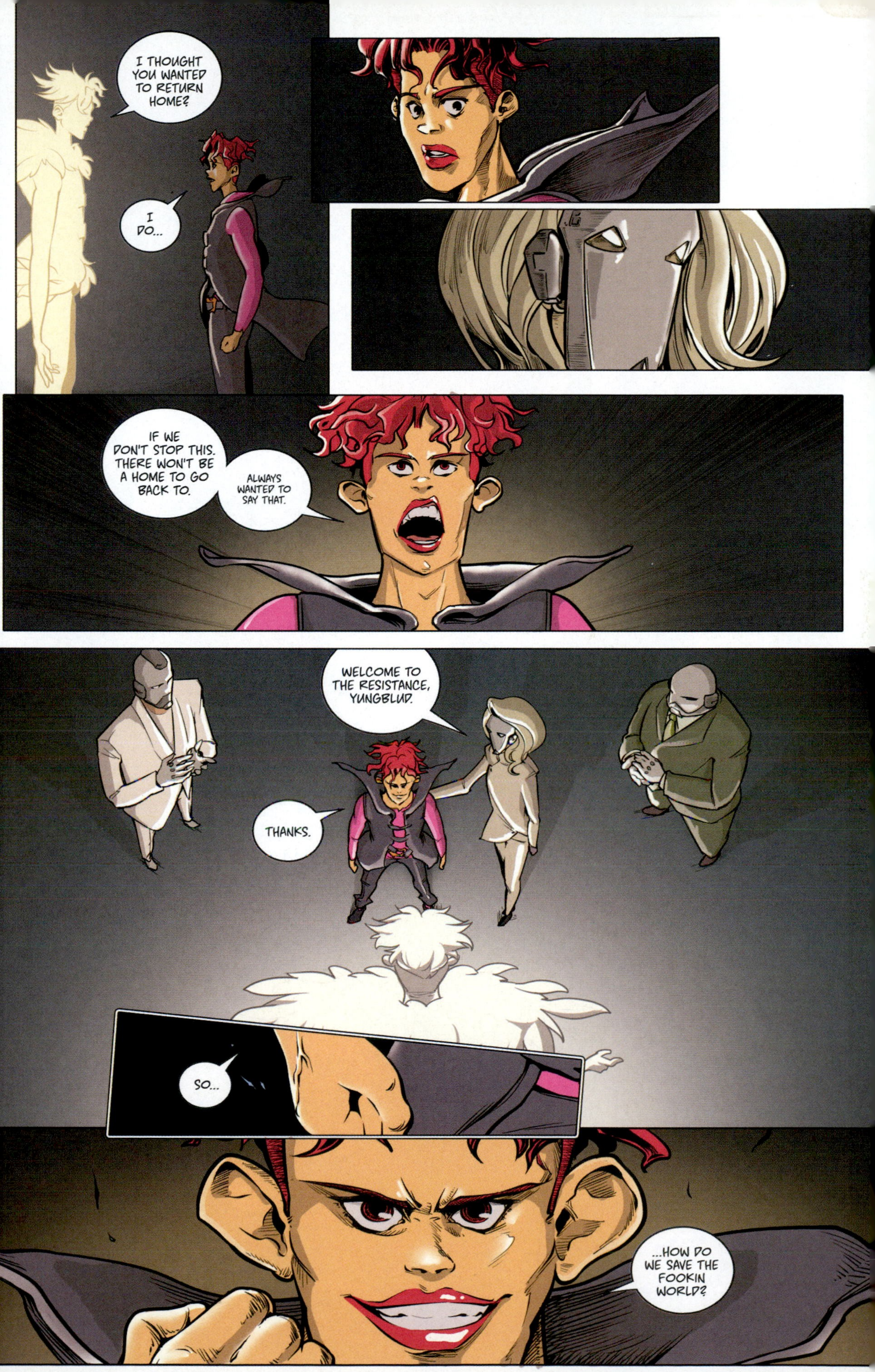
I THOUGHT YOU WANTED TO RETURN HOME?
I DO...
IF WE DON'T STOP THIS. THERE WON'T BE A HOME TO GO BACK TO.
ALWAYS WANTED TO SAY THAT.
WELCOME TO THE RESISTANCE, YUNGBLUD.
THANKS.
SO...
...HOW DO WE SAVE THE FOOKIN WORLD?

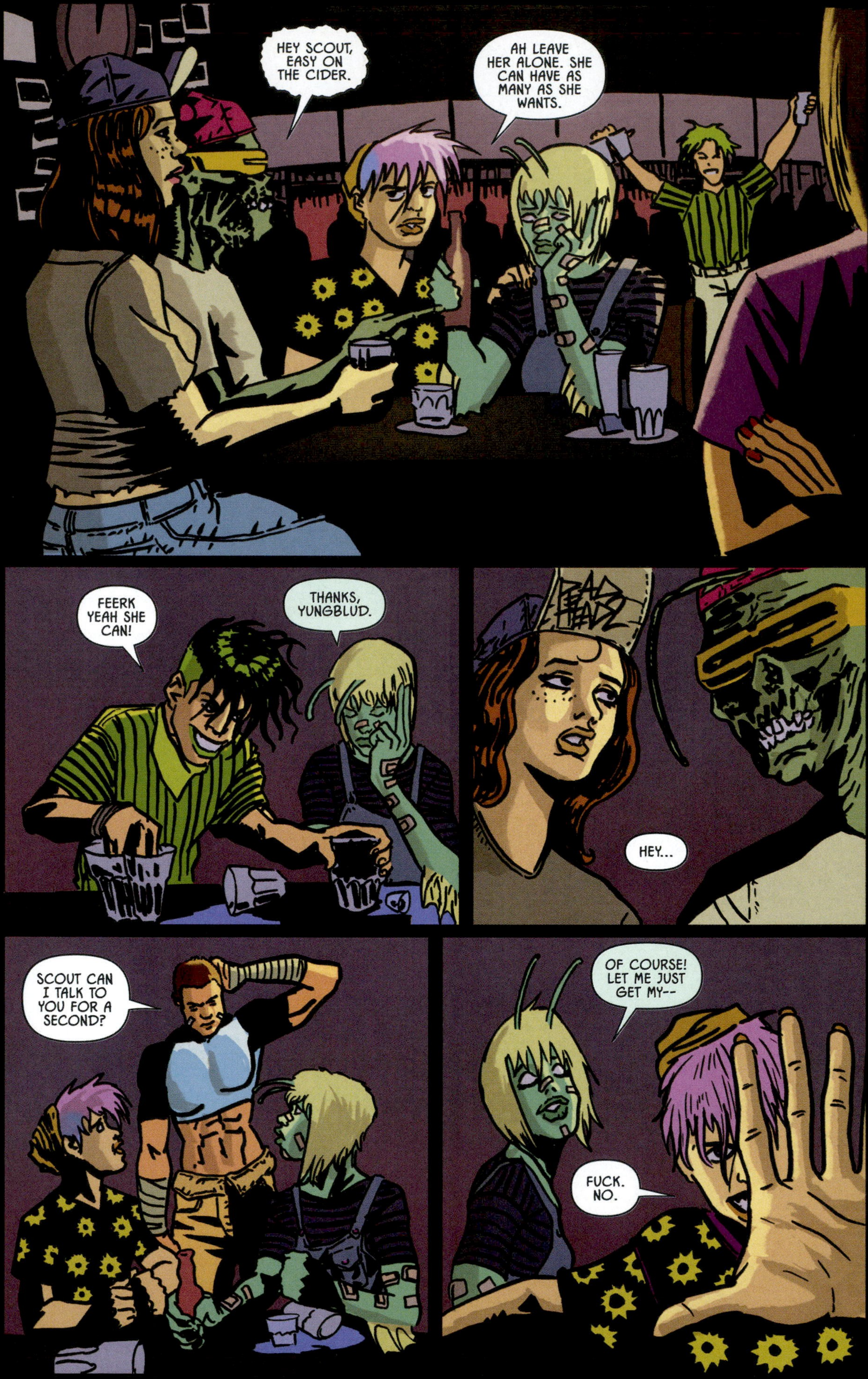
HEY SCOUT, EASY ON THE CIDER.
AH LEAVE HER ALONE. SHE CAN HAVE AS MANY AS SHE WANTS.
FEERK YEAH SHE CAN!
THANKS, YUNGBLUD.
HEY...
SCOUT CAN I TALK TO YOU FOR A SECOND?
OF COURSE! LET ME JUST GET MY--
FUCK. NO.

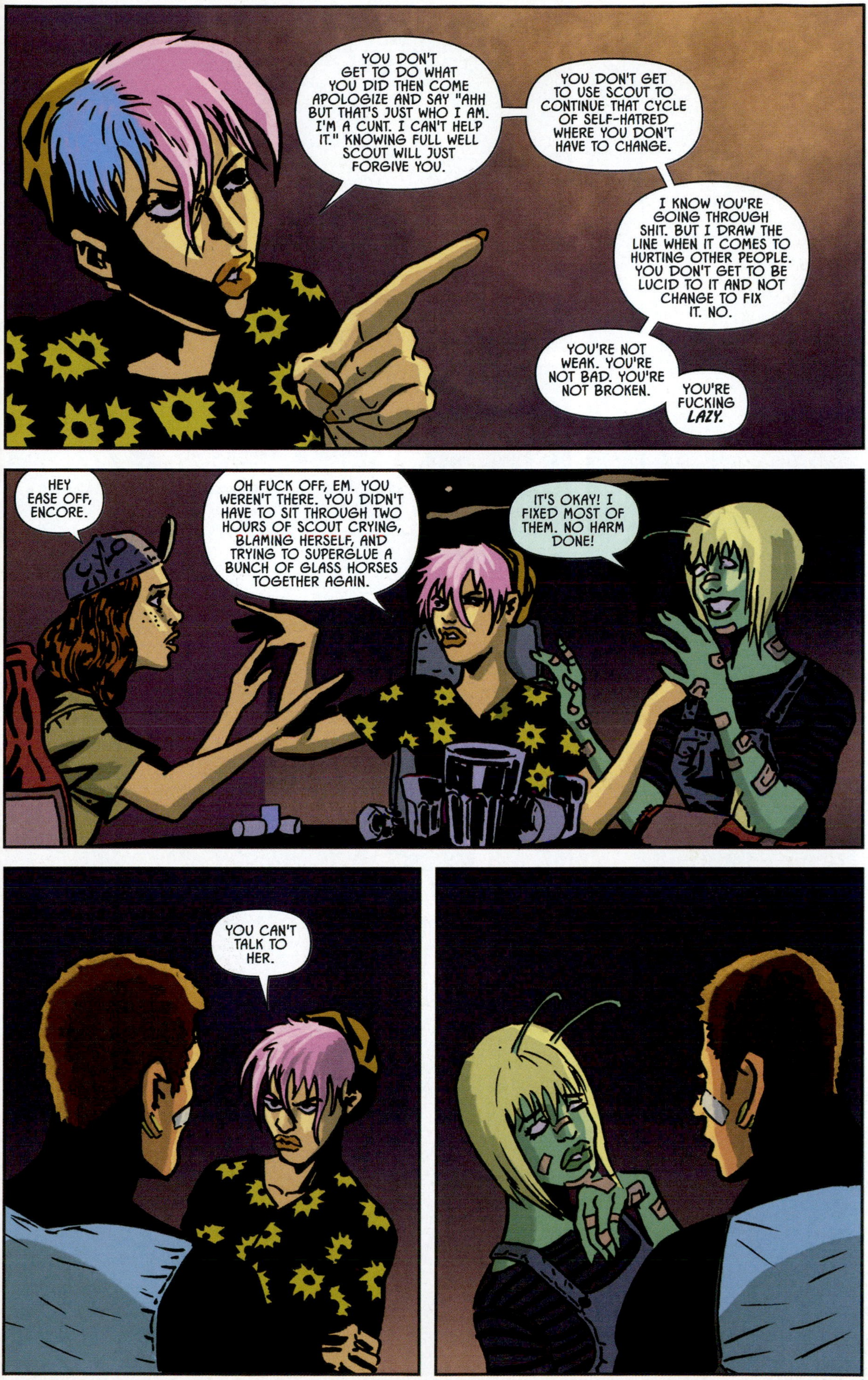
YOU DON'T GET TO DO WHAT YOU DID THEN COME APOLOGIZE AND SAY "AHH BUT THAT'S JUST WHO I AM. I'M A CUNT. I CAN'T HELP IT." KNOWING FULL WELL SCOUT WILL JUST FORGIVE YOU.
YOU DON'T GET TO USE SCOUT TO CONTINUE THAT CYCLE OF SELF-HATRED WHERE YOU DON'T HAVE TO CHANGE.
I KNOW YOU'RE GOING THROUGH SHIT. BUT I DRAW THE LINE WHEN IT COMES TO HURTING OTHER PEOPLE. YOU DON'T GET TO BE LUCID TO IT AND NOT CHANGE TO FIX IT. NO.
YOU'RE NOT WEAK. YOU'RE NOT BAD. YOU'RE NOT BROKEN.
YOU'RE FUCKING *LAZY.*
HEY EASE OFF, ENCORE.
OH FUCK OFF, EM. YOU WEREN'T THERE. YOU DIDN'T HAVE TO SIT THROUGH TWO HOURS OF SCOUT CRYING, BLAMING HERSELF, AND TRYING TO SUPERGLUE A BUNCH OF GLASS HORSES TOGETHER AGAIN.
IT'S OKAY! I FIXED MOST OF THEM. NO HARM DONE!
YOU CAN'T TALK TO HER.

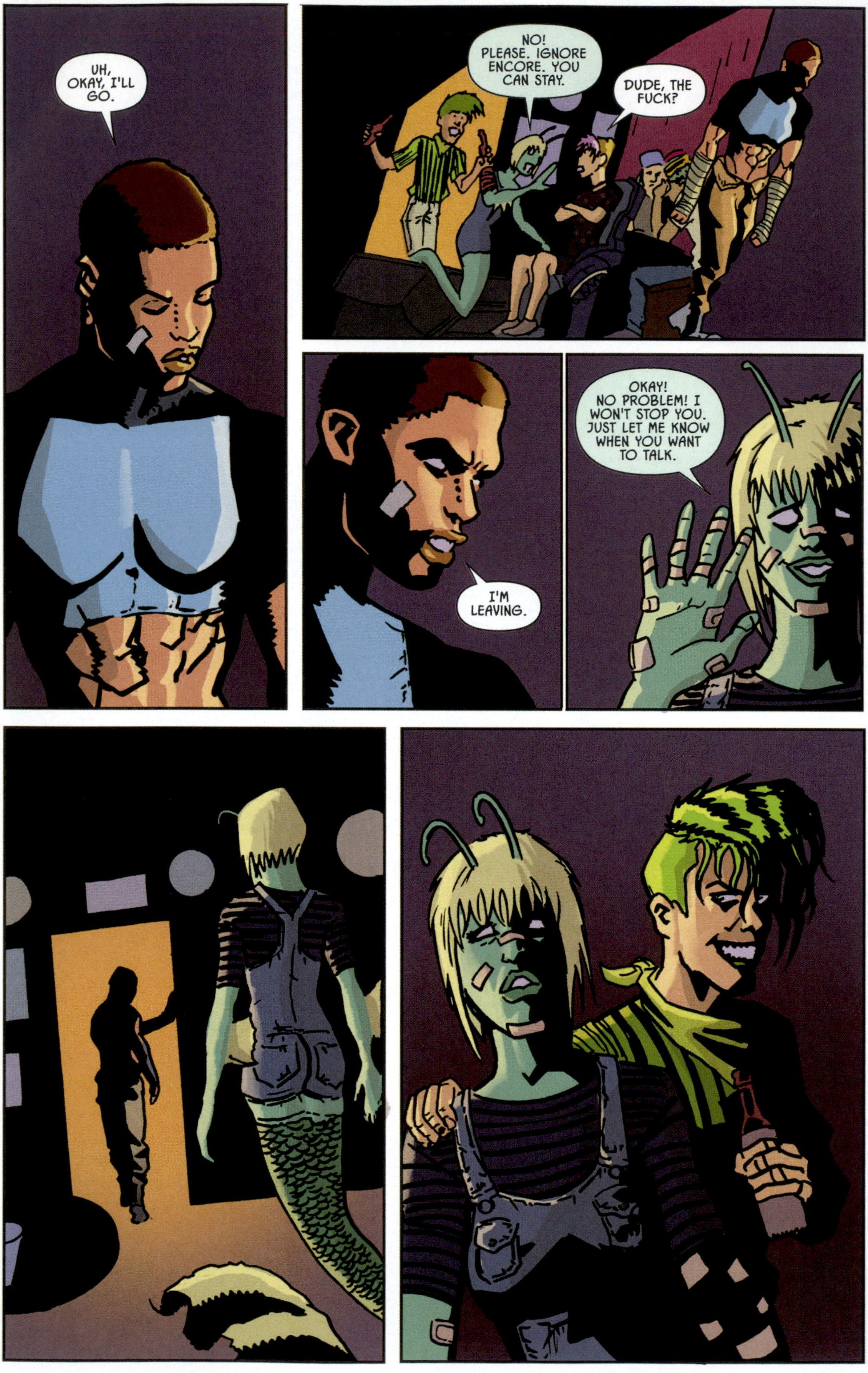

UH, OKAY, I'LL GO.
NO! PLEASE. IGNORE ENCORE. YOU CAN STAY.
DUDE, THE FUCK?
I'M LEAVING.
OKAY! NO PROBLEM! I WON'T STOP YOU. JUST LET ME KNOW WHEN YOU WANT TO TALK.

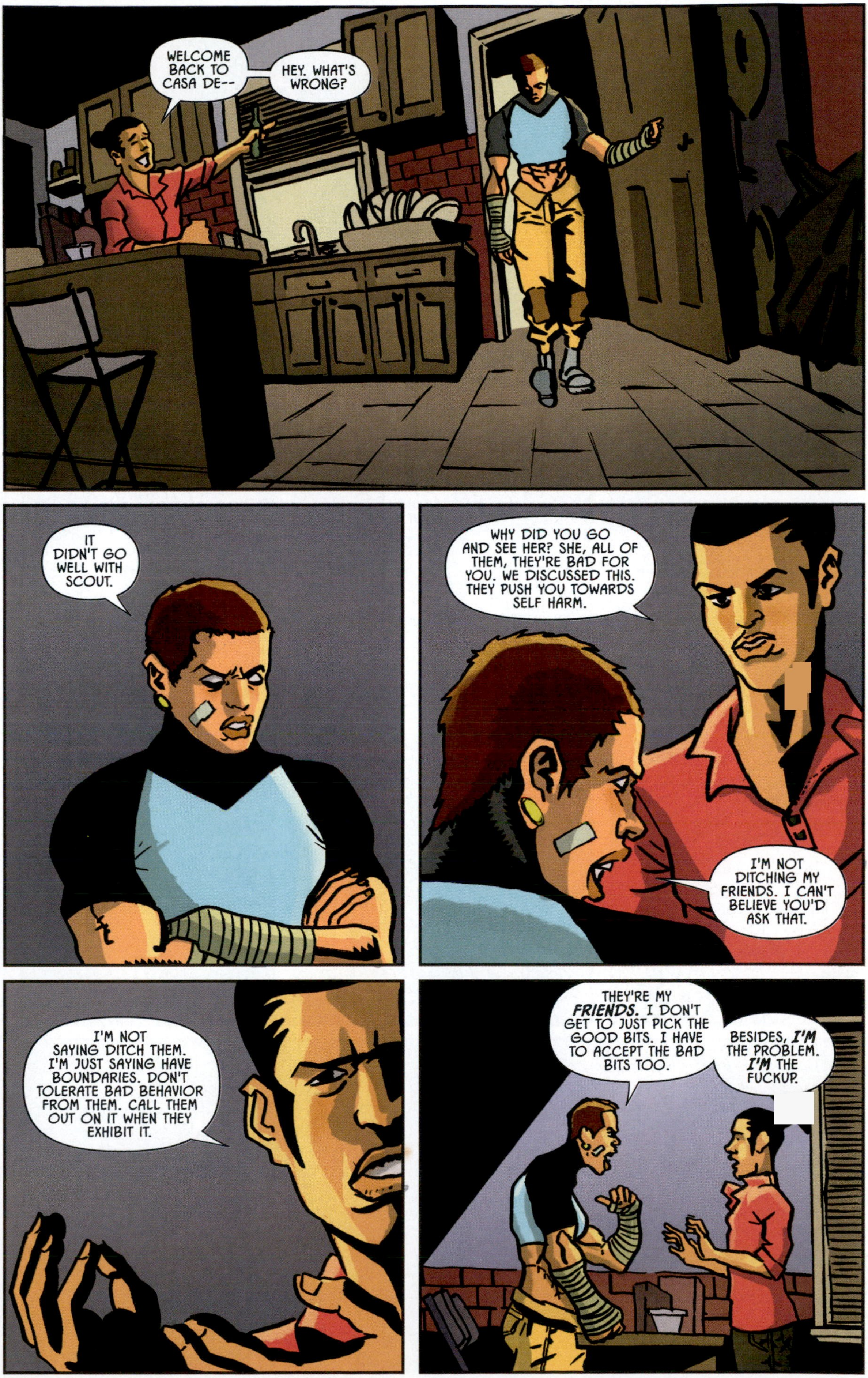

WELCOME BACK TO CASA DE--
HEY. WHAT'S WRONG?
IT DIDN'T GO WELL WITH SCOUT.
WHY DID YOU GO AND SEE HER? SHE, ALL OF THEM, THEY'RE BAD FOR YOU. WE DISCUSSED THIS. THEY PUSH YOU TOWARDS SELF HARM.
I'M NOT DITCHING MY FRIENDS. I CAN'T BELIEVE YOU'D ASK THAT.
I'M NOT SAYING DITCH THEM. I'M JUST SAYING HAVE BOUNDARIES. DON'T TOLERATE BAD BEHAVIOR FROM THEM. CALL THEM OUT ON IT WHEN THEY EXHIBIT IT.
THEY'RE MY ***FRIENDS.*** I DON'T GET TO JUST PICK THE GOOD BITS. I HAVE TO ACCEPT THE BAD BITS TOO.
BESIDES, ***I'M*** THE PROBLEM. ***I'M*** THE FUCKUP.

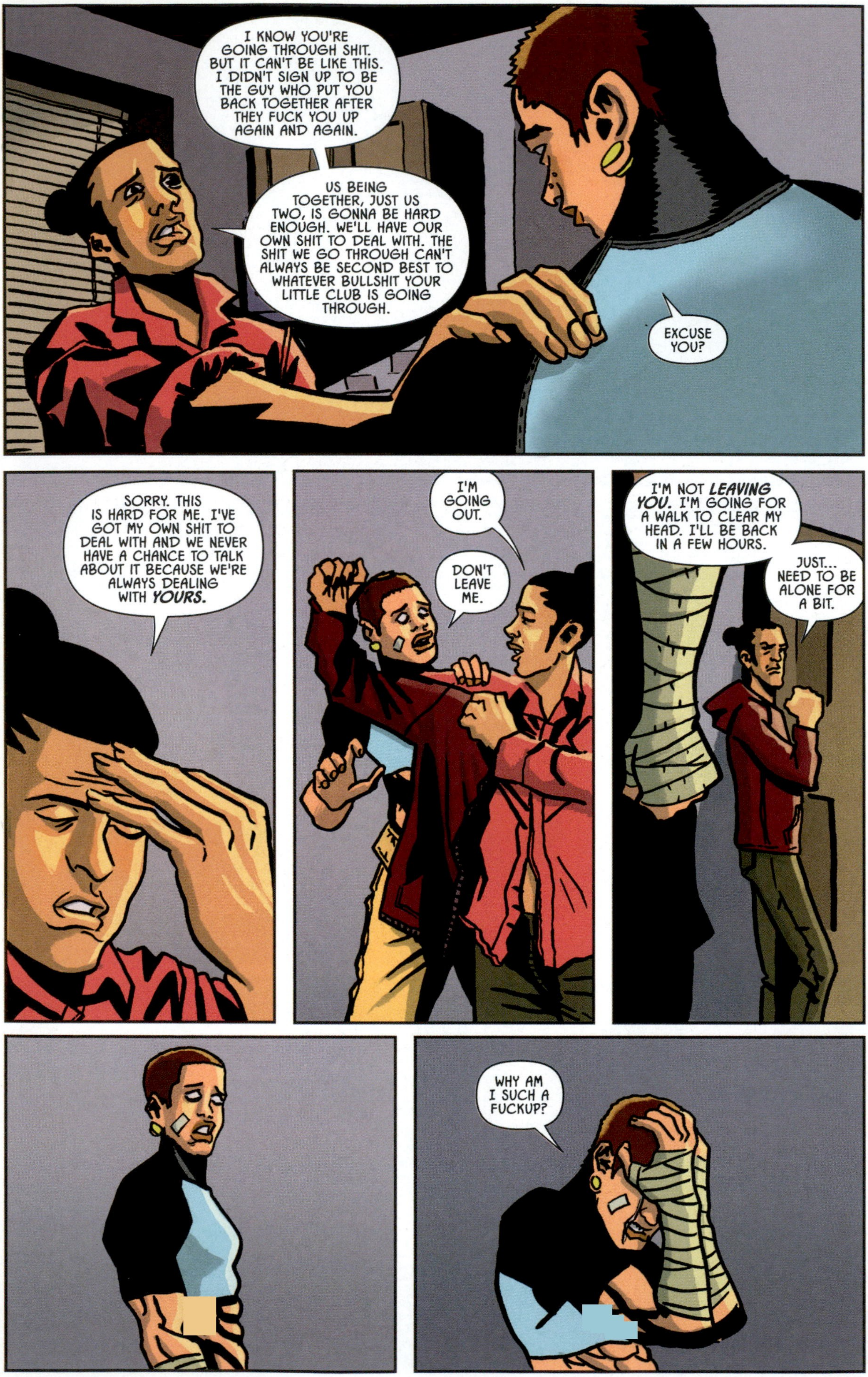
I KNOW YOU'RE GOING THROUGH SHIT. BUT IT CAN'T BE LIKE THIS. I DIDN'T SIGN UP TO BE THE GUY WHO PUT YOU BACK TOGETHER AFTER THEY FUCK YOU UP AGAIN AND AGAIN.
US BEING TOGETHER, JUST US TWO, IS GONNA BE HARD ENOUGH. WE'LL HAVE OUR OWN SHIT TO DEAL WITH. THE SHIT WE GO THROUGH CAN'T ALWAYS BE SECOND BEST TO WHATEVER BULLSHIT YOUR LITTLE CLUB IS GOING THROUGH.
EXCUSE YOU?
SORRY. THIS IS HARD FOR ME. I'VE GOT MY OWN SHIT TO DEAL WITH AND WE NEVER HAVE A CHANCE TO TALK ABOUT IT BECAUSE WE'RE ALWAYS DEALING WITH *YOURS.*
I'M GOING OUT.
DON'T LEAVE ME.
I'M NOT *LEAVING YOU.* I'M GOING FOR A WALK TO CLEAR MY HEAD. I'LL BE BACK IN A FEW HOURS.
JUST... NEED TO BE ALONE FOR A BIT.
WHY AM I SUCH A FUCKUP?

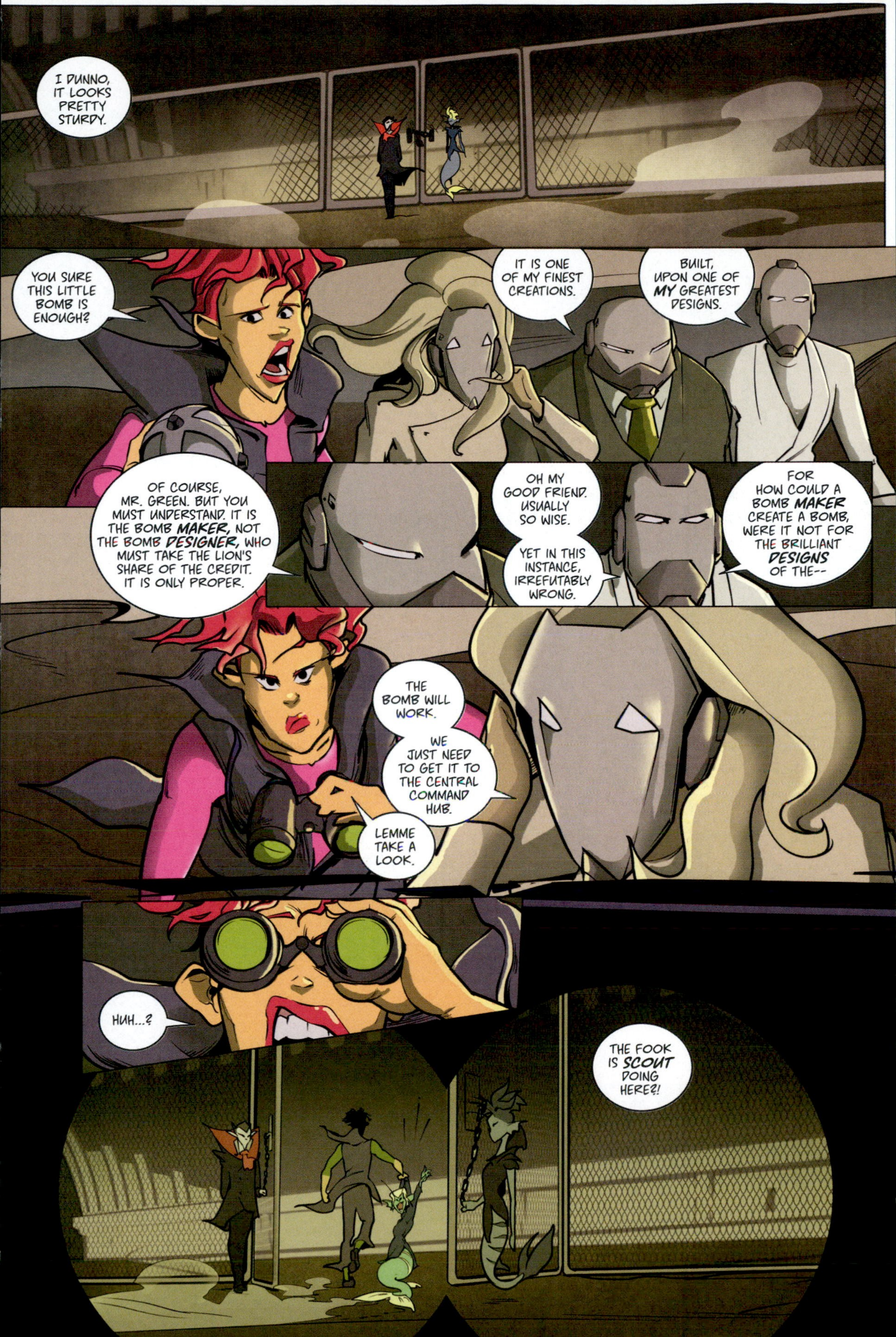
I DUNNO, IT LOOKS PRETTY STURDY.
YOU SURE THIS LITTLE BOMB IS ENOUGH?
IT IS ONE OF MY FINEST CREATIONS.
BUILT, UPON ONE OF MY GREATEST DESIGNS.
OF COURSE, MR. GREEN. BUT YOU MUST UNDERSTAND. IT IS THE BOMB MAKER, NOT THE BOMB DESIGNER, WHO MUST TAKE THE LION'S SHARE OF THE CREDIT. IT IS ONLY PROPER.
OH MY GOOD FRIEND. USUALLY SO WISE.
YET IN THIS INSTANCE, IRREFUTABLY WRONG.
FOR HOW COULD A BOMB MAKER CREATE A BOMB, WERE IT NOT FOR THE BRILLIANT DESIGNS OF THE--
THE BOMB WILL WORK.
WE JUST NEED TO GET IT TO THE CENTRAL COMMAND HUB.
LEMME TAKE A LOOK.
HUH...?
THE FOOK IS SCOUT DOING HERE?!

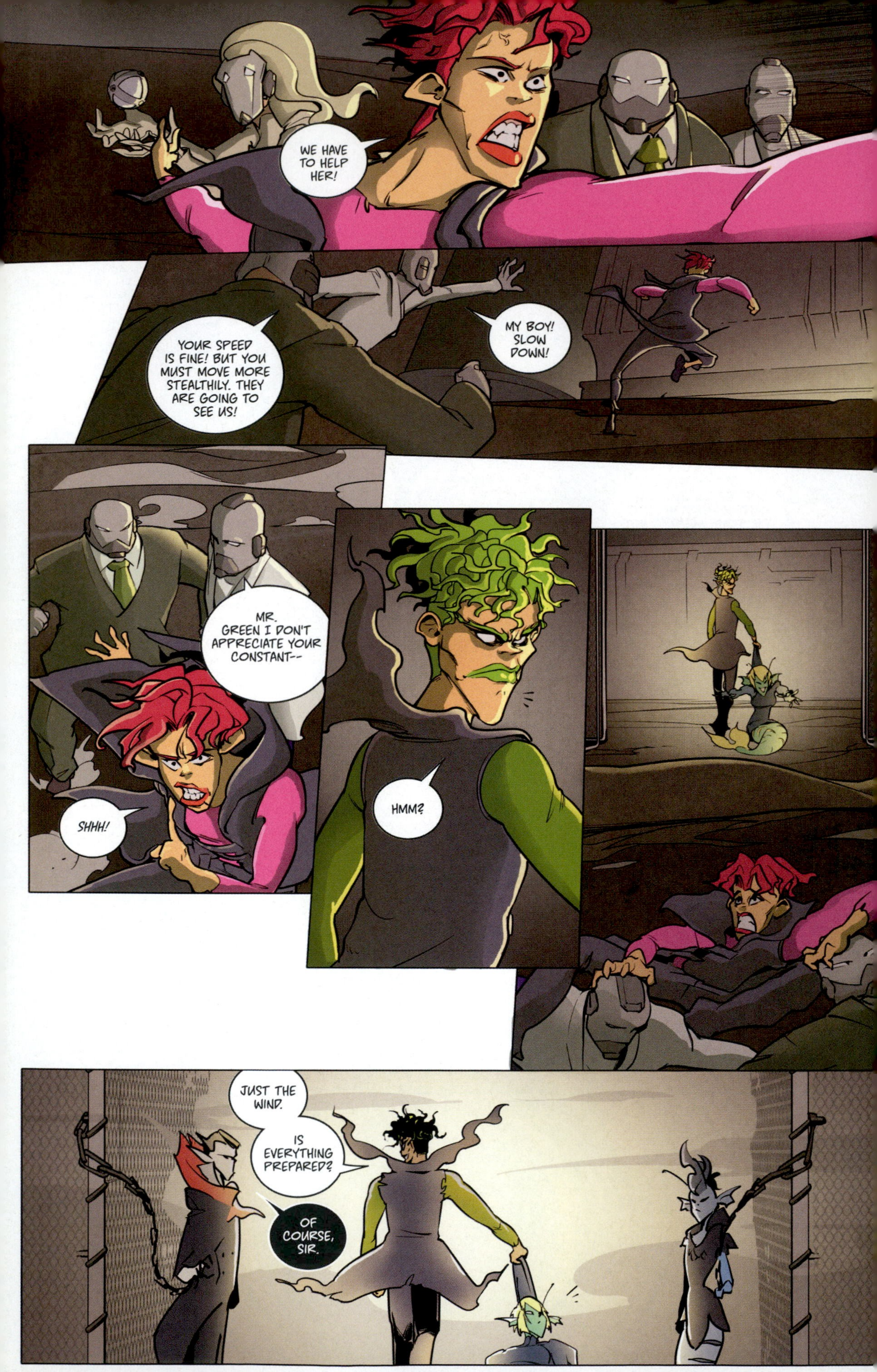
WE HAVE TO HELP HER!
YOUR SPEED IS FINE! BUT YOU MUST MOVE MORE STEALTHILY. THEY ARE GOING TO SEE US!
MY BOY! SLOW DOWN!
MR. GREEN I DON'T APPRECIATE YOUR CONSTANT--
SHHH!
HMM?
JUST THE WIND.
IS EVERYTHING PREPARED?
OF COURSE, SIR.

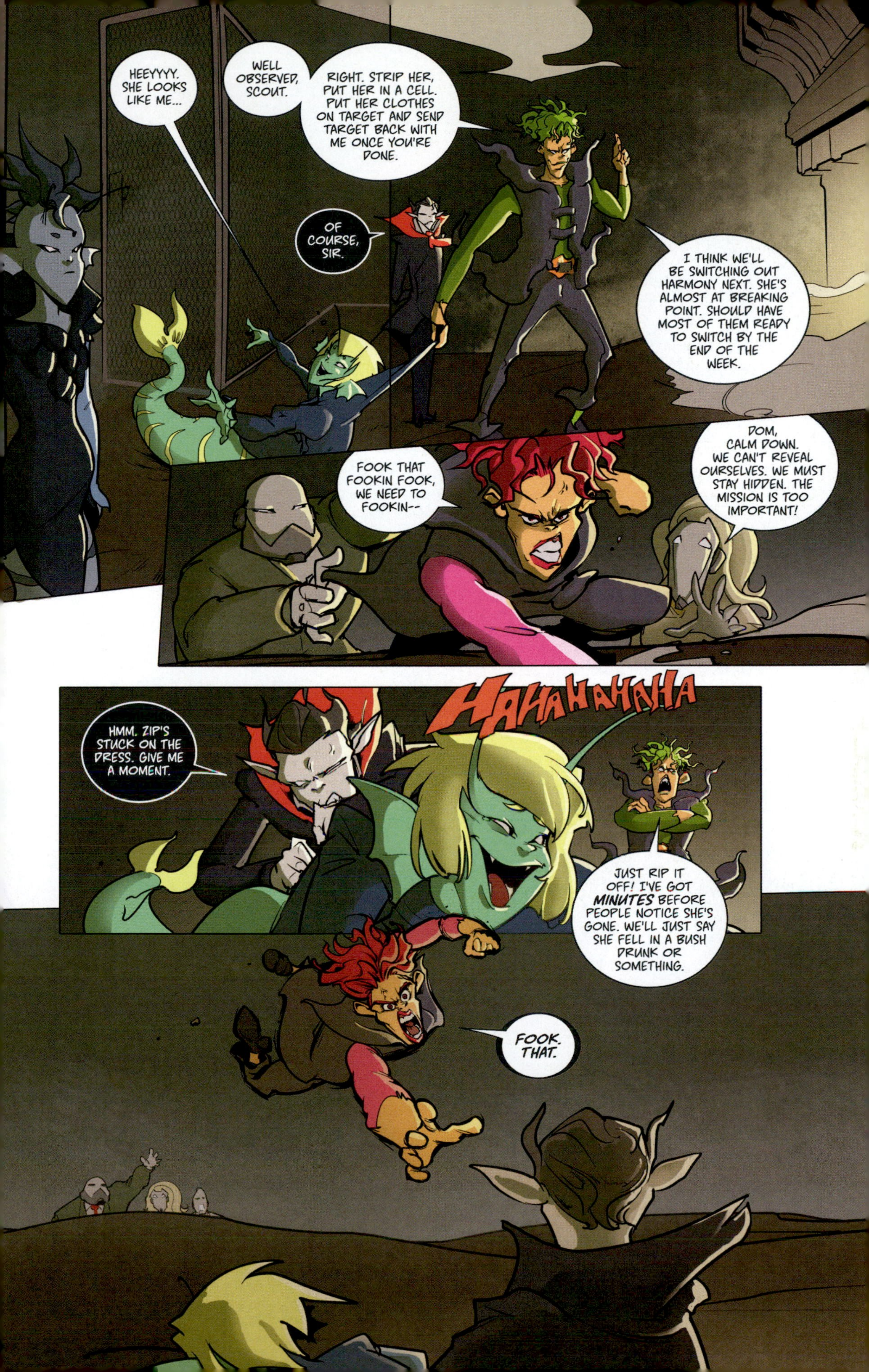
HEEYYYY. SHE LOOKS LIKE ME...
WELL OBSERVED, SCOUT.
RIGHT. STRIP HER, PUT HER IN A CELL. PUT HER CLOTHES ON TARGET AND SEND TARGET BACK WITH ME ONCE YOU'RE DONE.
OF COURSE, SIR.
I THINK WE'LL BE SWITCHING OUT HARMONY NEXT. SHE'S ALMOST AT BREAKING POINT. SHOULD HAVE MOST OF THEM READY TO SWITCH BY THE END OF THE WEEK.
FOOK THAT FOOKIN FOOK, WE NEED TO FOOKIN--
DOM, CALM DOWN. WE CAN'T REVEAL OURSELVES. WE MUST STAY HIDDEN. THE MISSION IS TOO IMPORTANT!
HAHAHAHAHA
HMM. ZIP'S STUCK ON THE DRESS. GIVE ME A MOMENT.
JUST RIP IT OFF! I'VE GOT MINUTES BEFORE PEOPLE NOTICE SHE'S GONE. WE'LL JUST SAY SHE FELL IN A BUSH DRUNK OR SOMETHING.
FOOK. THAT.

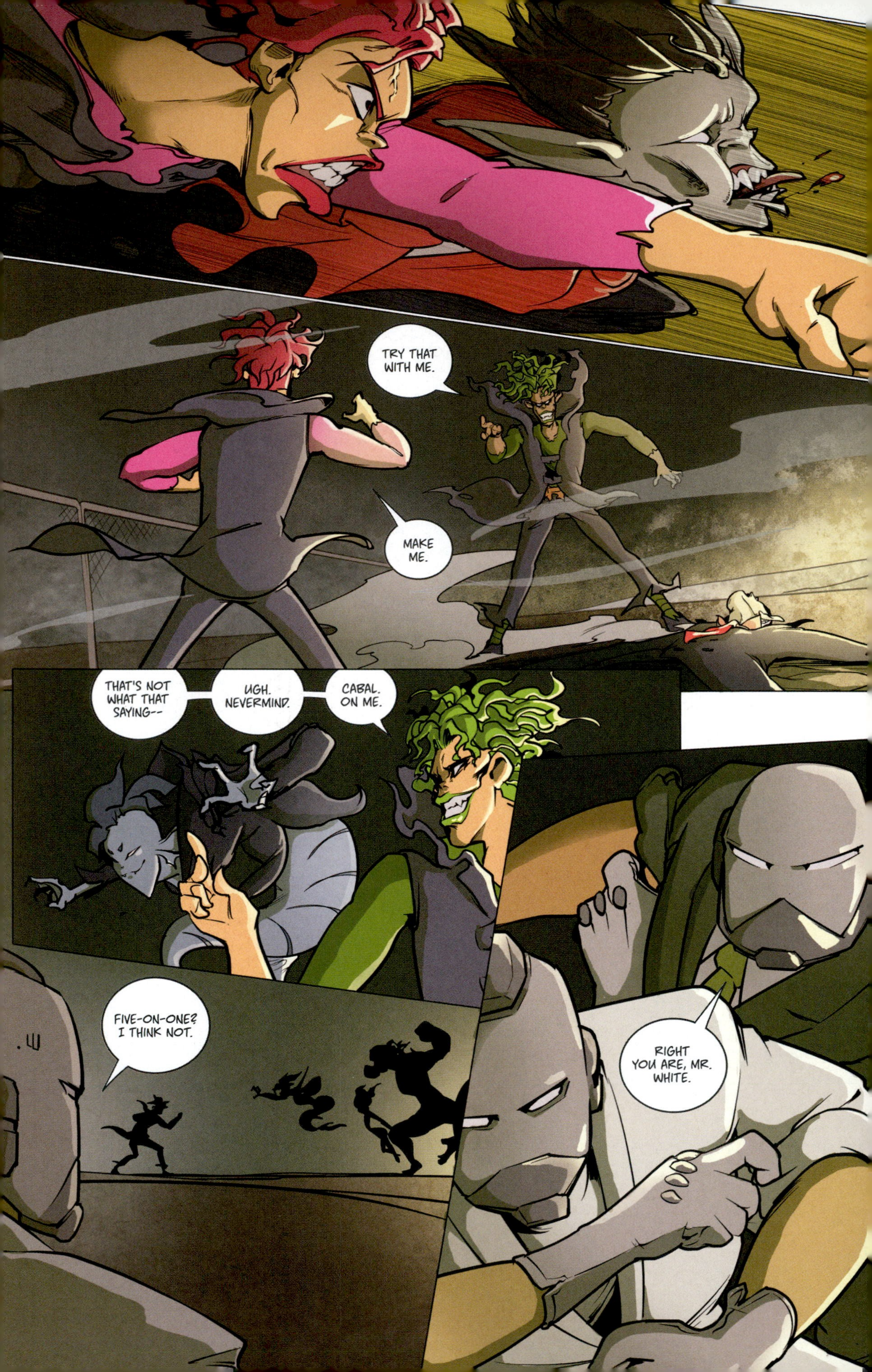
TRY THAT WITH ME.
MAKE ME.
THAT'S NOT WHAT THAT SAYING--
UGH. NEVERMIND.
CABAL. ON ME.
FIVE-ON-ONE? I THINK NOT.
RIGHT YOU ARE, MR. WHITE.

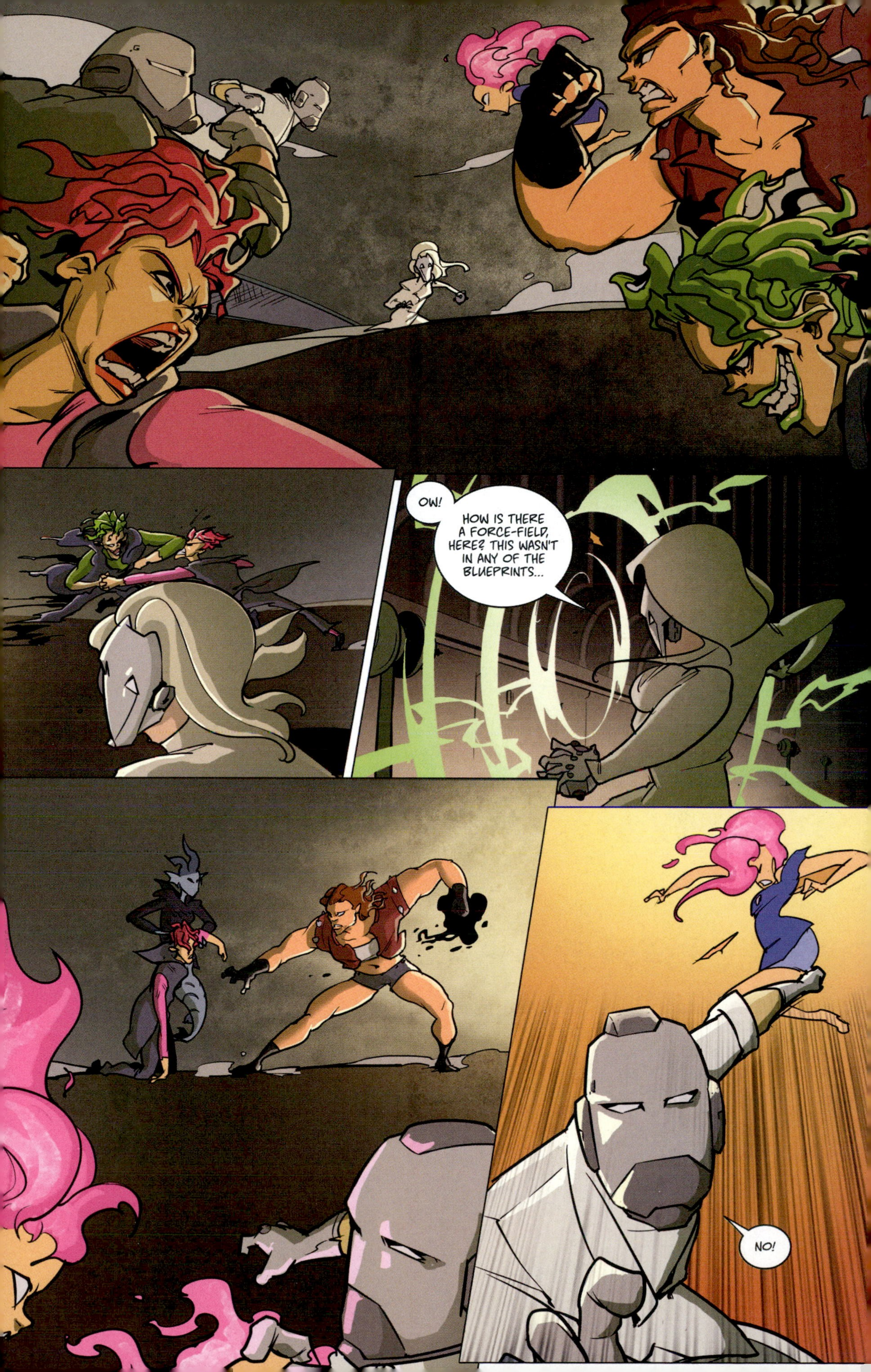
OW!
HOW IS THERE A FORCE-FIELD, HERE? THIS WASN'T IN ANY OF THE BLUEPRINTS...
NO!

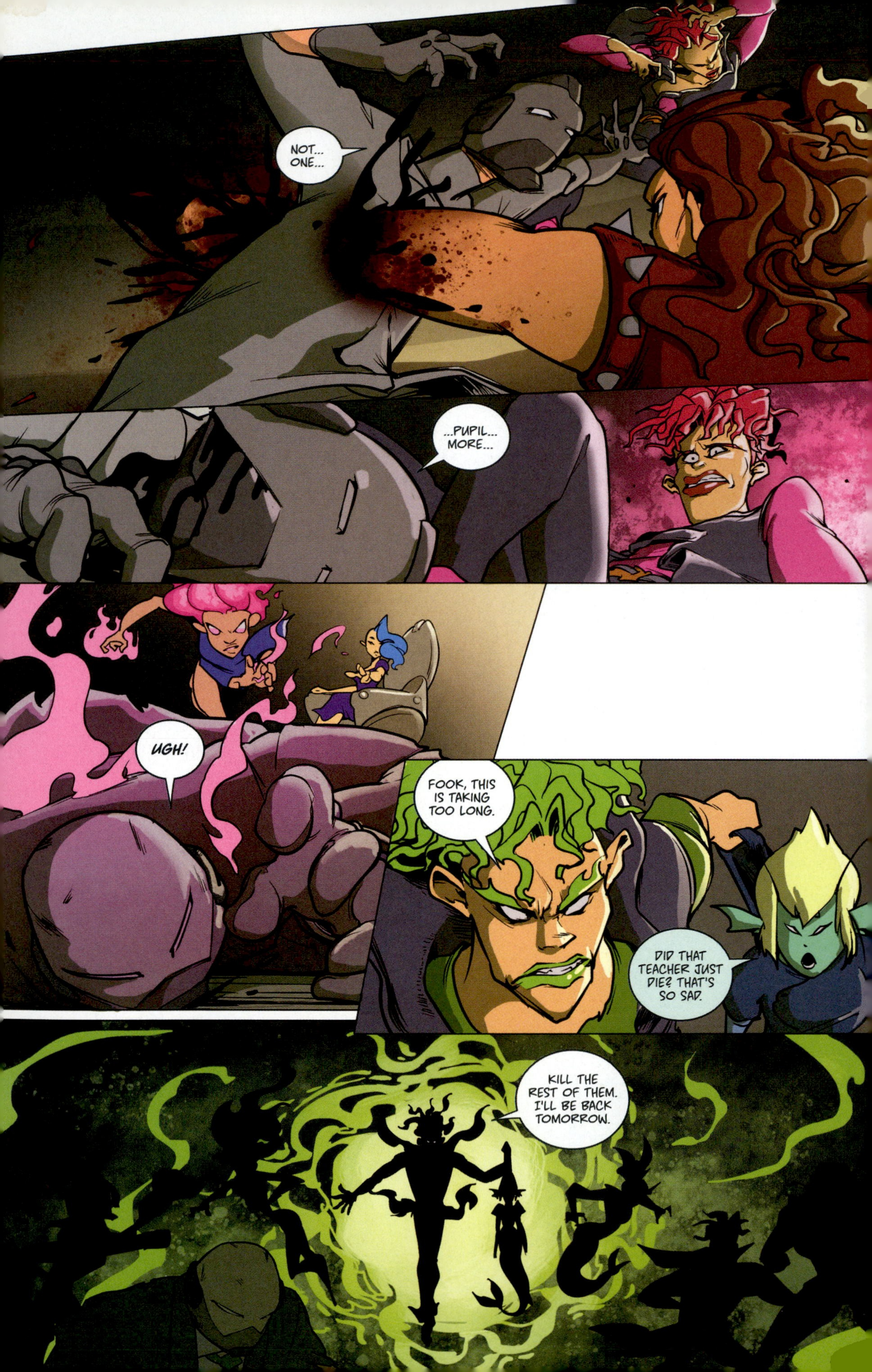
NOT... ONE...
...PUPIL... MORE...
UGH!
FOOK, THIS IS TAKING TOO LONG.
DID THAT TEACHER JUST DIE? THAT'S SO SAD.
KILL THE REST OF THEM. I'LL BE BACK TOMORROW.

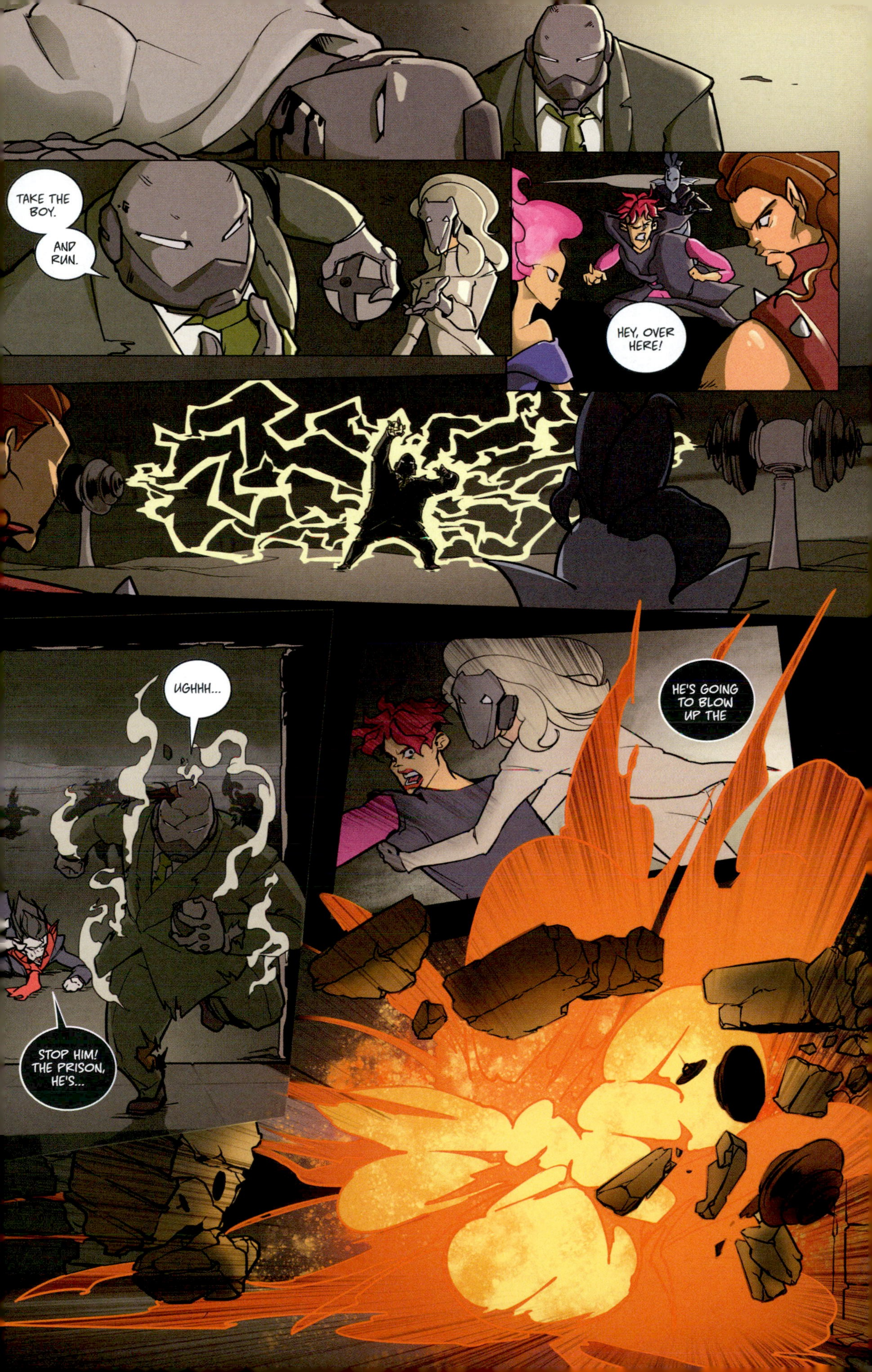
TAKE THE BOY.
AND RUN.
HEY, OVER HERE!
UGHHH...
STOP HIM! THE PRISON, HE'S...
HE'S GOING TO BLOW UP THE

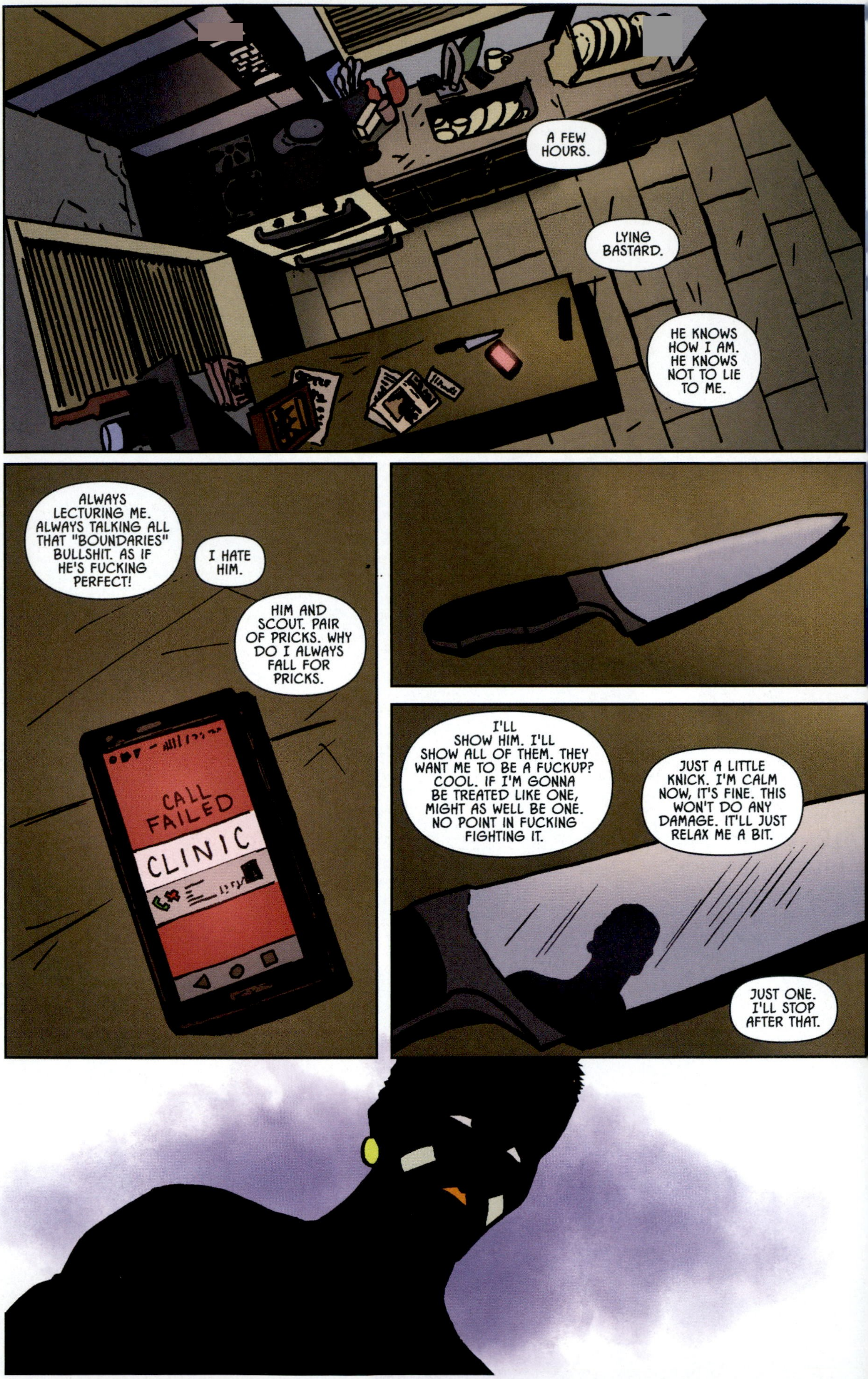
A FEW HOURS.
LYING BASTARD.
HE KNOWS HOW I AM. HE KNOWS NOT TO LIE TO ME.
ALWAYS LECTURING ME. ALWAYS TALKING ALL THAT "BOUNDARIES" BULLSHIT. AS IF HE'S FUCKING PERFECT!
I HATE HIM.
HIM AND SCOUT. PAIR OF PRICKS. WHY DO I ALWAYS FALL FOR PRICKS.
CALL FAILED
CLINIC
I'LL SHOW HIM. I'LL SHOW ALL OF THEM. THEY WANT ME TO BE A FUCKUP? COOL. IF I'M GONNA BE TREATED LIKE ONE, MIGHT AS WELL BE ONE. NO POINT IN FUCKING FIGHTING IT.
JUST A LITTLE KNICK. I'M CALM NOW, IT'S FINE. THIS WON'T DO ANY DAMAGE. IT'LL JUST RELAX ME A BIT.
JUST ONE. I'LL STOP AFTER THAT.

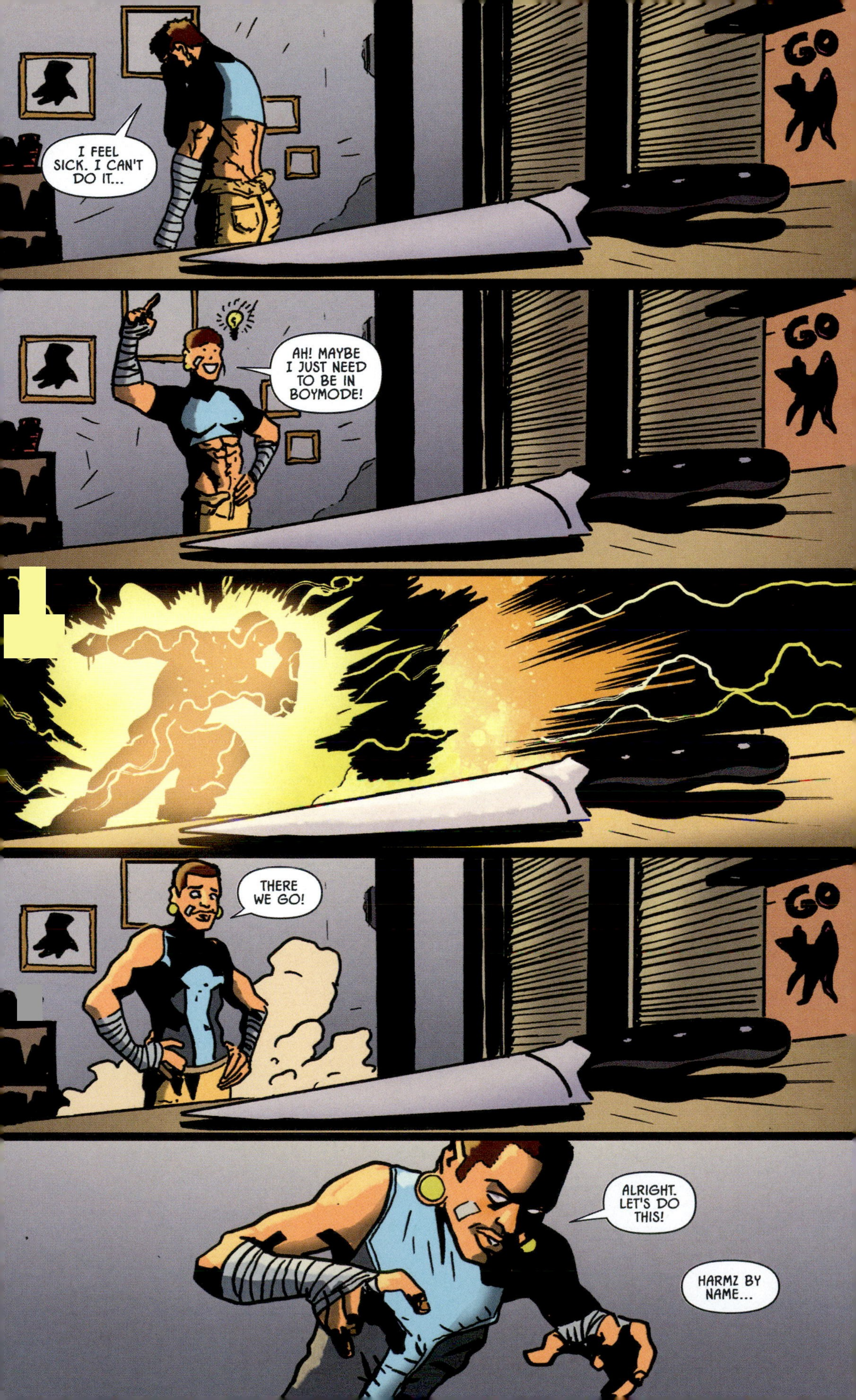
I FEEL SICK. I CAN'T DO IT...
GO
AH! MAYBE I JUST NEED TO BE IN BOYMODE!
GO
THERE WE GO!
GO
ALRIGHT. LET'S DO THIS!
HARMZ BY NAME...

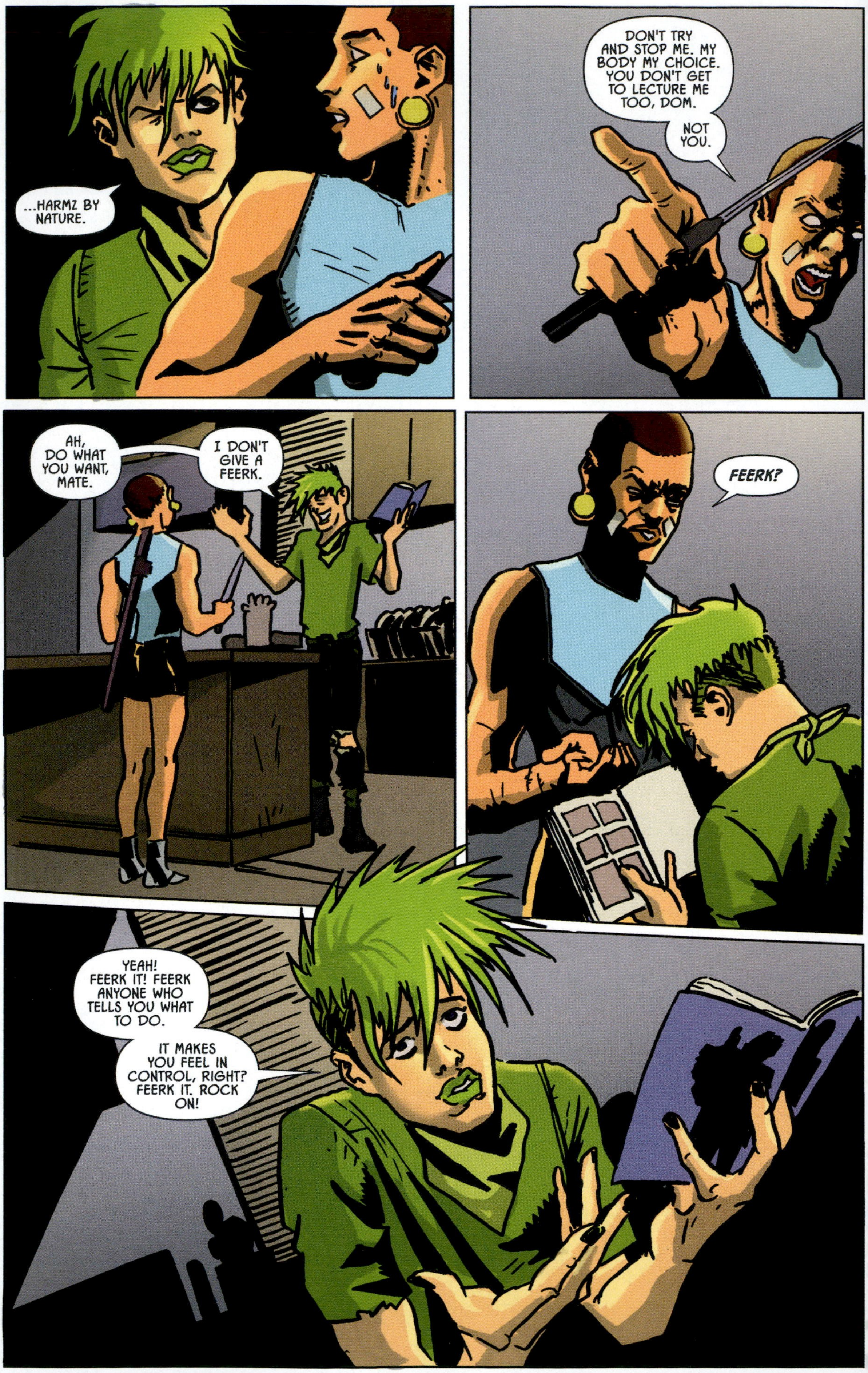
...HARMZ BY NATURE.
DON'T TRY AND STOP ME. MY BODY MY CHOICE. YOU DON'T GET TO LECTURE ME TOO, DOM.
NOT YOU.
AH, DO WHAT YOU WANT, MATE.
I DON'T GIVE A FEERK.
FEERK?
YEAH! FEERK IT! FEERK ANYONE WHO TELLS YOU WHAT TO DO.
IT MAKES YOU FEEL IN CONTROL, RIGHT? FEERK IT. ROCK ON!

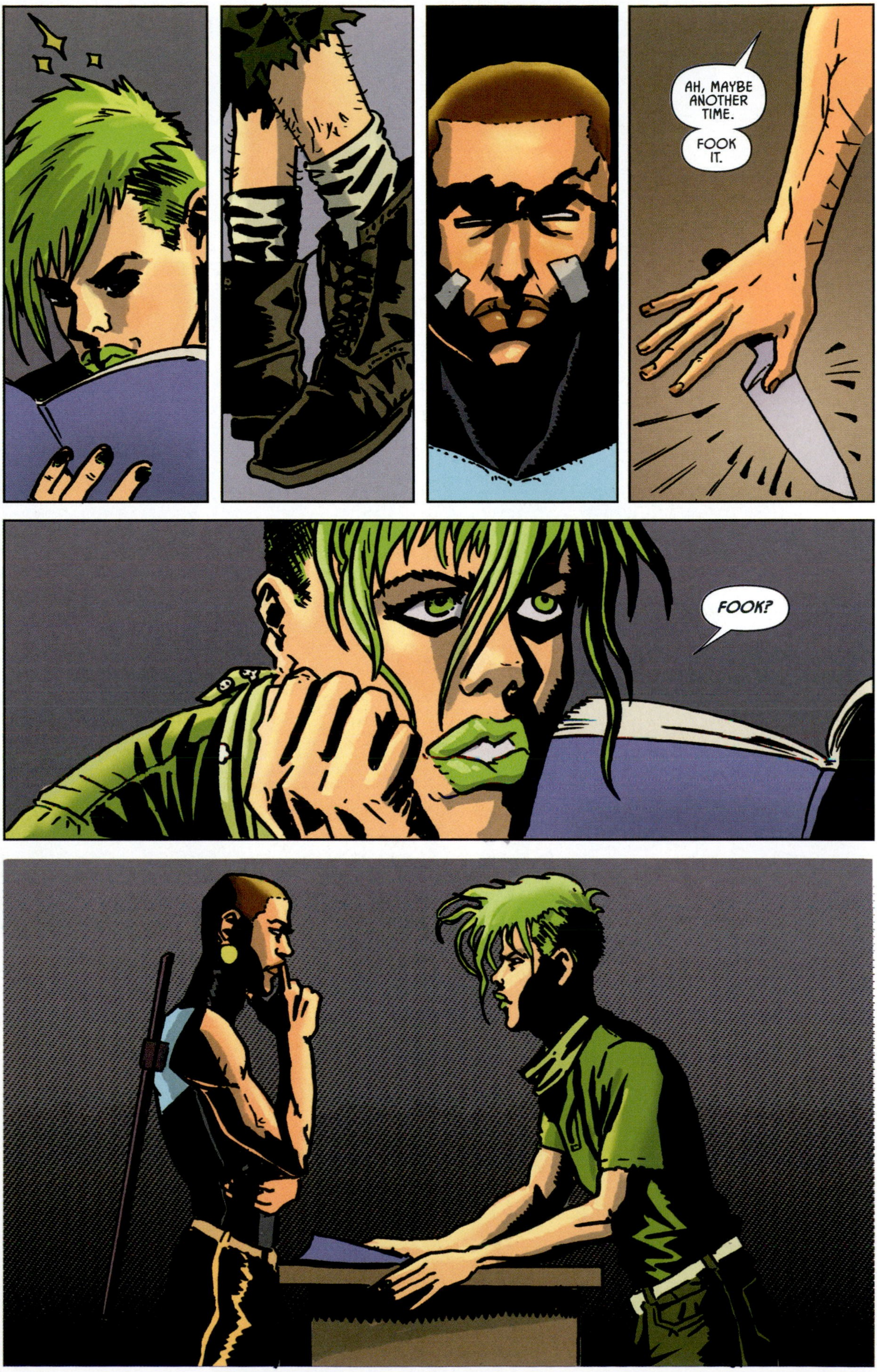
AH, MAYBE ANOTHER TIME.
FOOK IT.
FOOK?

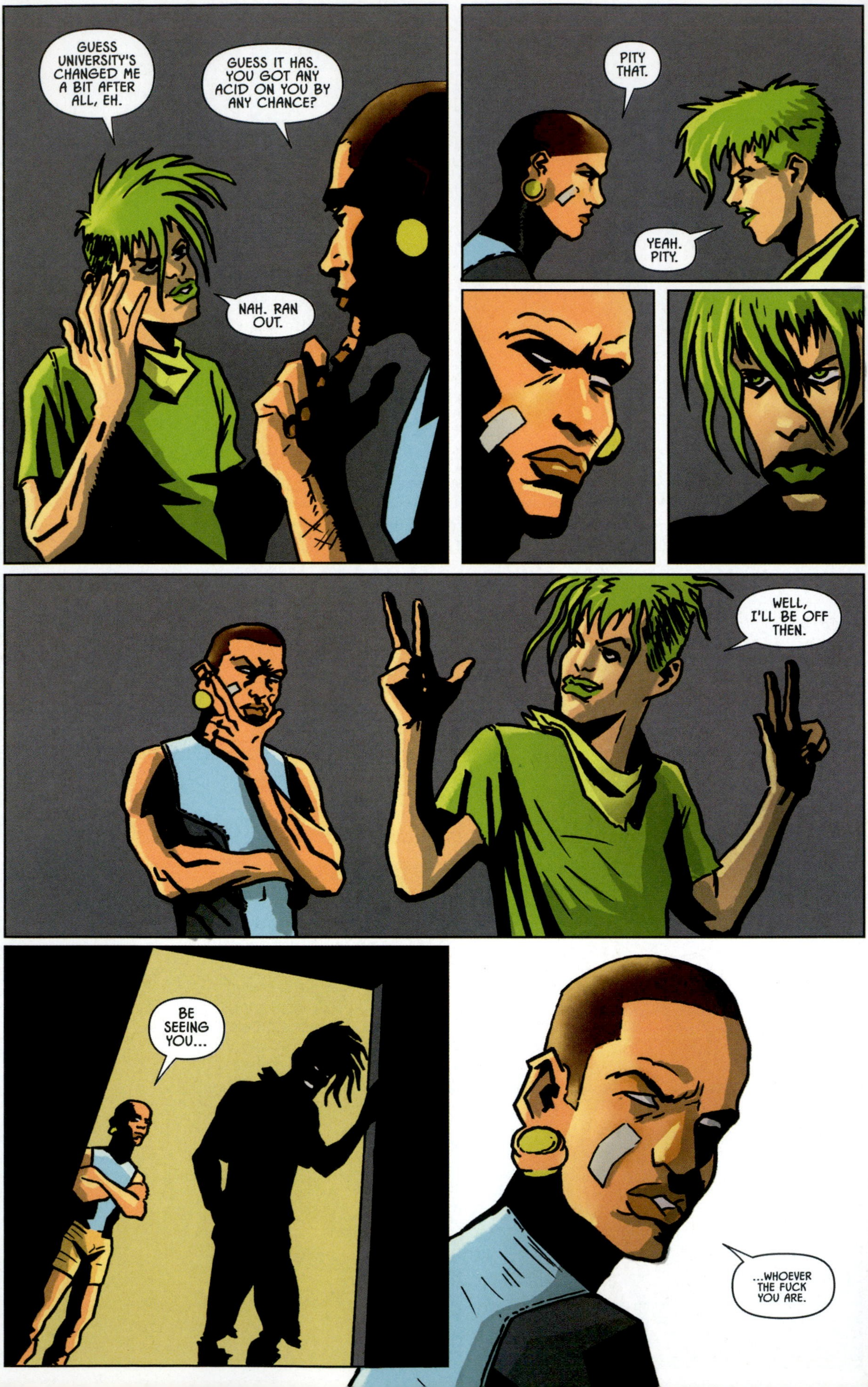
GUESS UNIVERSITY'S CHANGED ME A BIT AFTER ALL, EH.
GUESS IT HAS. YOU GOT ANY ACID ON YOU BY ANY CHANCE?
NAH. RAN OUT.
PITY THAT.
YEAH. PITY.
WELL, I'LL BE OFF THEN.
BE SEEING YOU...
...WHOEVER THE FUCK YOU ARE.

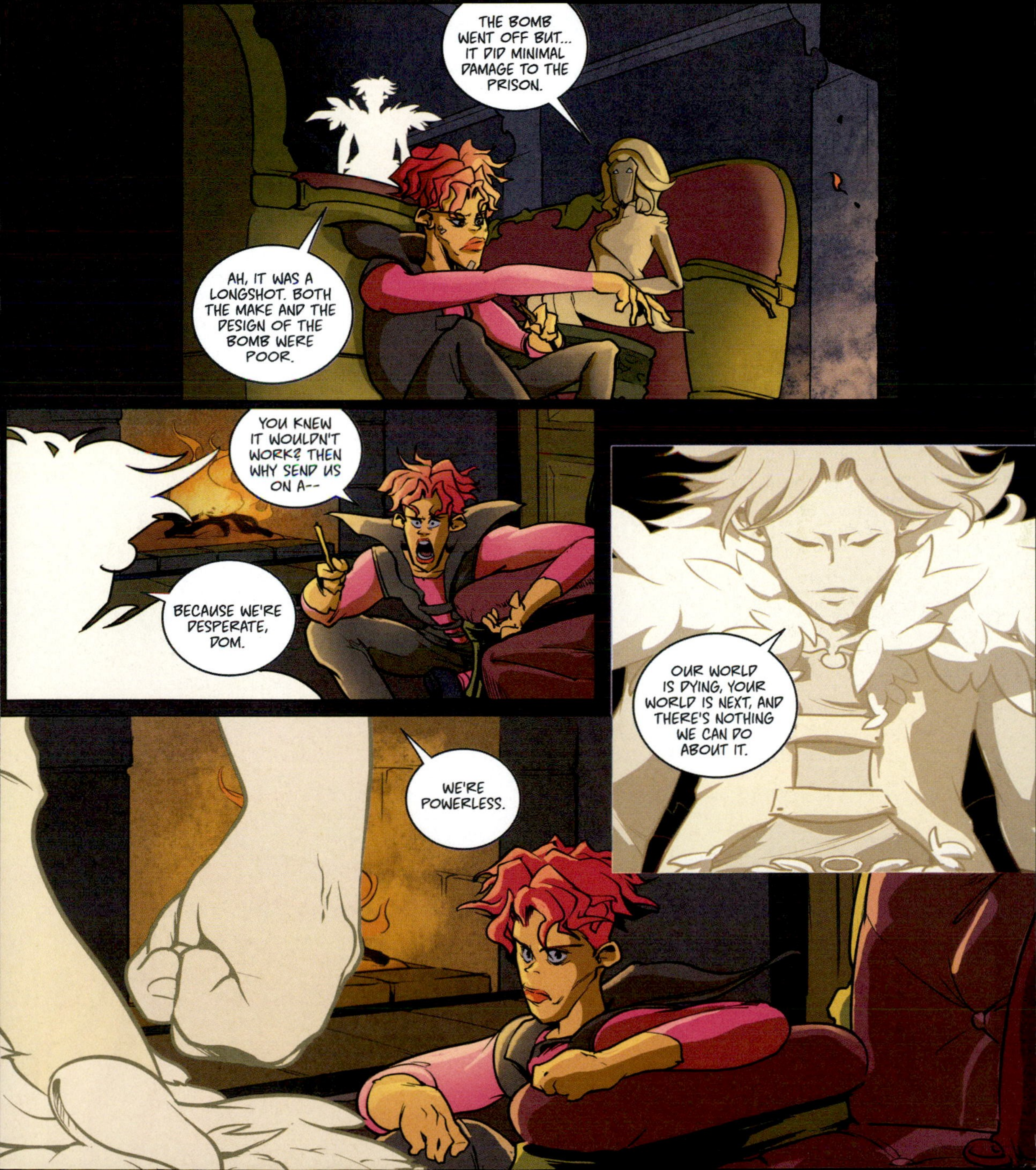
THE BOMB WENT OFF BUT... IT DID MINIMAL DAMAGE TO THE PRISON.
AH, IT WAS A LONGSHOT. BOTH THE MAKE AND THE DESIGN OF THE BOMB WERE POOR.
YOU KNEW IT WOULDN'T WORK? THEN WHY SEND US ON A--
BECAUSE WE'RE DESPERATE, DOM.
OUR WORLD IS DYING, YOUR WORLD IS NEXT, AND THERE'S NOTHING WE CAN DO ABOUT IT.
WE'RE POWERLESS.

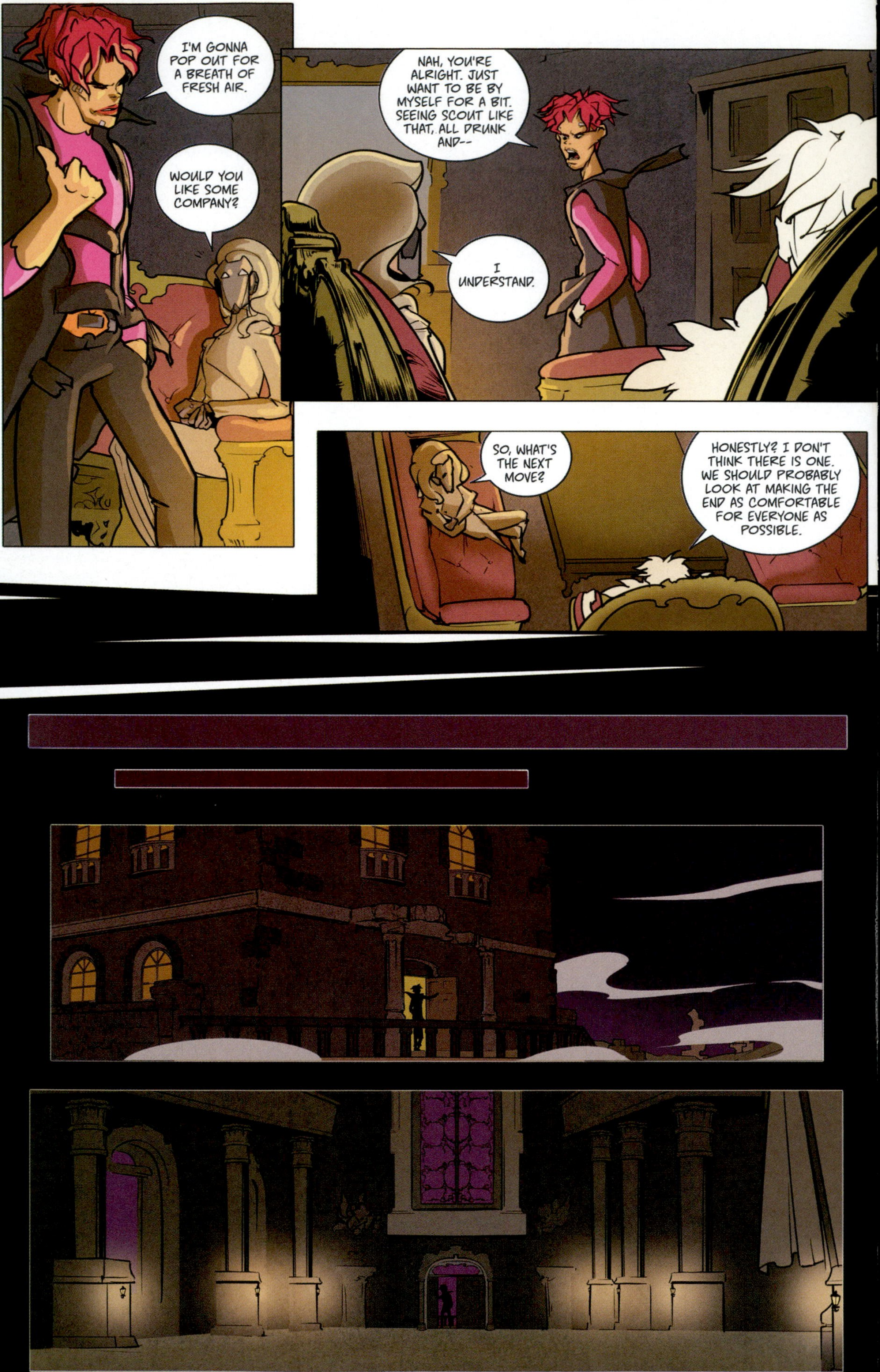
I'M GONNA POP OUT FOR A BREATH OF FRESH AIR.
WOULD YOU LIKE SOME COMPANY?
NAH, YOU'RE ALRIGHT. JUST WANT TO BE BY MYSELF FOR A BIT. SEEING SCOUT LIKE THAT, ALL DRUNK AND--
I UNDERSTAND.
SO, WHAT'S THE NEXT MOVE?
HONESTLY? I DON'T THINK THERE IS ONE. WE SHOULD PROBABLY LOOK AT MAKING THE END AS COMFORTABLE FOR EVERYONE AS POSSIBLE.

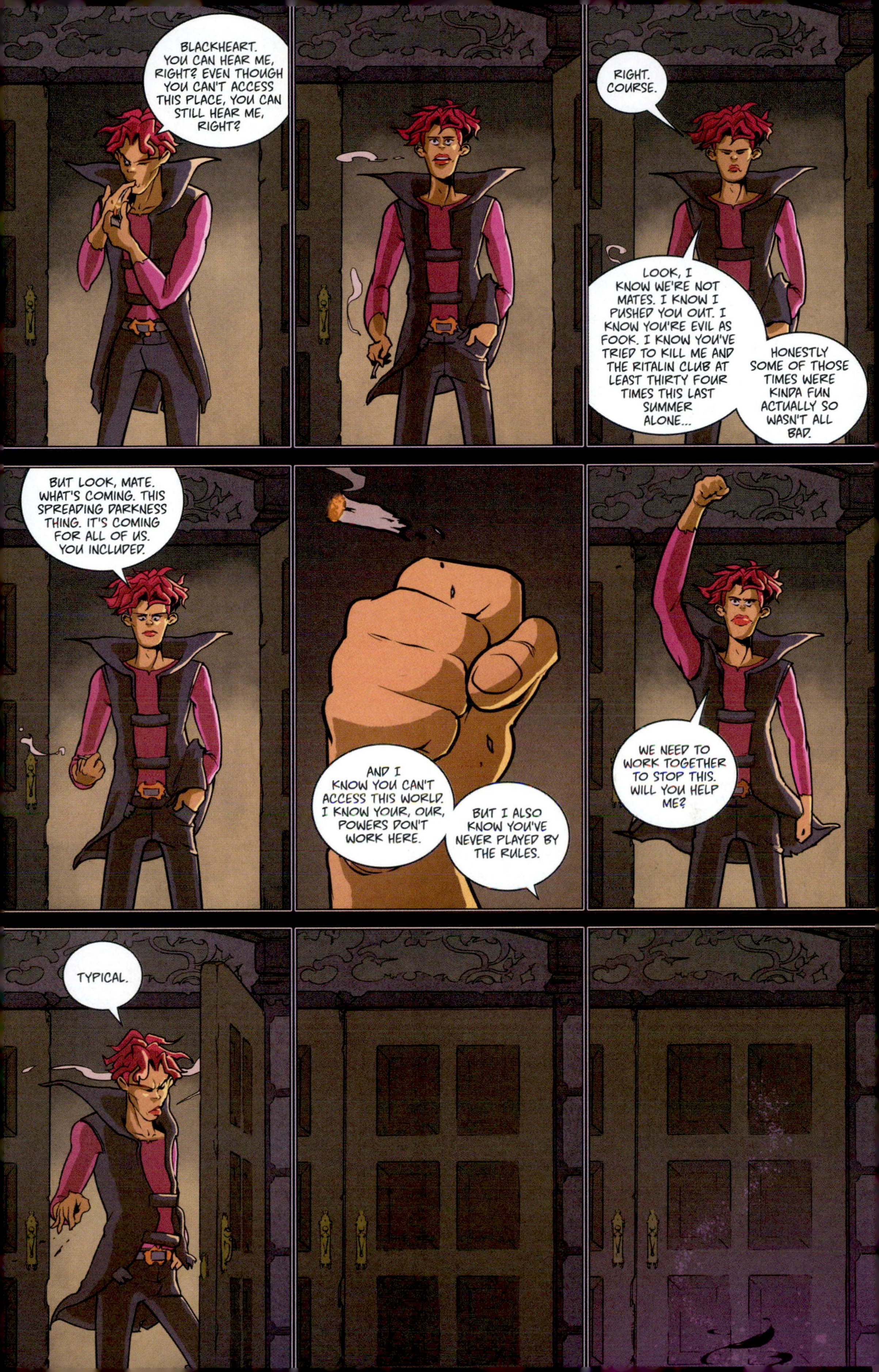
BLACKHEART. YOU CAN HEAR ME, RIGHT? EVEN THOUGH YOU CAN'T ACCESS THIS PLACE, YOU CAN STILL HEAR ME, RIGHT?
RIGHT. COURSE.
LOOK, I KNOW WE'RE NOT MATES. I KNOW I PUSHED YOU OUT. I KNOW YOU'RE EVIL AS FOOK. I KNOW YOU'VE TRIED TO KILL ME AND THE RITALIN CLUB AT LEAST THIRTY FOUR TIMES THIS LAST SUMMER ALONE...
HONESTLY SOME OF THOSE TIMES WERE KINDA FUN ACTUALLY SO WASN'T ALL BAD.
BUT LOOK, MATE. WHAT'S COMING. THIS SPREADING DARKNESS THING. IT'S COMING FOR ALL OF US. YOU INCLUDED.
AND I KNOW YOU CAN'T ACCESS THIS WORLD. I KNOW YOUR, OUR, POWERS DON'T WORK HERE.
BUT I ALSO KNOW YOU'VE NEVER PLAYED BY THE RULES.
WE NEED TO WORK TOGETHER TO STOP THIS. WILL YOU HELP ME?
TYPICAL.

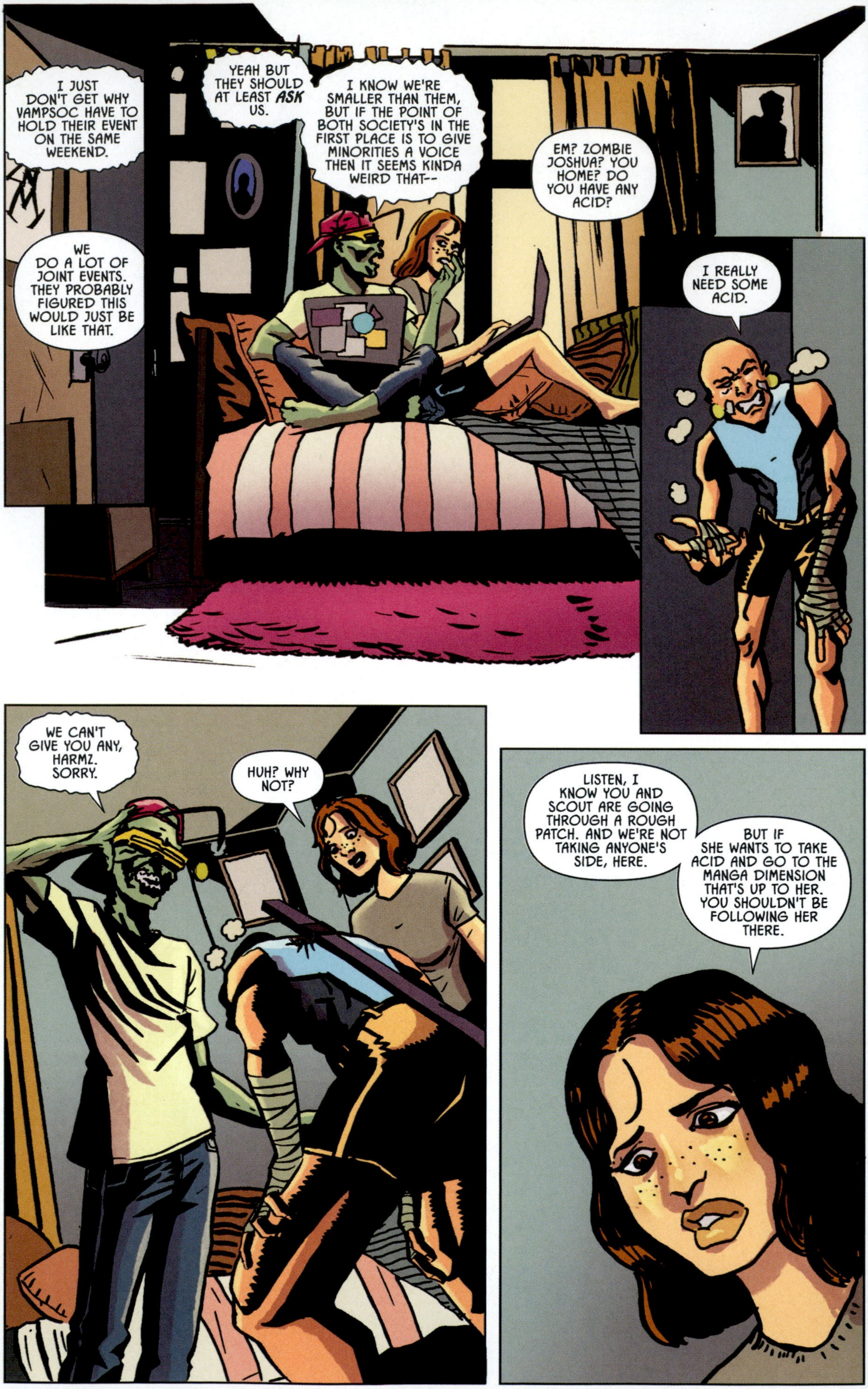
I JUST DON'T GET WHY VAMPSOC HAVE TO HOLD THEIR EVENT ON THE SAME WEEKEND.
YEAH BUT THEY SHOULD AT LEAST ASK US.
I KNOW WE'RE SMALLER THAN THEM, BUT IF THE POINT OF BOTH SOCIETY'S IN THE FIRST PLACE IS TO GIVE MINORITIES A VOICE THEN IT SEEMS KINDA WEIRD THAT--
WE DO A LOT OF JOINT EVENTS. THEY PROBABLY FIGURED THIS WOULD JUST BE LIKE THAT.
EM? ZOMBIE JOSHUA? YOU HOME? DO YOU HAVE ANY ACID?
I REALLY NEED SOME ACID.
WE CAN'T GIVE YOU ANY, HARMZ. SORRY.
HUH? WHY NOT?
LISTEN, I KNOW YOU AND SCOUT ARE GOING THROUGH A ROUGH PATCH. AND WE'RE NOT TAKING ANYONE'S SIDE, HERE.
BUT IF SHE WANTS TO TAKE ACID AND GO TO THE MANGA DIMENSION THAT'S UP TO HER. YOU SHOULDN'T BE FOLLOWING HER THERE.

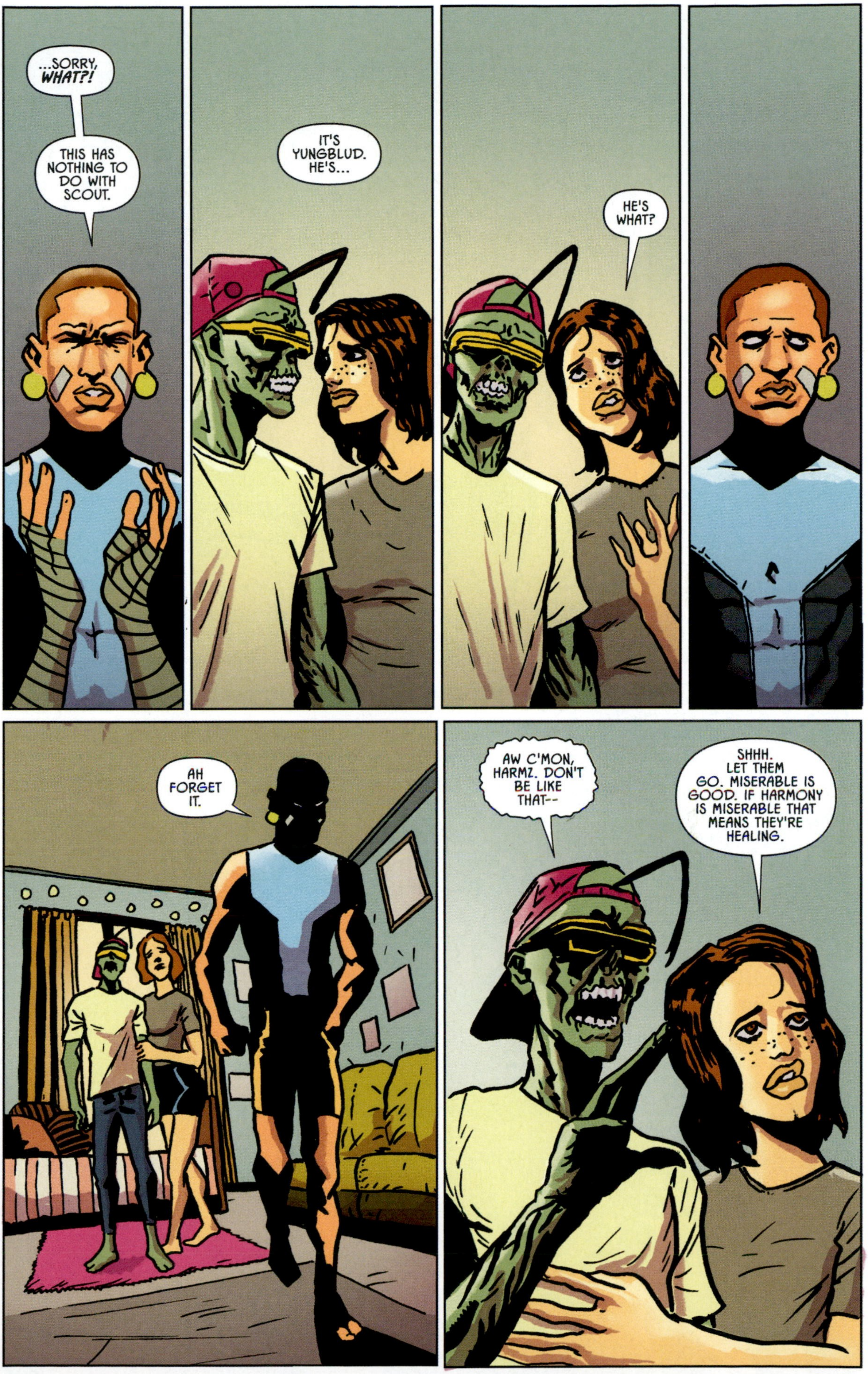
...SORRY, WHAT?!
THIS HAS NOTHING TO DO WITH SCOUT.
IT'S YUNGBLUD. HE'S...
HE'S WHAT?
AH FORGET IT.
AW C'MON, HARMZ. DON'T BE LIKE THAT--
SHHH. LET THEM GO. MISERABLE IS GOOD. IF HARMONY IS MISERABLE THAT MEANS THEY'RE HEALING.

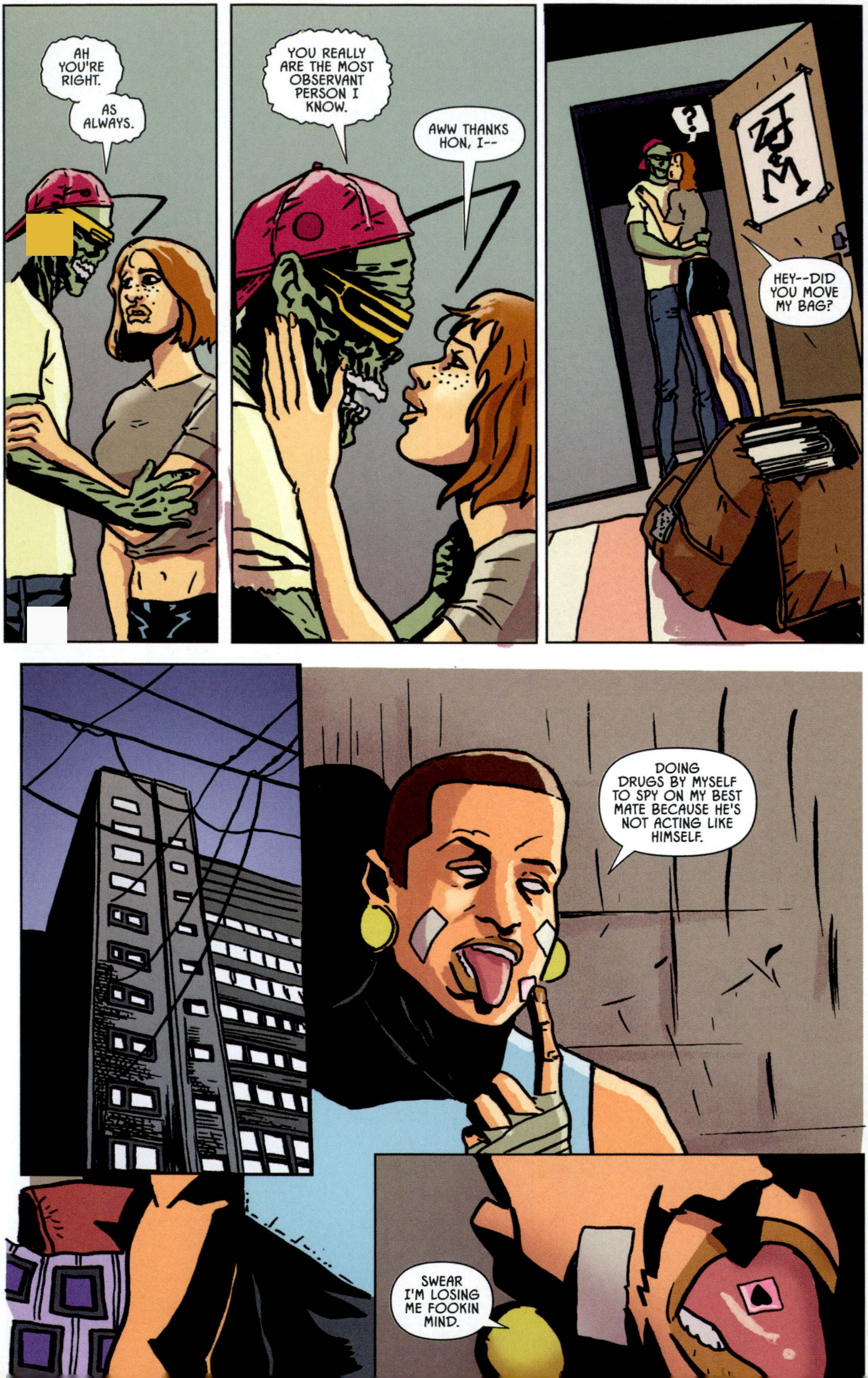
AH YOU'RE RIGHT.
AS ALWAYS.
YOU REALLY ARE THE MOST OBSERVANT PERSON I KNOW.
AWW THANKS HON, I--
?
HEY--DID YOU MOVE MY BAG?
DOING DRUGS BY MYSELF TO SPY ON MY BEST MATE BECAUSE HE'S NOT ACTING LIKE HIMSELF.
SWEAR I'M LOSING ME FOOKIN MIND.

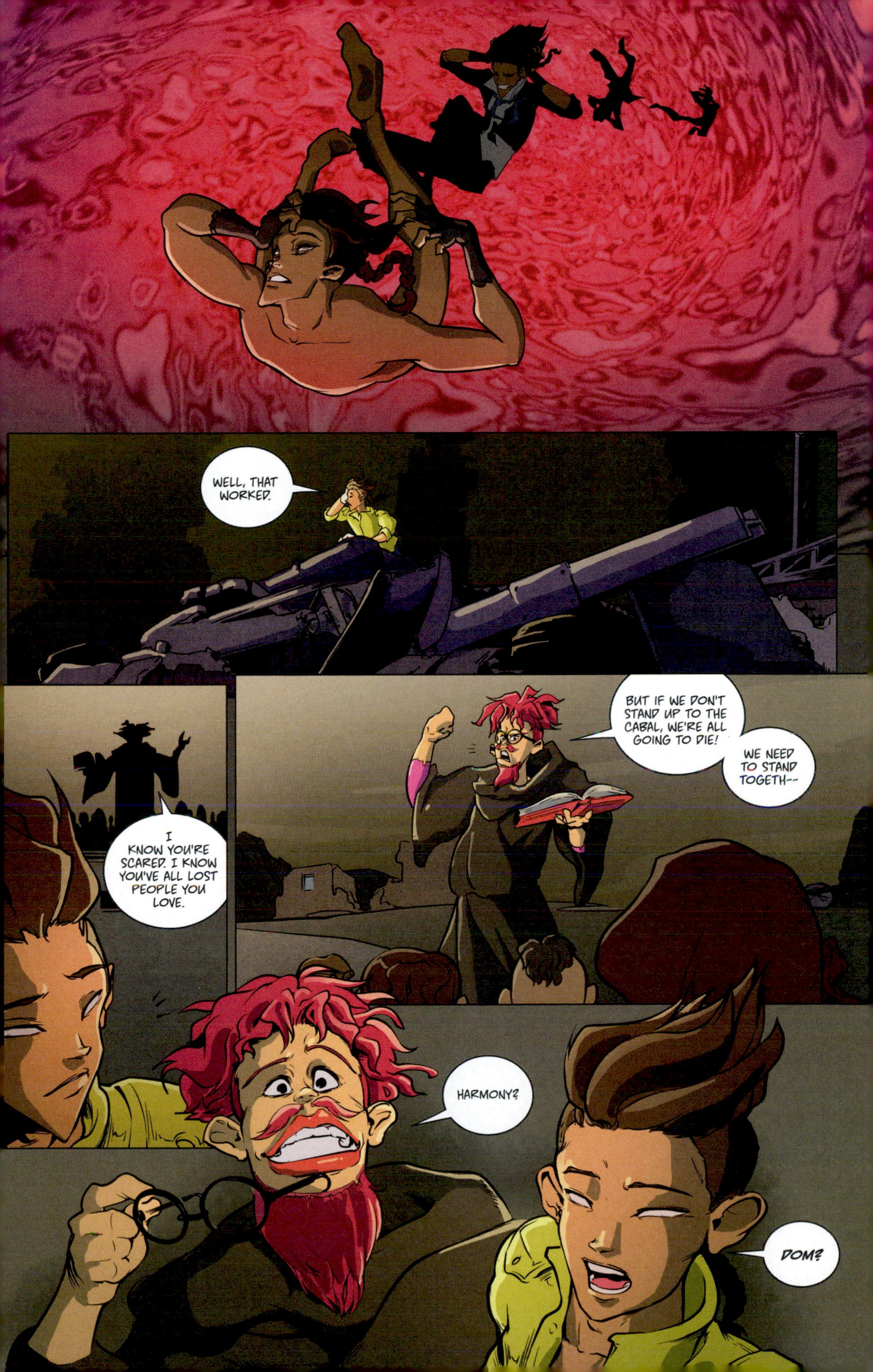
WELL, THAT WORKED.
I KNOW YOU'RE SCARED. I KNOW YOU'VE ALL LOST PEOPLE YOU LOVE.
BUT IF WE DON'T STAND UP TO THE CABAL, WE'RE ALL GOING TO DIE!
WE NEED TO STAND TOGETH--
HARMONY?
DOM?

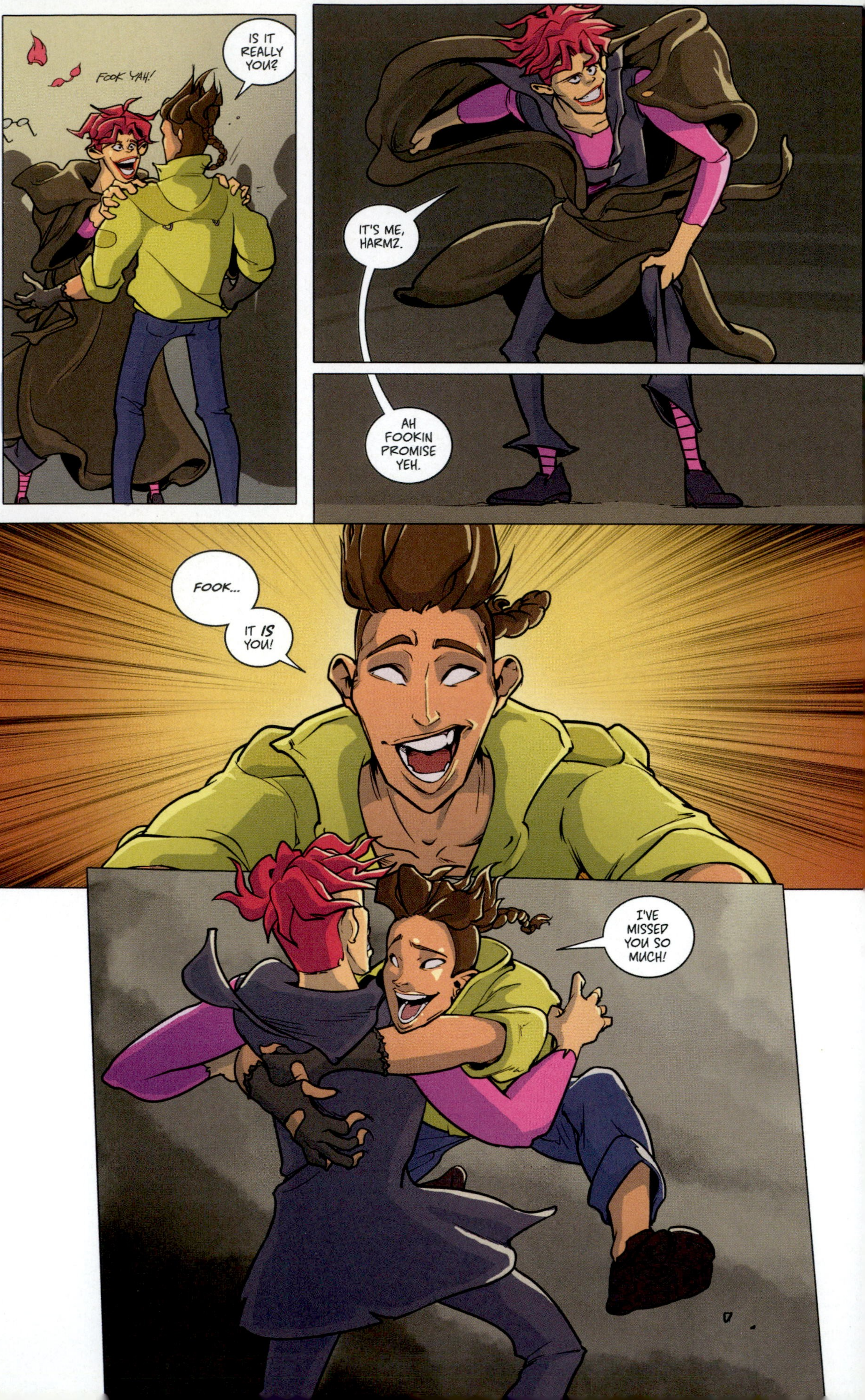
FOOK YAH!
IS IT REALLY YOU?
IT'S ME, HARMZ.
AH FOOKIN PROMISE YEH.
FOOK...
IT *IS* YOU!
I'VE MISSED YOU SO MUCH!

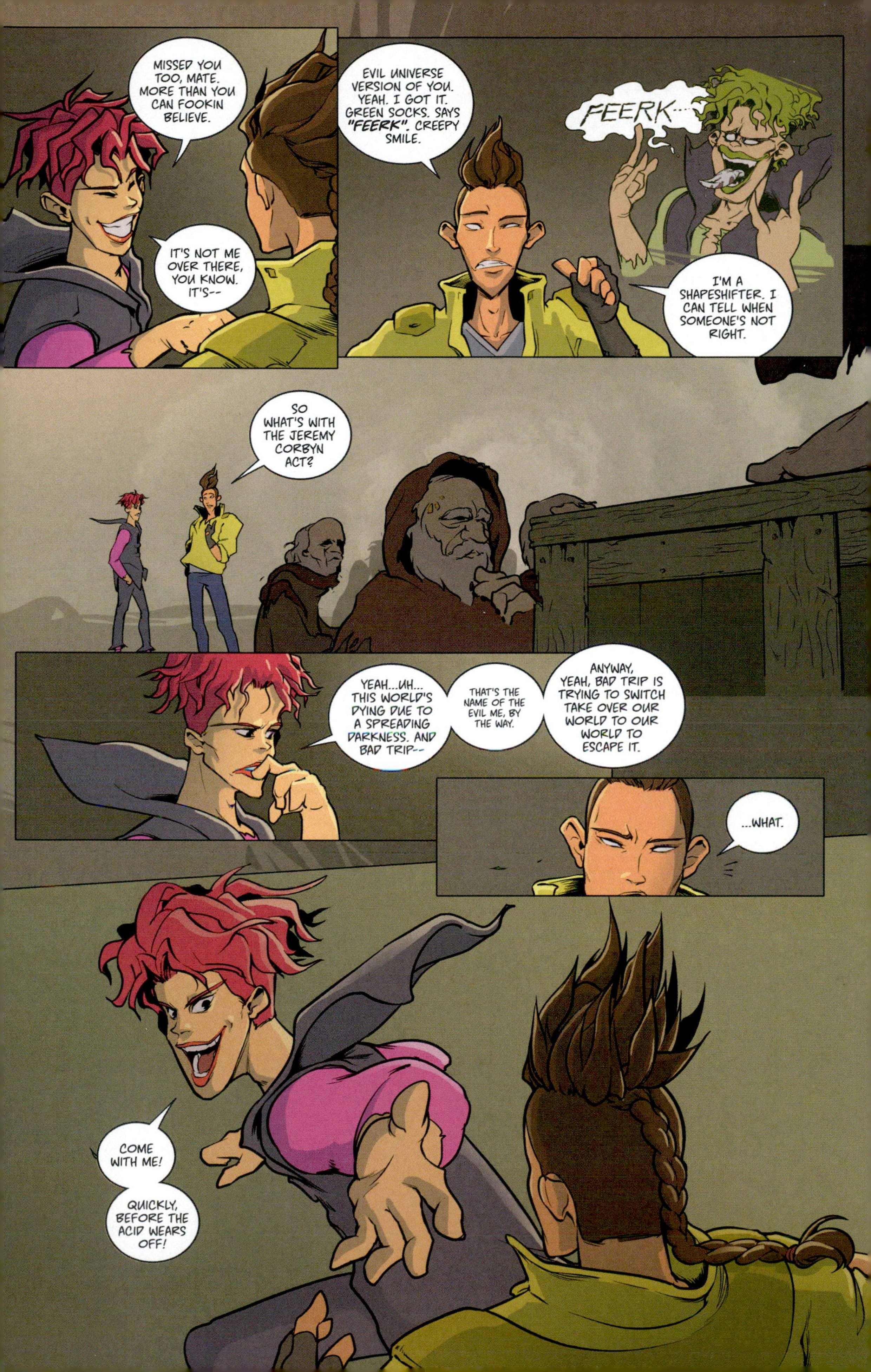
MISSED YOU TOO, MATE. MORE THAN YOU CAN FOOKIN BELIEVE.
IT'S NOT ME OVER THERE, YOU KNOW. IT'S--
EVIL UNIVERSE VERSION OF YOU. YEAH. I GOT IT. GREEN SOCKS. SAYS "FEERK". CREEPY SMILE.
FEERK...
I'M A SHAPESHIFTER. I CAN TELL WHEN SOMEONE'S NOT RIGHT.
SO WHAT'S WITH THE JEREMY CORBYN ACT?
YEAH...UH... THIS WORLD'S DYING DUE TO A SPREADING DARKNESS. AND BAD TRIP--
THAT'S THE NAME OF THE EVIL ME, BY THE WAY.
ANYWAY, YEAH, BAD TRIP IS TRYING TO SWITCH TAKE OVER OUR WORLD TO OUR WORLD TO ESCAPE IT.
...WHAT.
COME WITH ME!
QUICKLY, BEFORE THE ACID WEARS OFF!

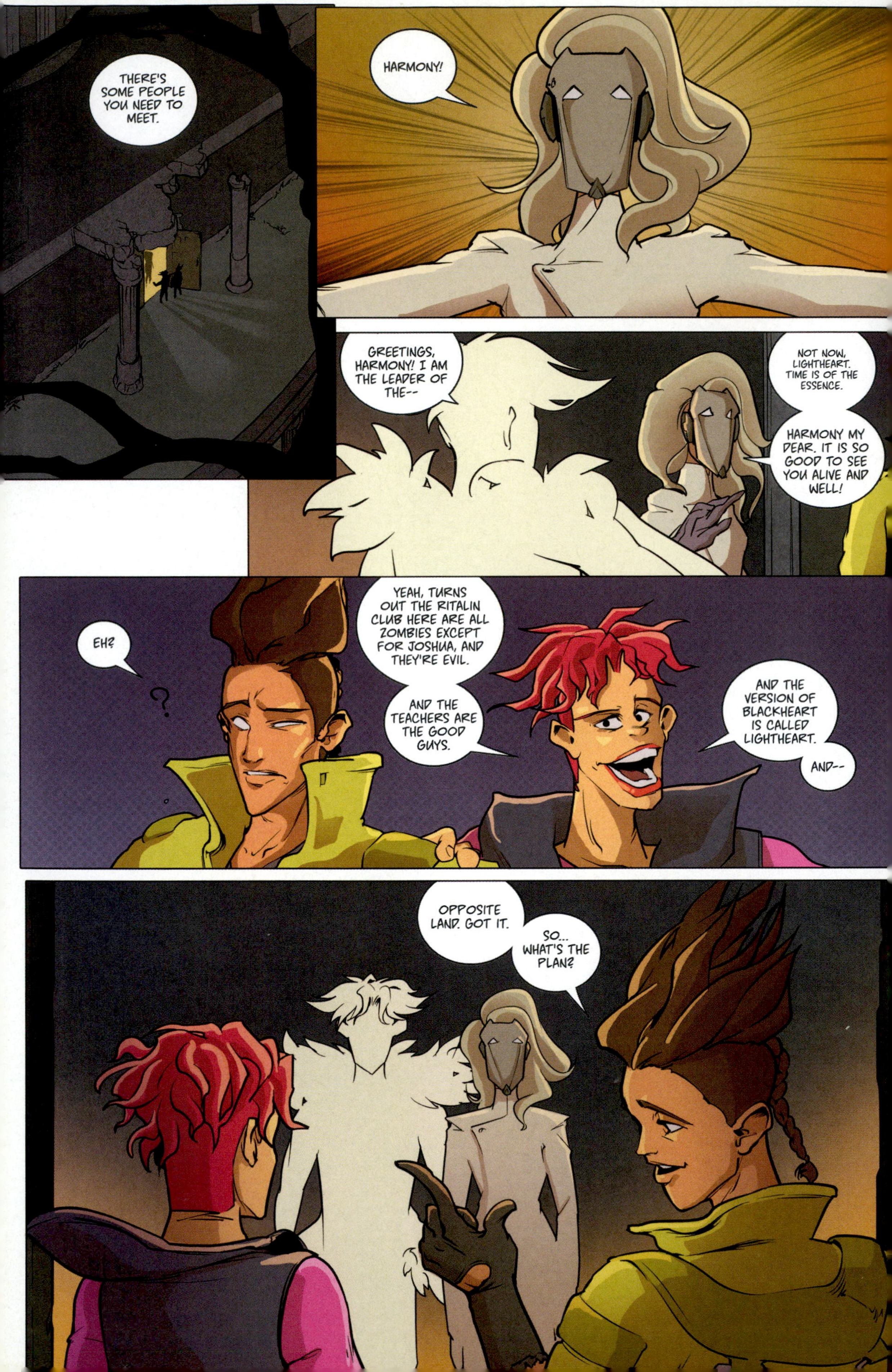
THERE'S SOME PEOPLE YOU NEED TO MEET.
HARMONY!
GREETINGS, HARMONY! I AM THE LEADER OF THE--
NOT NOW, LIGHTHEART. TIME IS OF THE ESSENCE.
HARMONY MY DEAR. IT IS SO GOOD TO SEE YOU ALIVE AND WELL!
EH?
YEAH, TURNS OUT THE RITALIN CLUB HERE ARE ALL ZOMBIES EXCEPT FOR JOSHUA, AND THEY'RE EVIL.
AND THE TEACHERS ARE THE GOOD GUYS.
AND THE VERSION OF BLACKHEART IS CALLED LIGHTHEART.
AND--
OPPOSITE LAND. GOT IT.
SO... WHAT'S THE PLAN?

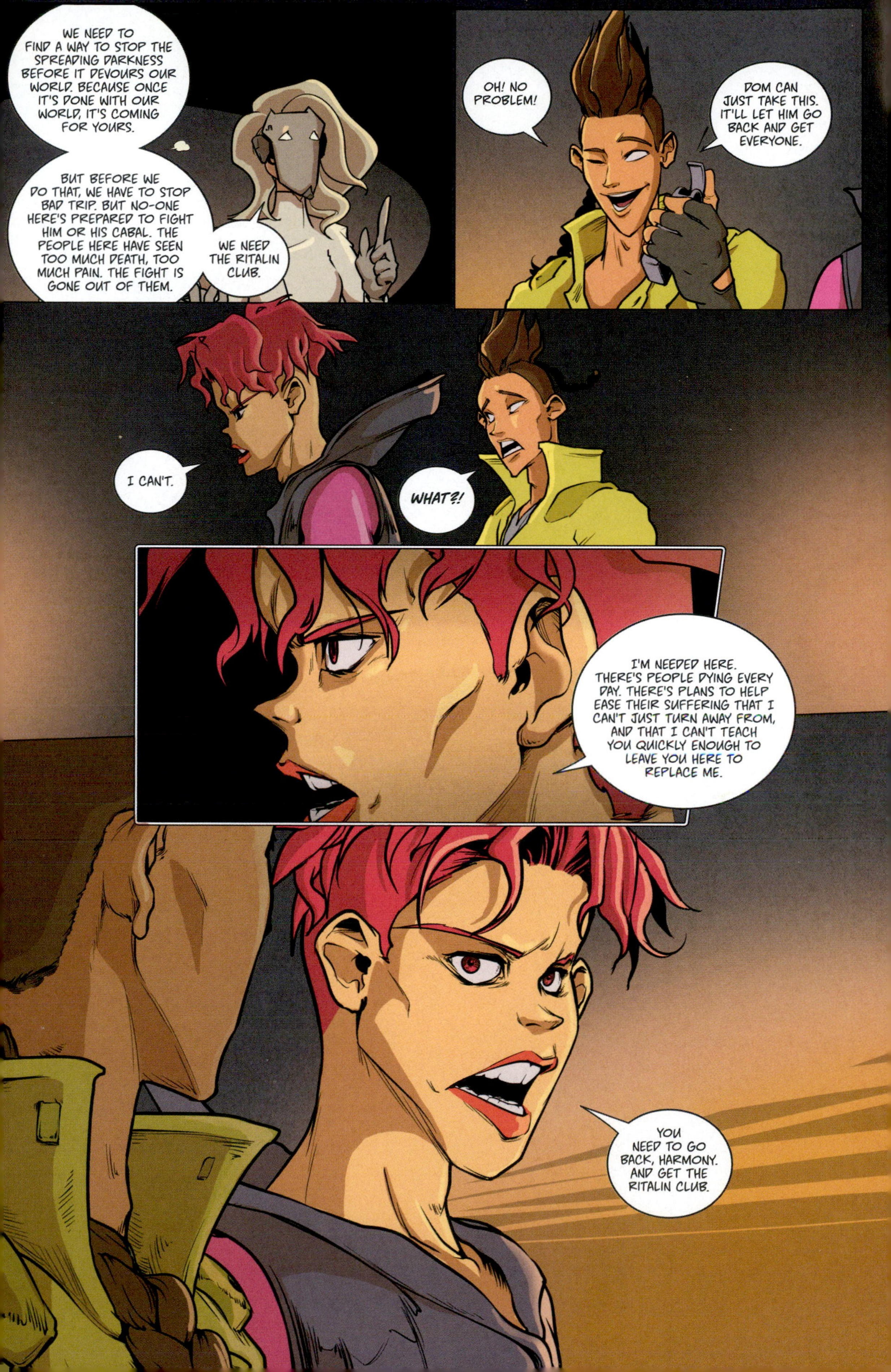
WE NEED TO FIND A WAY TO STOP THE SPREADING DARKNESS BEFORE IT DEVOURS OUR WORLD. BECAUSE ONCE IT'S DONE WITH OUR WORLD, IT'S COMING FOR YOURS.
BUT BEFORE WE DO THAT, WE HAVE TO STOP BAD TRIP. BUT NO-ONE HERE'S PREPARED TO FIGHT HIM OR HIS CABAL. THE PEOPLE HERE HAVE SEEN TOO MUCH DEATH, TOO MUCH PAIN. THE FIGHT IS GONE OUT OF THEM.
WE NEED THE RITALIN CLUB.
OH! NO PROBLEM!
DOM CAN JUST TAKE THIS. IT'LL LET HIM GO BACK AND GET EVERYONE.
I CAN'T.
WHAT?!
I'M NEEDED HERE. THERE'S PEOPLE DYING EVERY DAY. THERE'S PLANS TO HELP EASE THEIR SUFFERING THAT I CAN'T JUST TURN AWAY FROM, AND THAT I CAN'T TEACH YOU QUICKLY ENOUGH TO LEAVE YOU HERE TO REPLACE ME.
YOU NEED TO GO BACK, HARMONY. AND GET THE RITALIN CLUB.

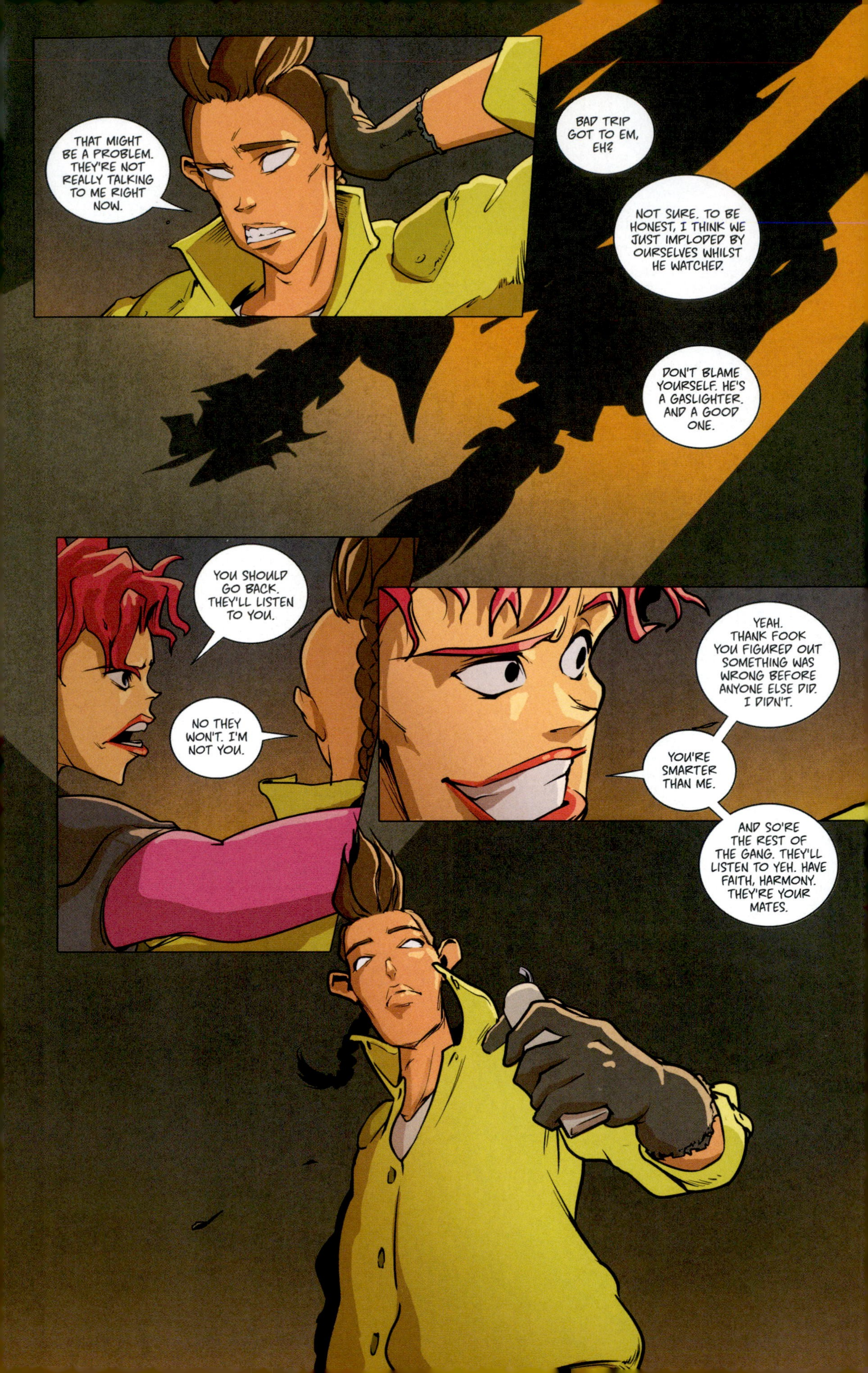
THAT MIGHT BE A PROBLEM. THEY'RE NOT REALLY TALKING TO ME RIGHT NOW.
BAD TRIP GOT TO EM, EH?
NOT SURE. TO BE HONEST, I THINK WE JUST IMPLODED BY OURSELVES WHILST HE WATCHED.
DON'T BLAME YOURSELF. HE'S A GASLIGHTER. AND A GOOD ONE.
YOU SHOULD GO BACK. THEY'LL LISTEN TO YOU.
NO THEY WON'T. I'M NOT YOU.
YEAH. THANK FOOK YOU FIGURED OUT SOMETHING WAS WRONG BEFORE ANYONE ELSE DID. I DIDN'T.
YOU'RE SMARTER THAN ME.
AND SO'RE THE REST OF THE GANG. THEY'LL LISTEN TO YEH. HAVE FAITH, HARMONY. THEY'RE YOUR MATES.

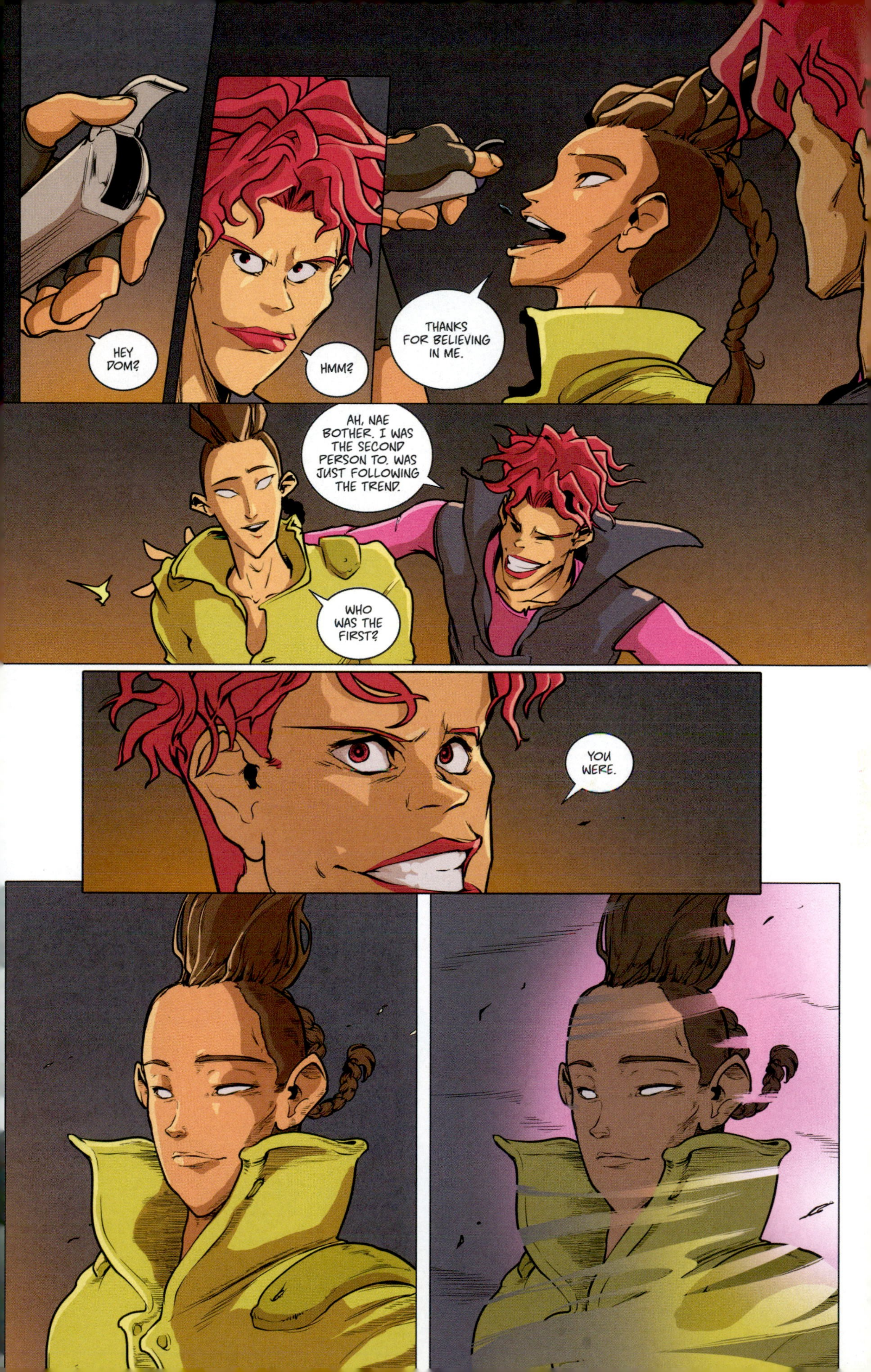
HEY DOM?
HMM?
THANKS FOR BELIEVING IN ME.
AH, NAE BOTHER. I WAS THE SECOND PERSON TO. WAS JUST FOLLOWING THE TREND.
WHO WAS THE FIRST?
YOU WERE.

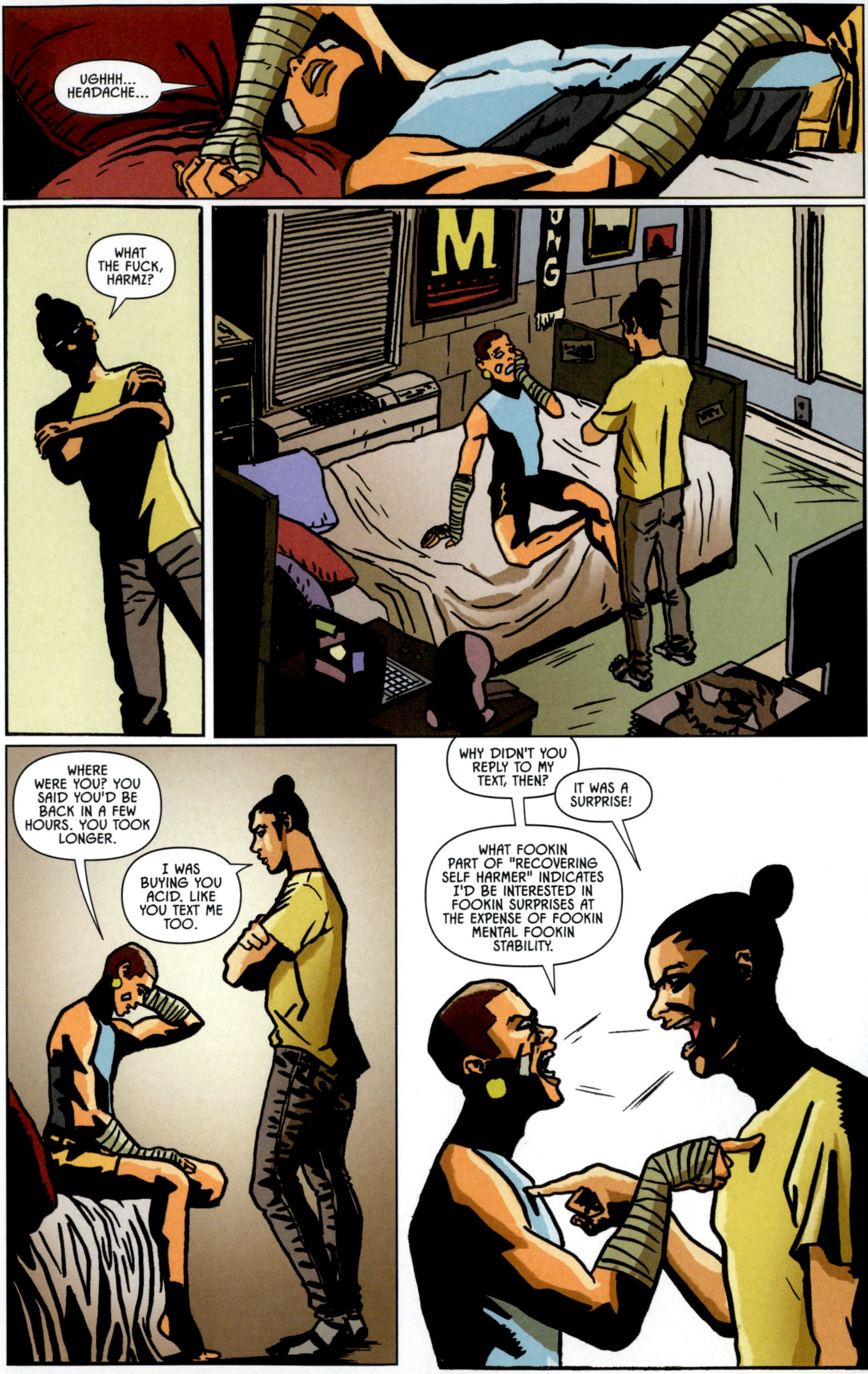
UGHHH... HEADACHE...
WHAT THE FUCK, HARMZ?
WHERE WERE YOU? YOU SAID YOU'D BE BACK IN A FEW HOURS. YOU TOOK LONGER.
I WAS BUYING YOU ACID. LIKE YOU TEXT ME TOO.
WHY DIDN'T YOU REPLY TO MY TEXT, THEN?
IT WAS A SURPRISE!
WHAT FOOKIN PART OF "RECOVERING SELF HARMER" INDICATES I'D BE INTERESTED IN FOOKIN SURPRISES AT THE EXPENSE OF FOOKIN MENTAL FOOKIN STABILITY.

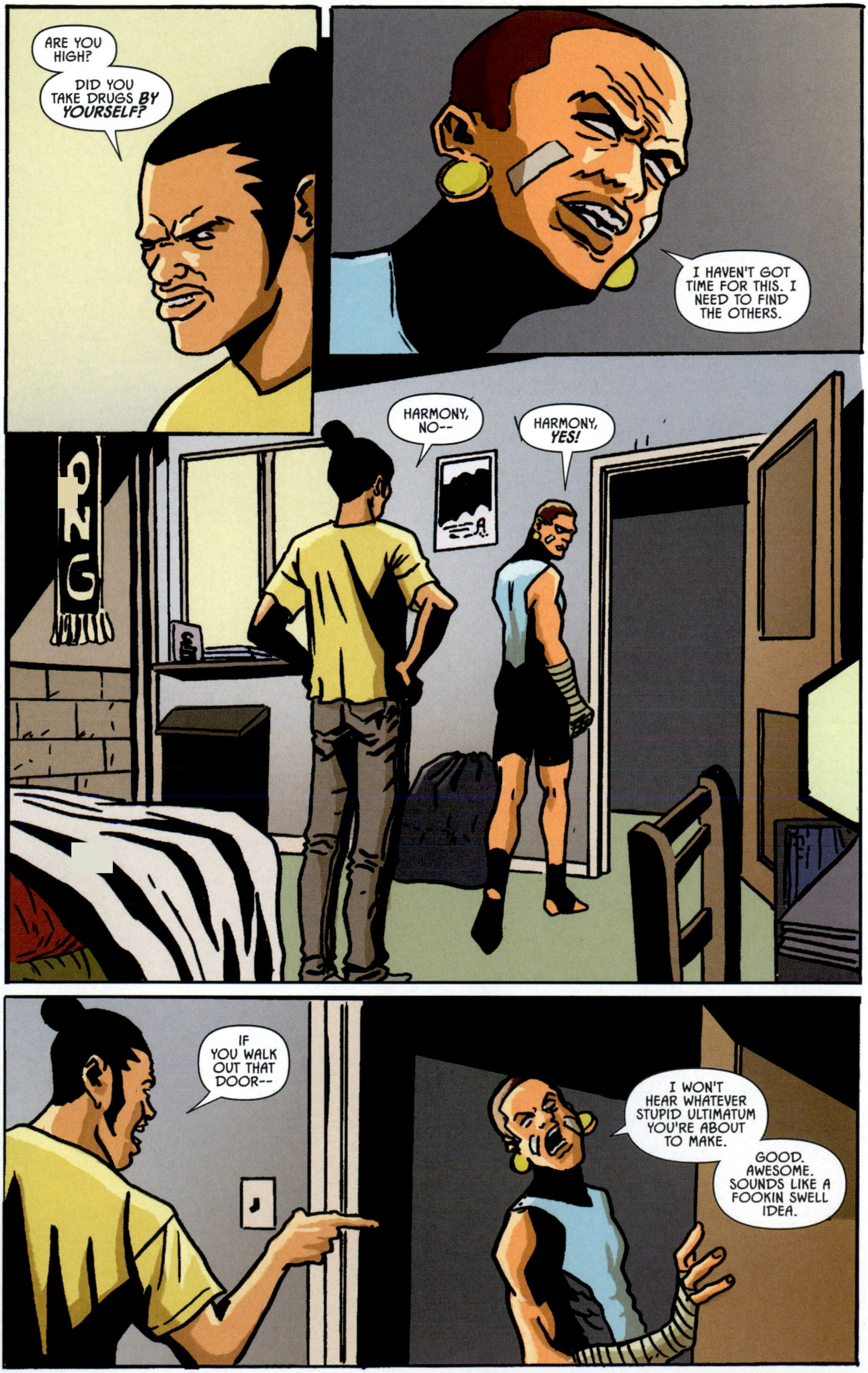
ARE YOU HIGH?
DID YOU TAKE DRUGS *BY YOURSELF?*
I HAVEN'T GOT TIME FOR THIS. I NEED TO FIND THE OTHERS.
HARMONY, NO--
HARMONY, *YES!*
IF YOU WALK OUT THAT DOOR--
I WON'T HEAR WHATEVER STUPID ULTIMATUM YOU'RE ABOUT TO MAKE.
GOOD. AWESOME. SOUNDS LIKE A FOOKIN SWELL IDEA.

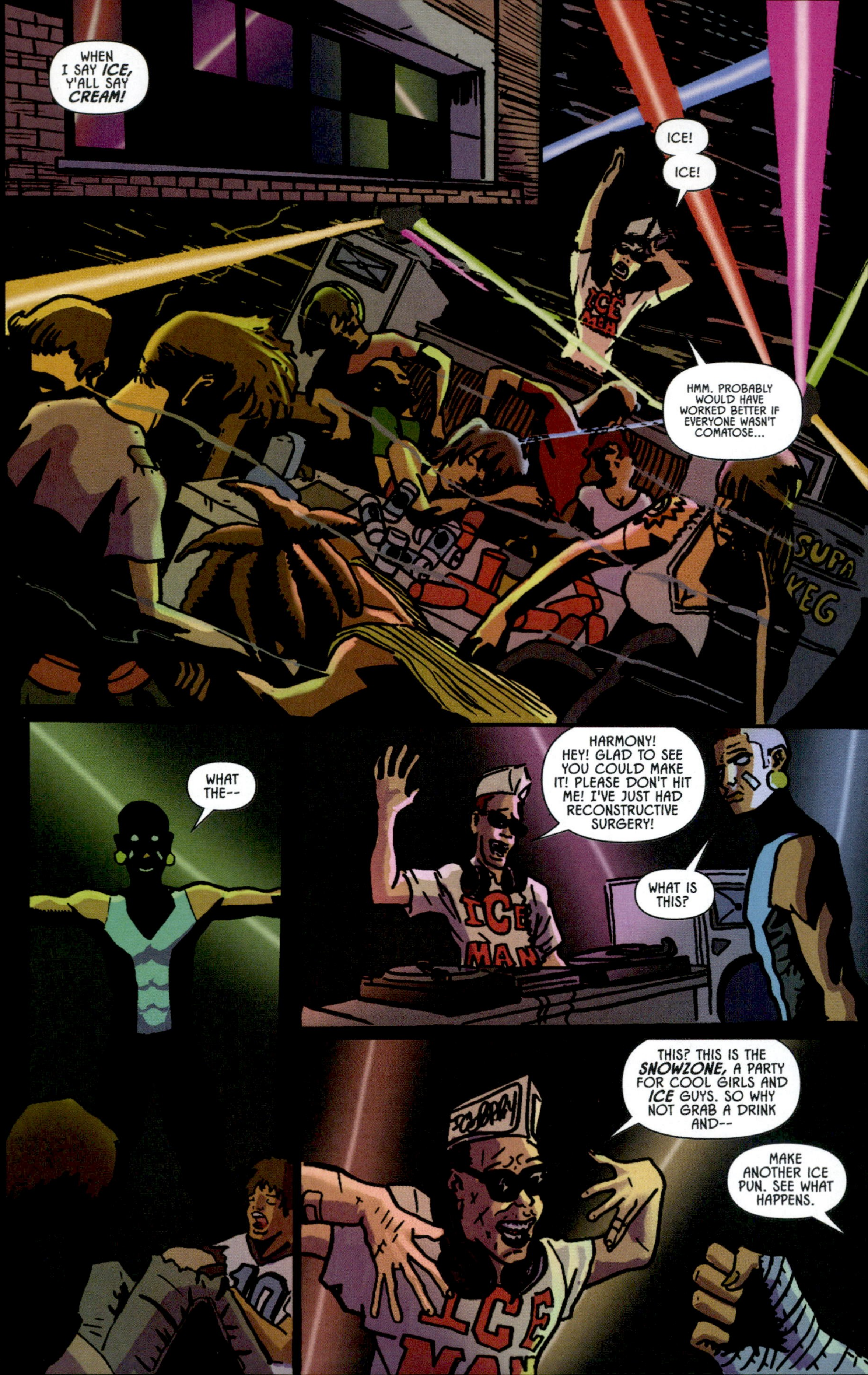
WHEN I SAY ICE, Y'ALL SAY CREAM!
ICE!
ICE!
HMM. PROBABLY WOULD HAVE WORKED BETTER IF EVERYONE WASN'T COMATOSE...
SUPA KEG
WHAT THE--
HARMONY! HEY! GLAD TO SEE YOU COULD MAKE IT! PLEASE DON'T HIT ME! I'VE JUST HAD RECONSTRUCTIVE SURGERY!
WHAT IS THIS?
THIS? THIS IS THE SNOWZONE, A PARTY FOR COOL GIRLS AND ICE GUYS. SO WHY NOT GRAB A DRINK AND--
MAKE ANOTHER ICE PUN. SEE WHAT HAPPENS.

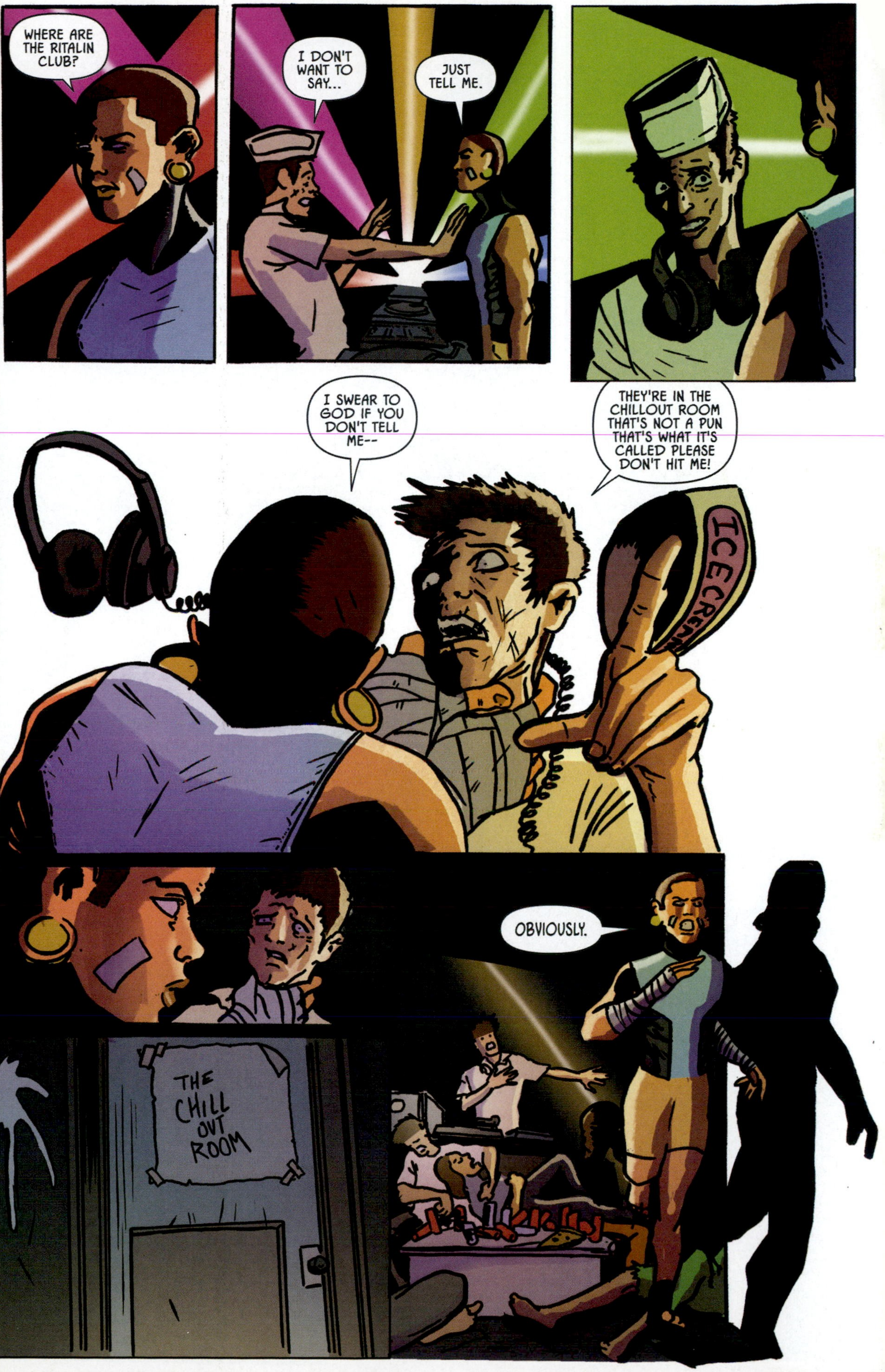
WHERE ARE THE RITALIN CLUB?
I DON'T WANT TO SAY...
JUST TELL ME.
I SWEAR TO GOD IF YOU DON'T TELL ME--
THEY'RE IN THE CHILLOUT ROOM THAT'S NOT A PUN THAT'S WHAT IT'S CALLED PLEASE DON'T HIT ME!
ICE CREAM
THE CHILL OUT ROOM
OBVIOUSLY.

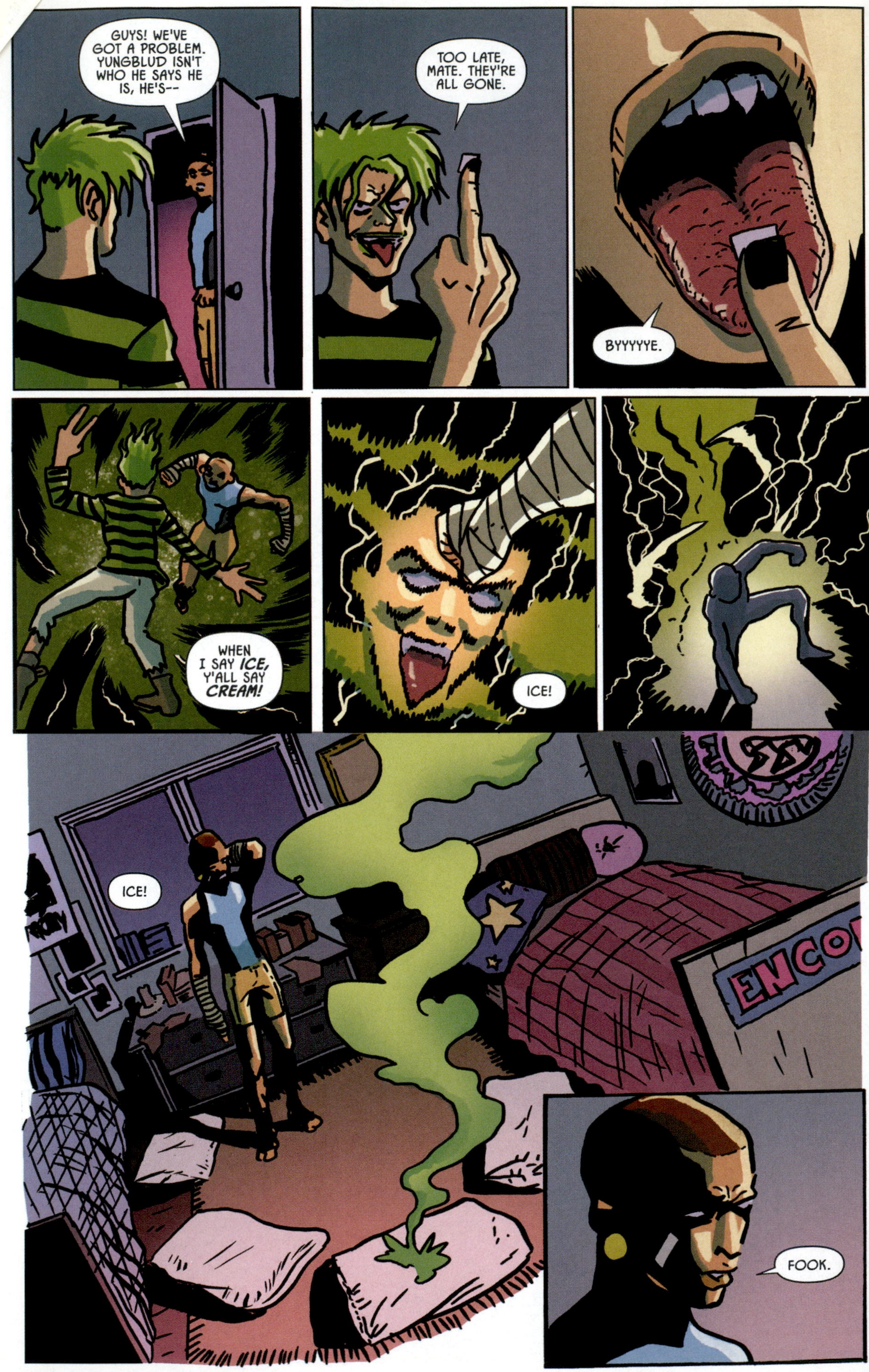
GUYS! WE'VE GOT A PROBLEM. YUNGBLUD ISN'T WHO HE SAYS HE IS, HE'S--
TOO LATE, MATE. THEY'RE ALL GONE.
BYYYYYE.
WHEN I SAY *ICE,* Y'ALL SAY ***CREAM!***
ICE!
ICE!
FOOK.
ENCO

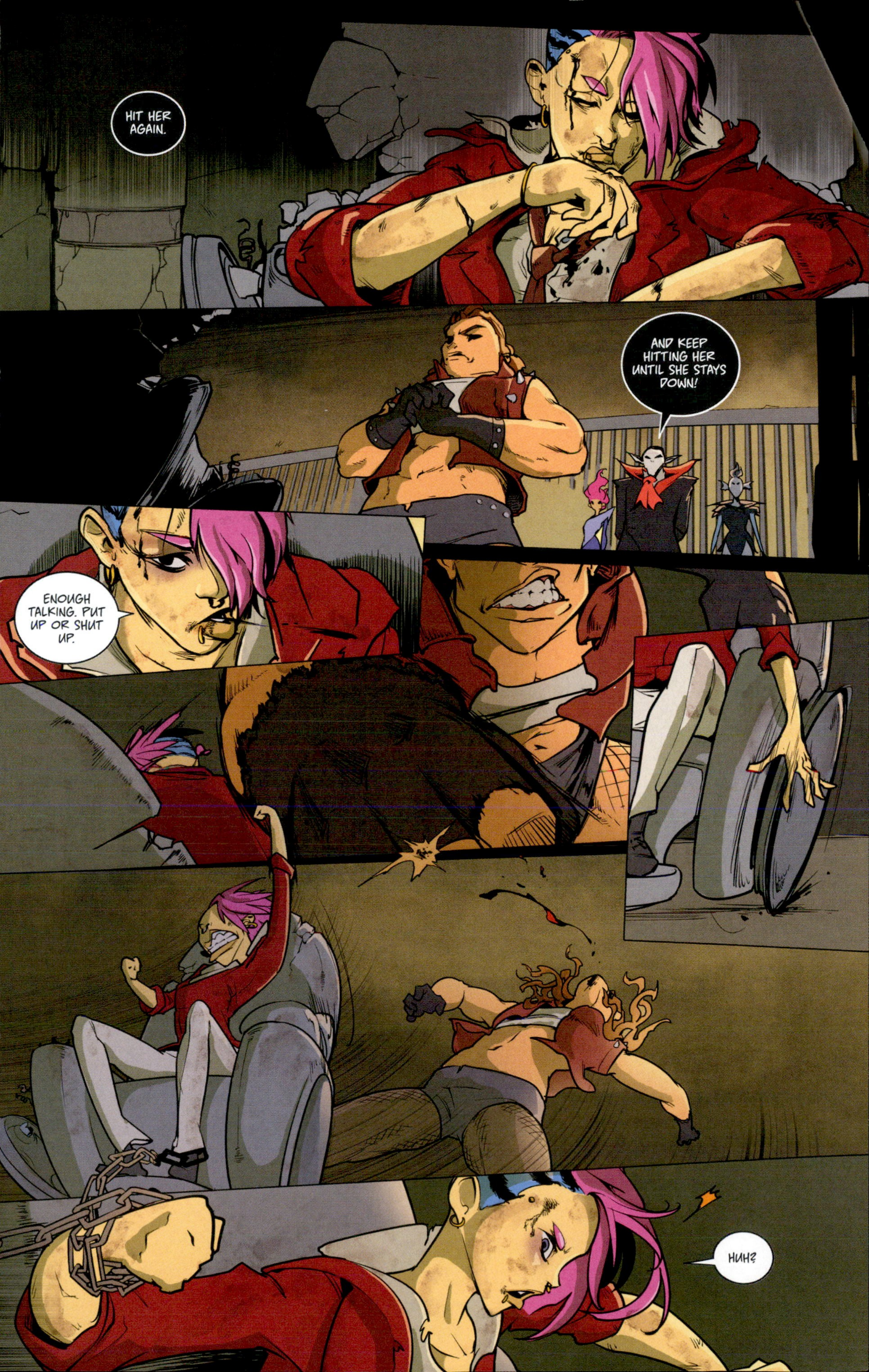
HIT HER AGAIN.
AND KEEP HITTING HER UNTIL SHE STAYS DOWN!
ENOUGH TALKING. PUT UP OR SHUT UP.
HUH?

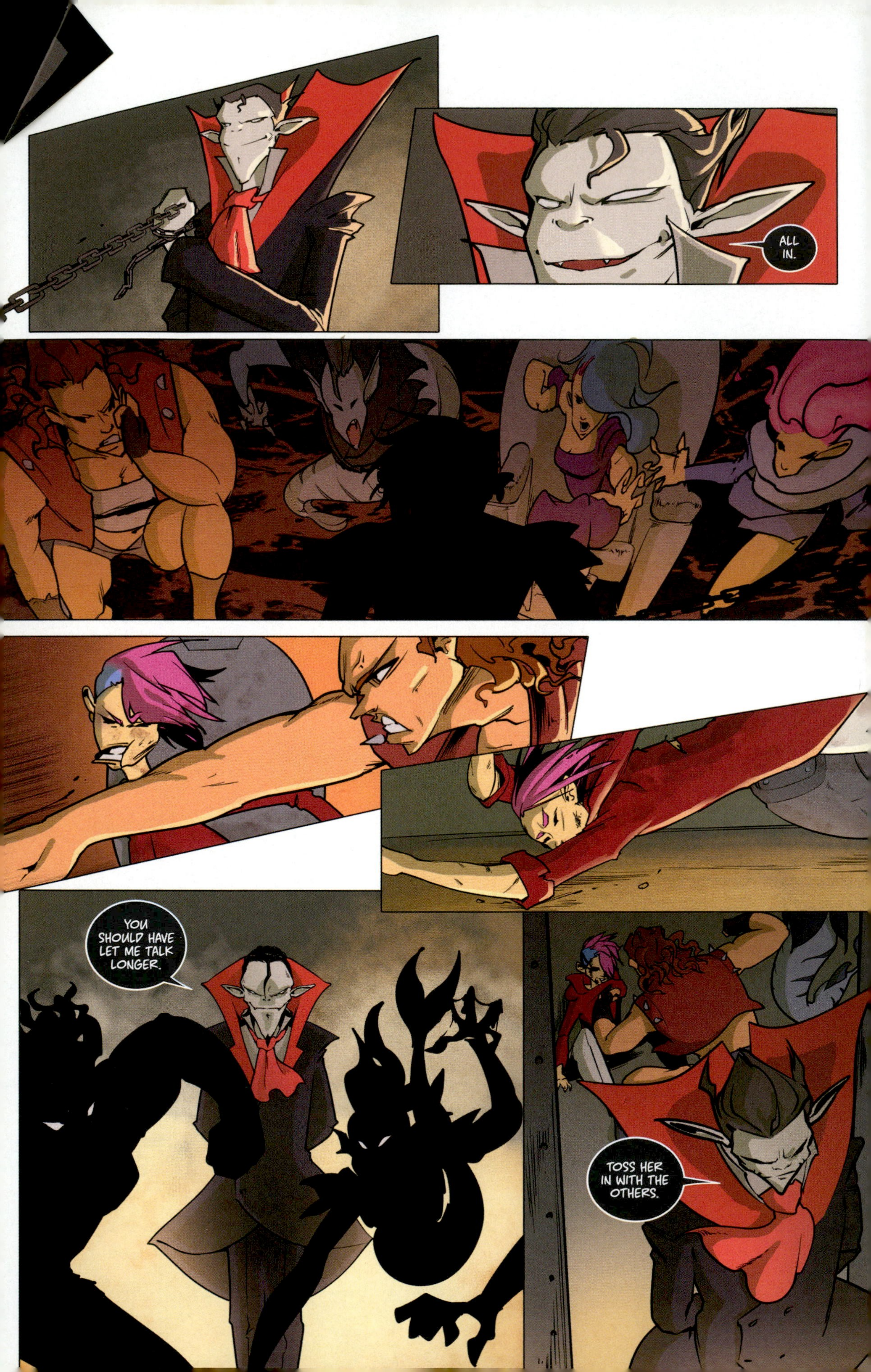
ALL IN.
YOU SHOULD HAVE LET ME TALK LONGER.
TOSS HER IN WITH THE OTHERS.

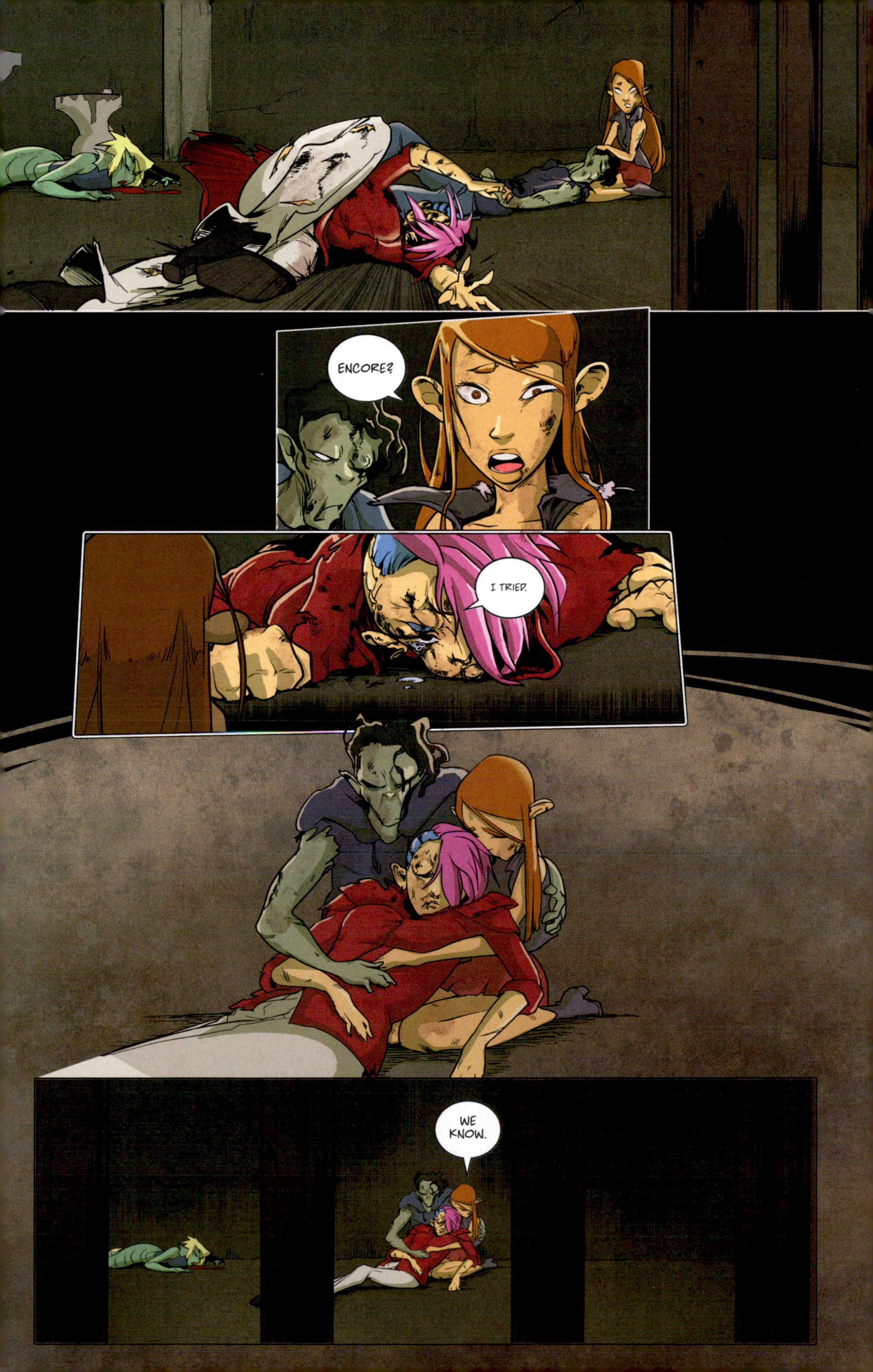
ENCORE?
I TRIED.
WE KNOW.

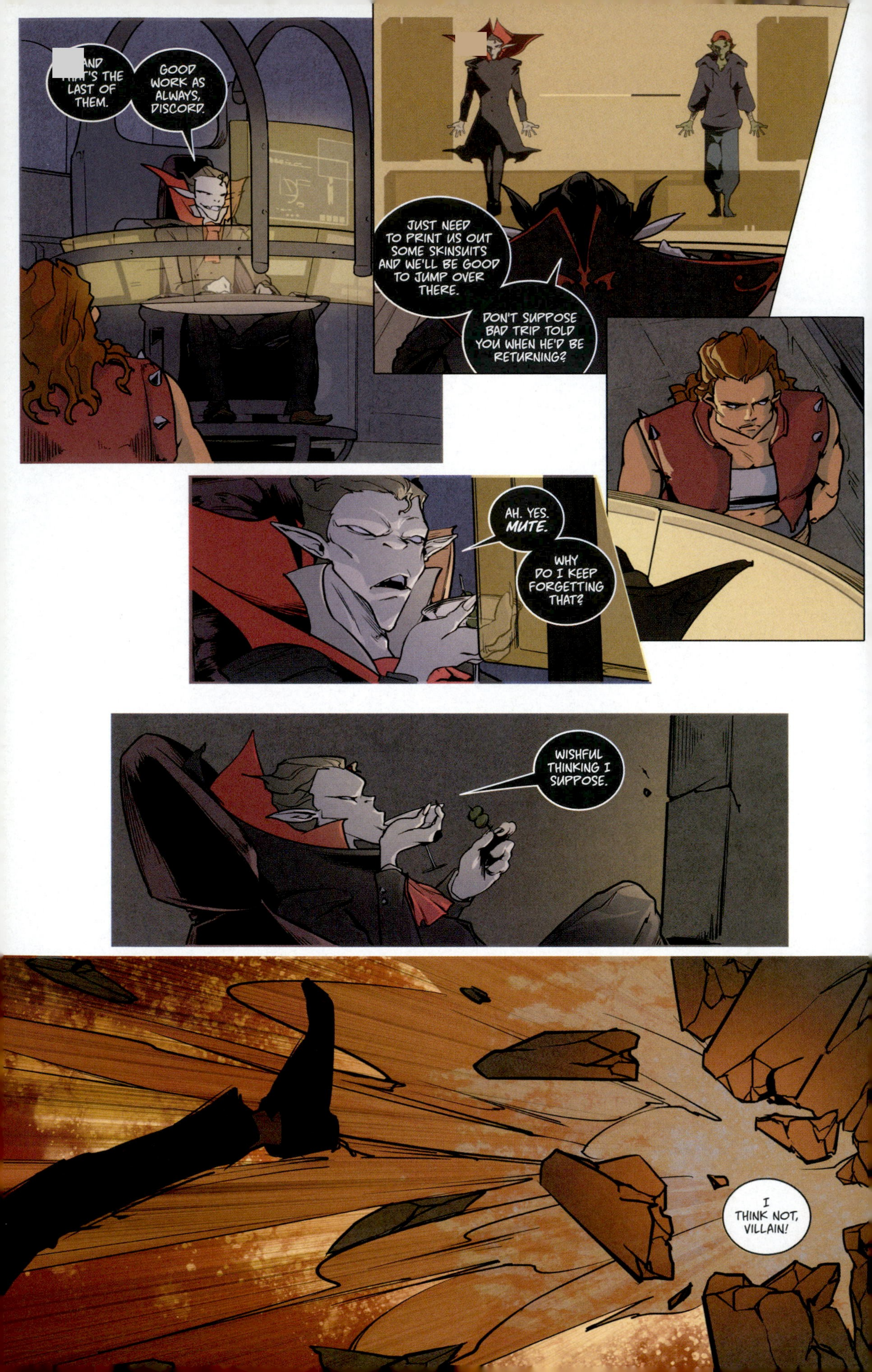
AND THAT'S THE LAST OF THEM.
GOOD WORK AS ALWAYS, DISCORD.
JUST NEED TO PRINT US OUT SOME SKINSUITS AND WE'LL BE GOOD TO JUMP OVER THERE.
DON'T SUPPOSE BAD TRIP TOLD YOU WHEN HE'D BE RETURNING?
AH. YES. ***MUTE.***
WHY DO I KEEP FORGETTING THAT?
WISHFUL THINKING I SUPPOSE.
I THINK NOT, VILLAIN!

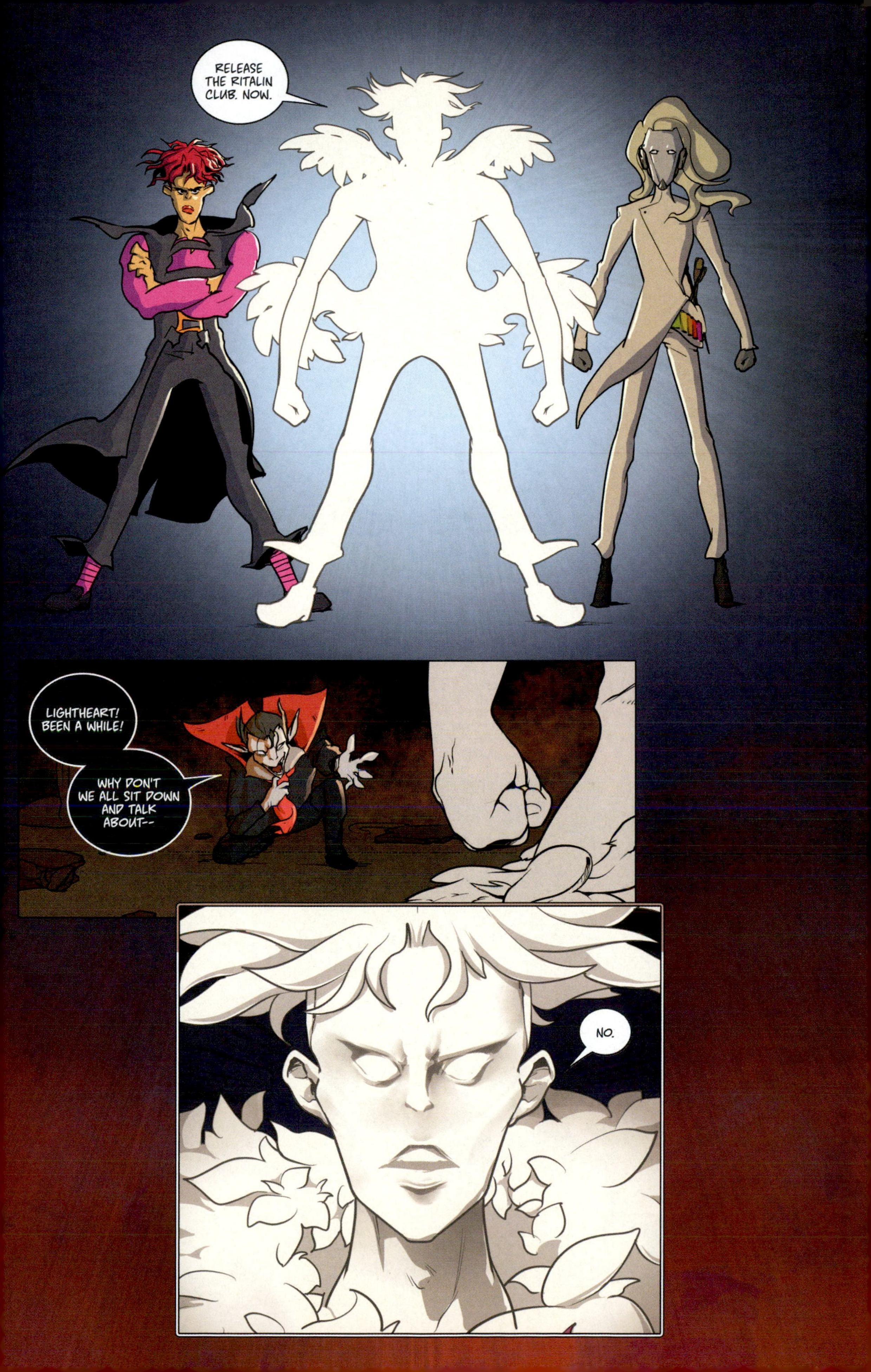
RELEASE THE RITALIN CLUB. NOW.
LIGHTHEART! BEEN A WHILE!
WHY DON'T WE ALL SIT DOWN AND TALK ABOUT--
NO.

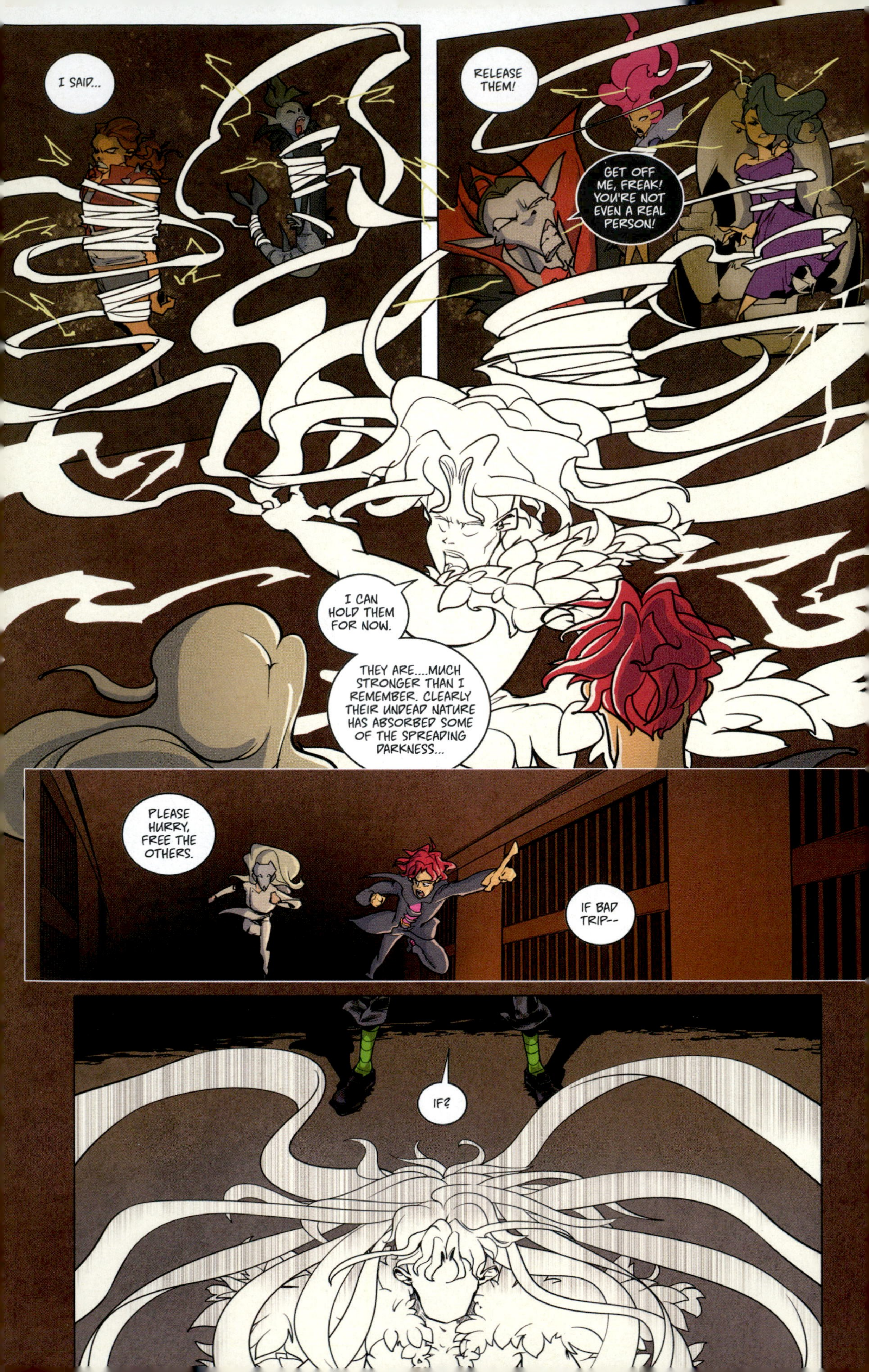
I SAID...
RELEASE THEM!
GET OFF ME, FREAK! YOU'RE NOT EVEN A REAL PERSON!
I CAN HOLD THEM FOR NOW.
THEY ARE....MUCH STRONGER THAN I REMEMBER. CLEARLY THEIR UNDEAD NATURE HAS ABSORBED SOME OF THE SPREADING DARKNESS...
PLEASE HURRY, FREE THE OTHERS.
IF BAD TRIP--
IF?

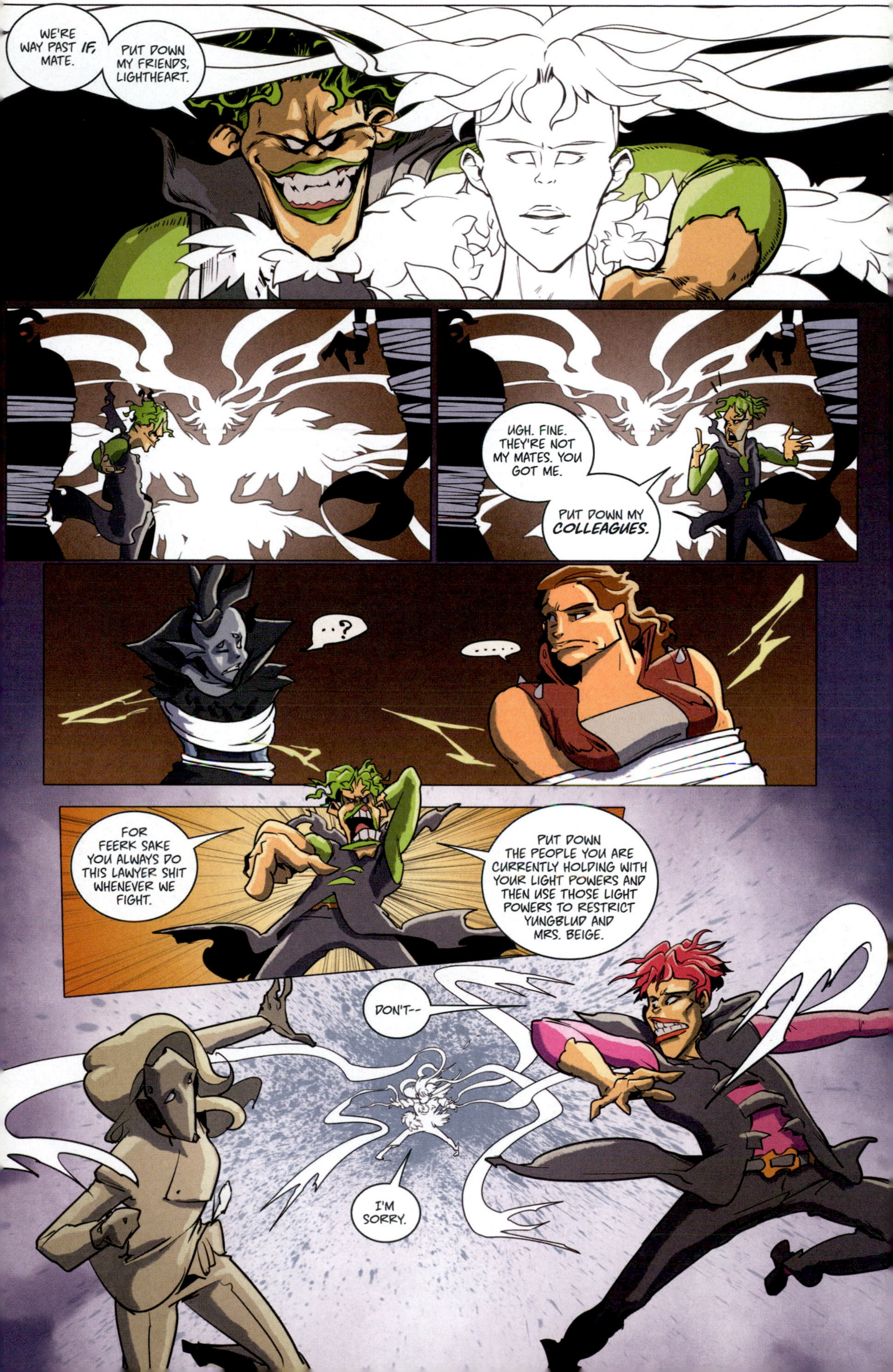
WE'RE WAY PAST IF, MATE.
PUT DOWN MY FRIENDS, LIGHTHEART.
UGH. FINE. THEY'RE NOT MY MATES. YOU GOT ME.
PUT DOWN MY COLLEAGUES.
...?
.....
FOR FEERK SAKE YOU ALWAYS DO THIS LAWYER SHIT WHENEVER WE FIGHT.
PUT DOWN THE PEOPLE YOU ARE CURRENTLY HOLDING WITH YOUR LIGHT POWERS AND THEN USE THOSE LIGHT POWERS TO RESTRICT YUNGBLUD AND MRS. BEIGE.
DON'T--
I'M SORRY.

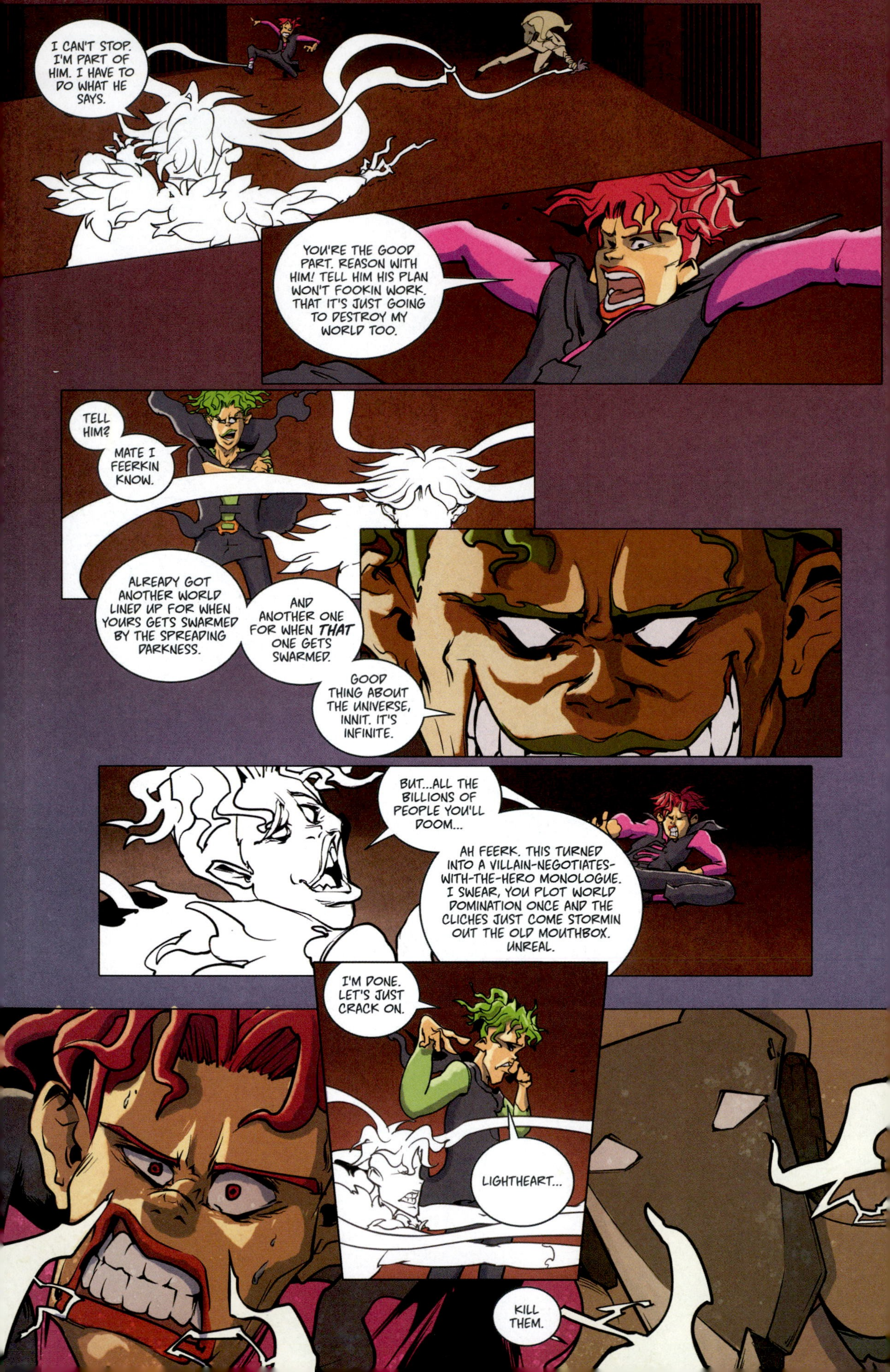
I CAN'T STOP. I'M PART OF HIM. I HAVE TO DO WHAT HE SAYS.
YOU'RE THE GOOD PART. REASON WITH HIM! TELL HIM HIS PLAN WON'T FOOKIN WORK. THAT IT'S JUST GOING TO DESTROY MY WORLD TOO.
TELL HIM?
MATE I FEERKIN KNOW.
ALREADY GOT ANOTHER WORLD LINED UP FOR WHEN YOURS GETS SWARMED BY THE SPREADING DARKNESS.
AND ANOTHER ONE FOR WHEN *THAT* ONE GETS SWARMED.
GOOD THING ABOUT THE UNIVERSE, INNIT. IT'S INFINITE.
BUT...ALL THE BILLIONS OF PEOPLE YOU'LL DOOM...
AH FEERK. THIS TURNED INTO A VILLAIN-NEGOTIATES-WITH-THE-HERO MONOLOGUE. I SWEAR, YOU PLOT WORLD DOMINATION ONCE AND THE CLICHES JUST COME STORMIN OUT THE OLD MOUTHBOX. UNREAL.
I'M DONE. LET'S JUST CRACK ON.
LIGHTHEART...
KILL THEM.

WHERE IS IT?

WHERE'S THE ACID?!

I HID IT.

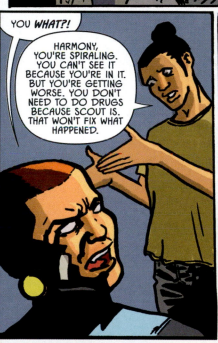

YOU **WHAT?!**

HARMONY, YOU'RE SPIRALING. YOU CAN'T SEE IT BECAUSE YOU'RE IN IT. BUT YOU'RE GETTING WORSE. YOU DON'T NEED TO DO DRUGS BECAUSE SCOUT IS. THAT WON'T FIX WHAT HAPPENED.

WHAT. THE. **FUCK.** ARE YOU TALKING ABOUT?

I...I'M NOT SURE I CAN DO THIS.

COOL. DON'T DO IT THEN. WHATEVER IT IS. GIVE ME THE ACID.

LISTEN TO YOURSELF! YOU SOUND LIKE A MANIAC!

THERE IS AN EVIL VERSION OF YUNGBLUD FROM A DIMENSION MADE OUT OF MANGA AND HE IS THREATENING TO TAKE OVER OUR WORLD.

IF I DON'T GET THE ACID, I CAN'T GO BACK THERE AND STOP HIM FROM SWITCHING MY FRIENDS WITH A BUNCH OF EVIL ZOMBIES.

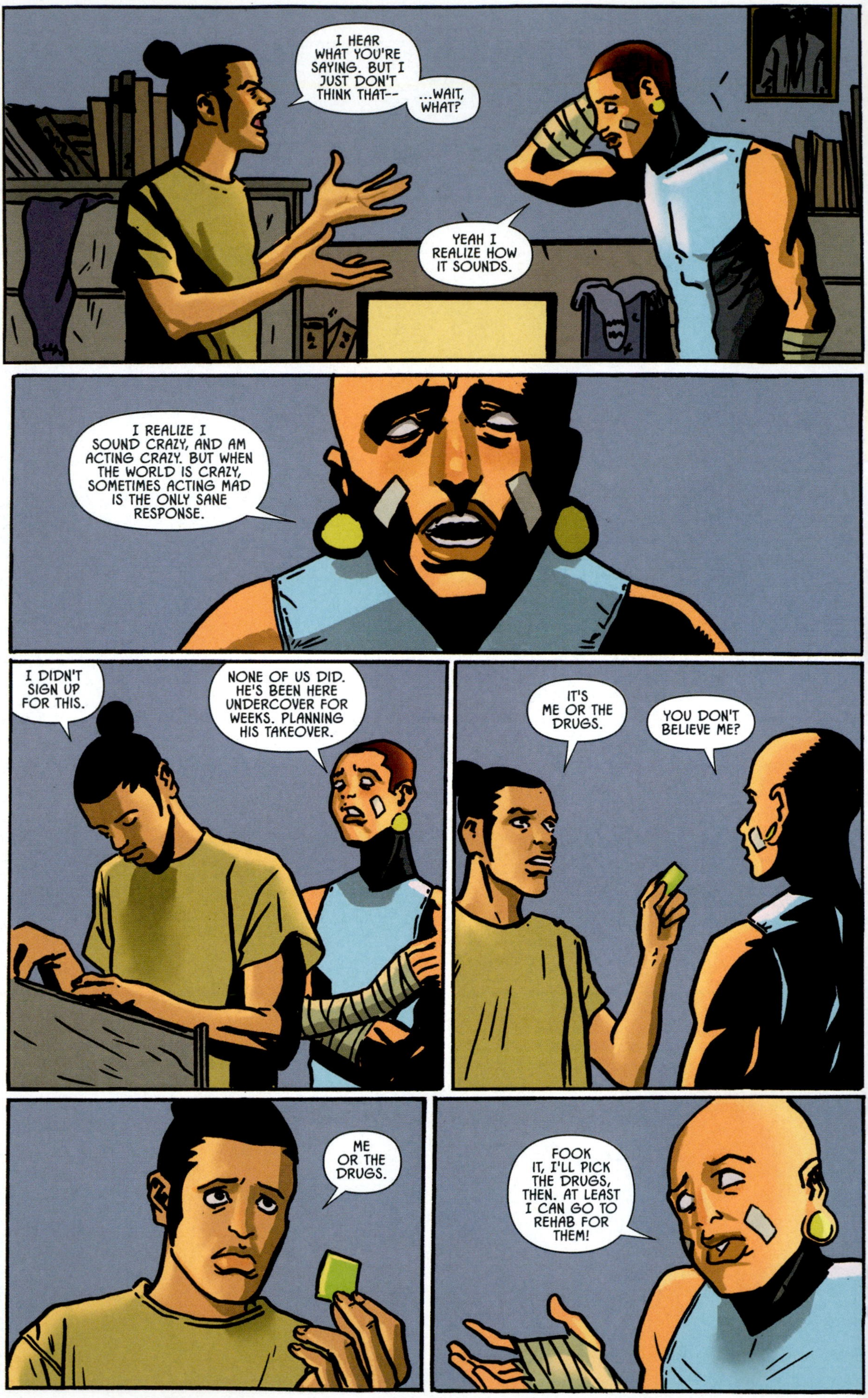
I HEAR WHAT YOU'RE SAYING. BUT I JUST DON'T THINK THAT--
...WAIT, WHAT?
YEAH I REALIZE HOW IT SOUNDS.
I REALIZE I SOUND CRAZY, AND AM ACTING CRAZY. BUT WHEN THE WORLD IS CRAZY, SOMETIMES ACTING MAD IS THE ONLY SANE RESPONSE.
I DIDN'T SIGN UP FOR THIS.
NONE OF US DID. HE'S BEEN HERE UNDERCOVER FOR WEEKS. PLANNING HIS TAKEOVER.
IT'S ME OR THE DRUGS.
YOU DON'T BELIEVE ME?
ME OR THE DRUGS.
FOOK IT, I'LL PICK THE DRUGS, THEN. AT LEAST I CAN GO TO REHAB FOR THEM!

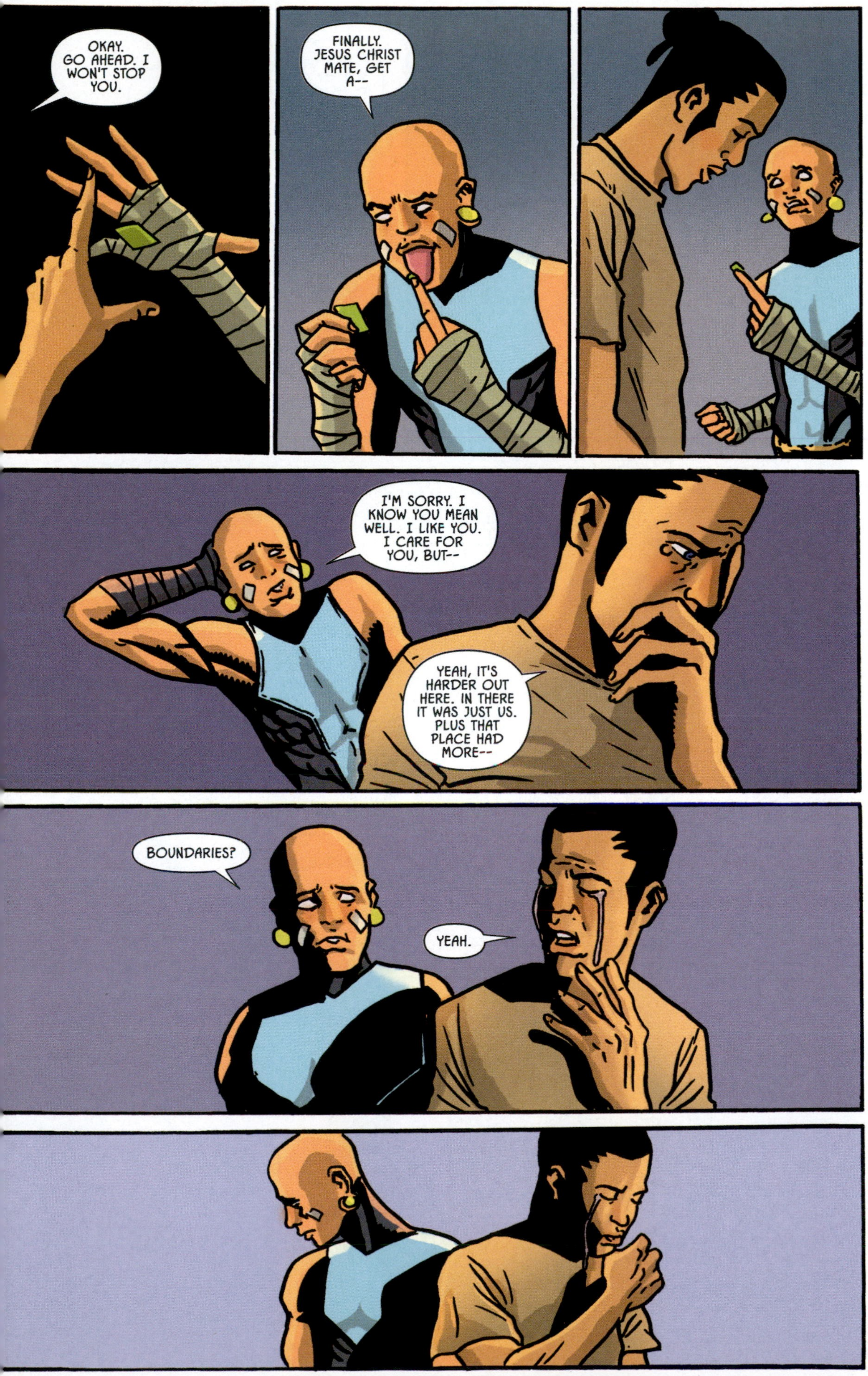
OKAY. GO AHEAD. I WON'T STOP YOU.
FINALLY. JESUS CHRIST MATE, GET A--
I'M SORRY. I KNOW YOU MEAN WELL. I LIKE YOU. I CARE FOR YOU, BUT--
YEAH, IT'S HARDER OUT HERE. IN THERE IT WAS JUST US. PLUS THAT PLACE HAD MORE--
BOUNDARIES?
YEAH.

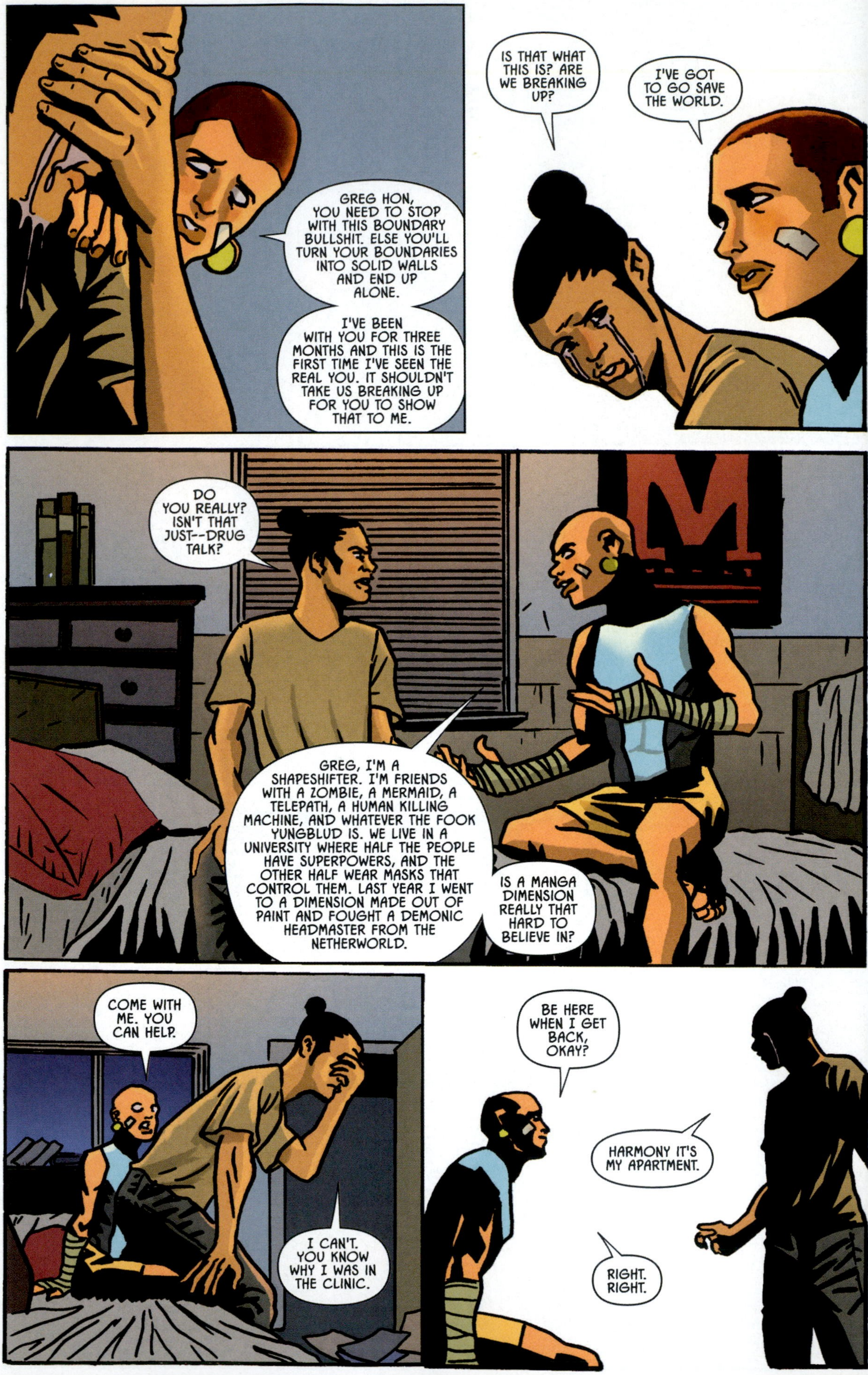
GREG HON, YOU NEED TO STOP WITH THIS BOUNDARY BULLSHIT. ELSE YOU'LL TURN YOUR BOUNDARIES INTO SOLID WALLS AND END UP ALONE.
I'VE BEEN WITH YOU FOR THREE MONTHS AND THIS IS THE FIRST TIME I'VE SEEN THE REAL YOU. IT SHOULDN'T TAKE US BREAKING UP FOR YOU TO SHOW THAT TO ME.
IS THAT WHAT THIS IS? ARE WE BREAKING UP?
I'VE GOT TO GO SAVE THE WORLD.
DO YOU REALLY? ISN'T THAT JUST--DRUG TALK?
GREG, I'M A SHAPESHIFTER. I'M FRIENDS WITH A ZOMBIE, A MERMAID, A TELEPATH, A HUMAN KILLING MACHINE, AND WHATEVER THE FOOK YUNGBLUD IS. WE LIVE IN A UNIVERSITY WHERE HALF THE PEOPLE HAVE SUPERPOWERS, AND THE OTHER HALF WEAR MASKS THAT CONTROL THEM. LAST YEAR I WENT TO A DIMENSION MADE OUT OF PAINT AND FOUGHT A DEMONIC HEADMASTER FROM THE NETHERWORLD.
IS A MANGA DIMENSION REALLY THAT HARD TO BELIEVE IN?
COME WITH ME. YOU CAN HELP.
I CAN'T. YOU KNOW WHY I WAS IN THE CLINIC.
BE HERE WHEN I GET BACK, OKAY?
HARMONY IT'S MY APARTMENT.
RIGHT. RIGHT.

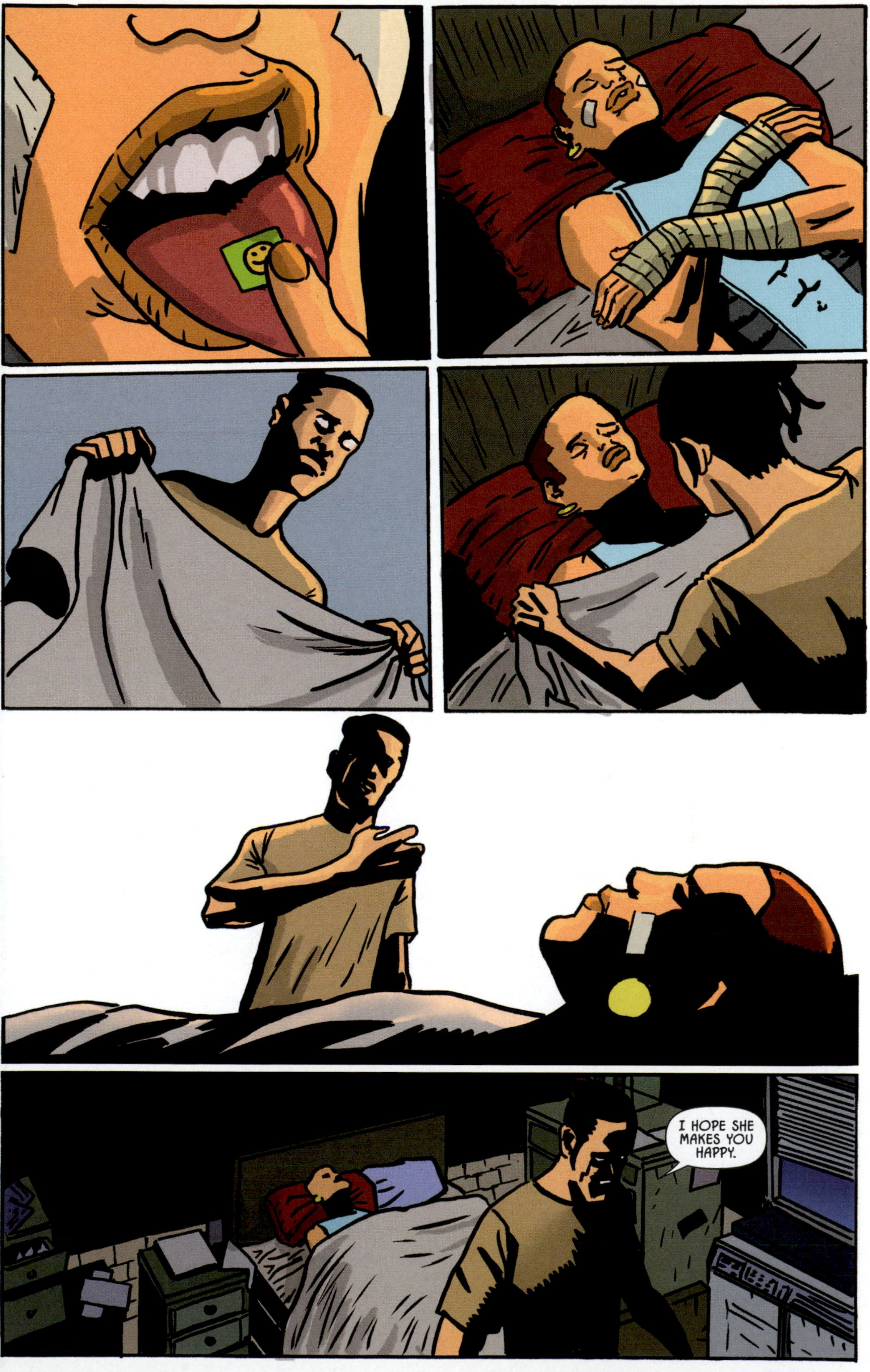
I HOPE SHE MAKES YOU HAPPY.

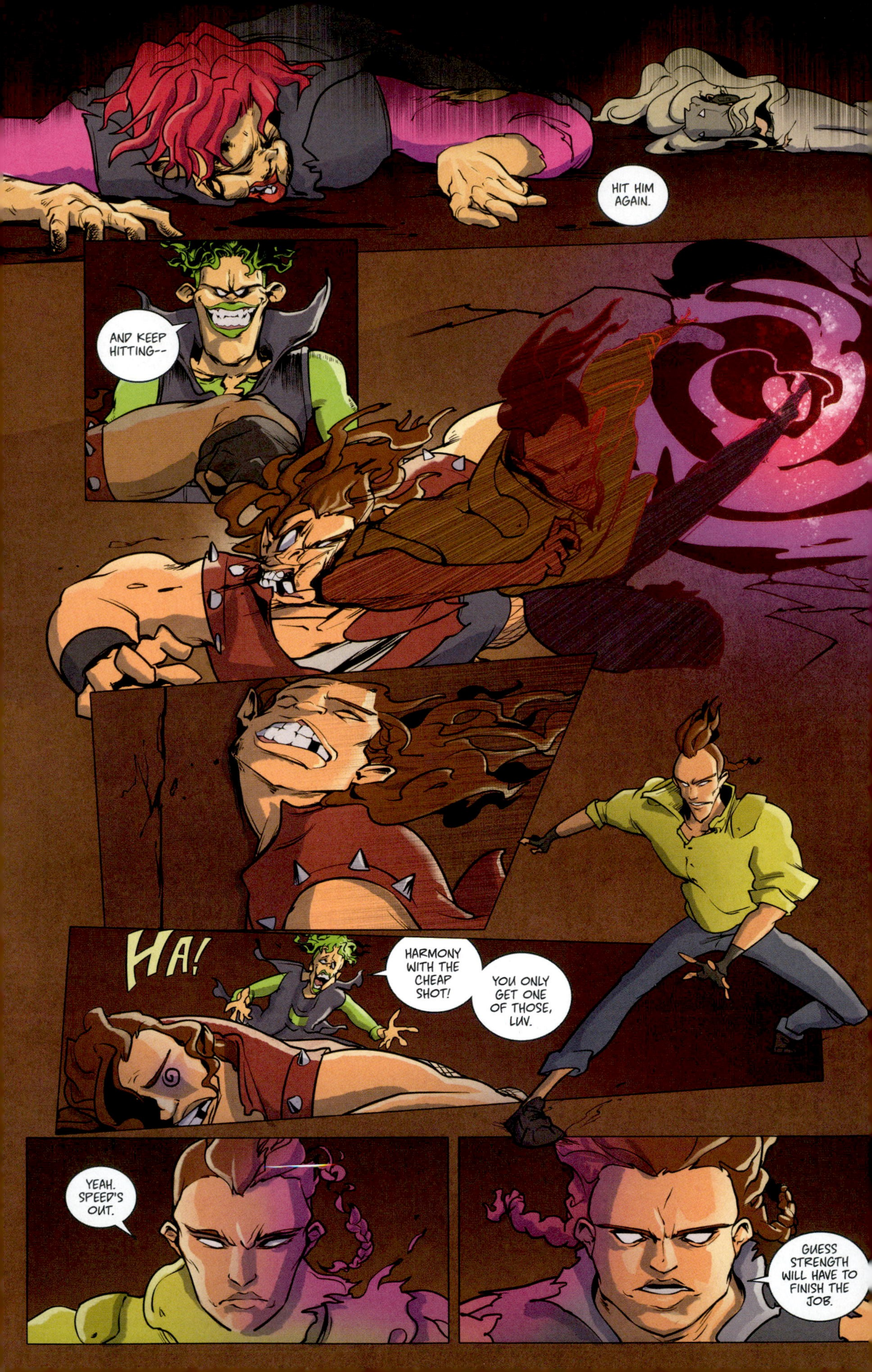
HIT HIM AGAIN.
AND KEEP HITTING--
HA!
HARMONY WITH THE CHEAP SHOT!
YOU ONLY GET ONE OF THOSE, LUV.
YEAH. SPEED'S OUT.
GUESS STRENGTH WILL HAVE TO FINISH THE JOB.

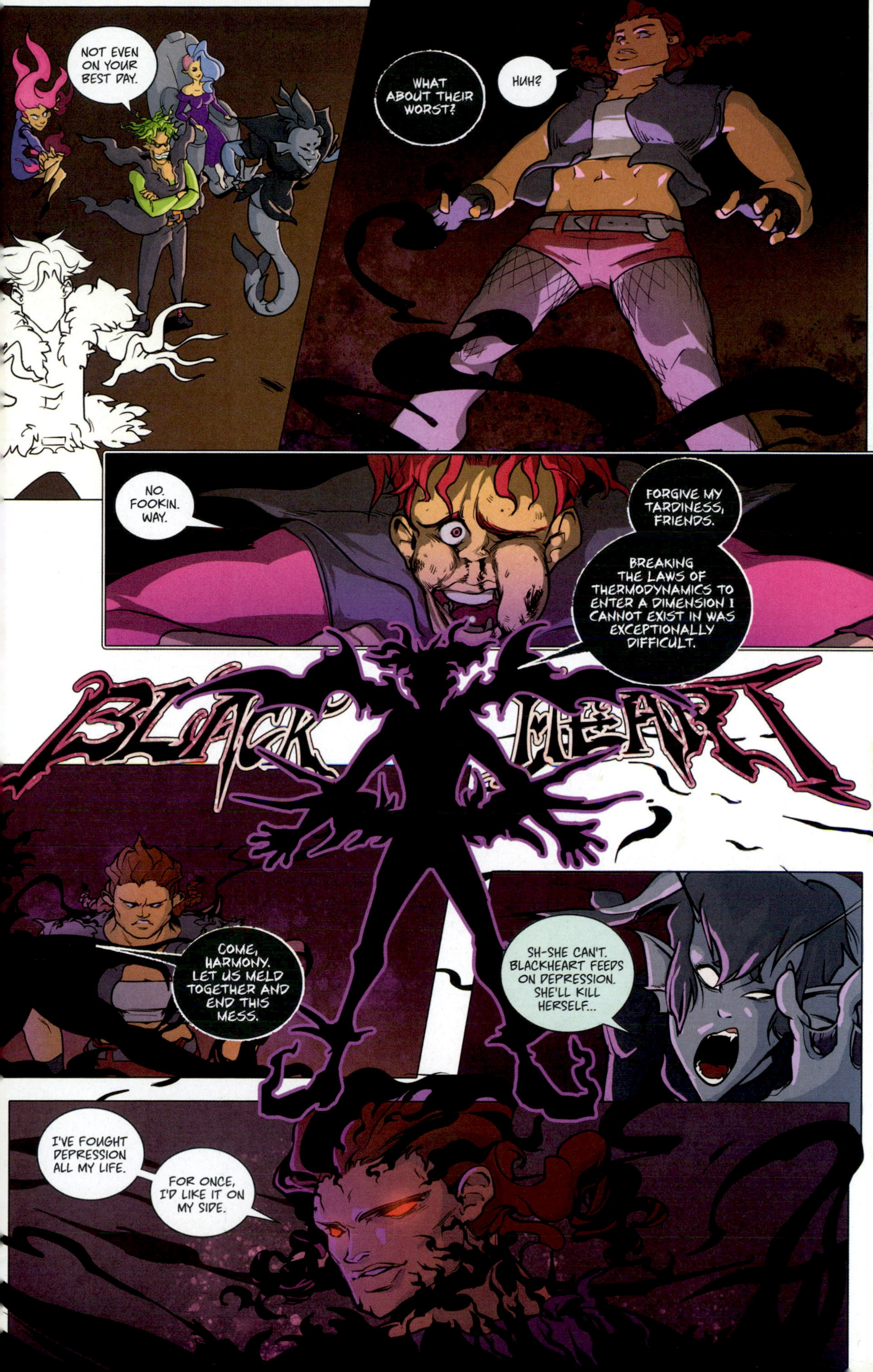
NOT EVEN ON YOUR BEST DAY.
WHAT ABOUT THEIR WORST?
HUH?
NO. FOOKIN. WAY.
FORGIVE MY TARDINESS, FRIENDS.
BREAKING THE LAWS OF THERMODYNAMICS TO ENTER A DIMENSION I CANNOT EXIST IN WAS EXCEPTIONALLY DIFFICULT.
BLACK HEART
COME, HARMONY. LET US MELD TOGETHER AND END THIS MESS.
SH-SHE CAN'T. BLACKHEART FEEDS ON DEPRESSION. SHE'LL KILL HERSELF...
I'VE FOUGHT DEPRESSION ALL MY LIFE.
FOR ONCE, I'D LIKE IT ON MY SIDE.

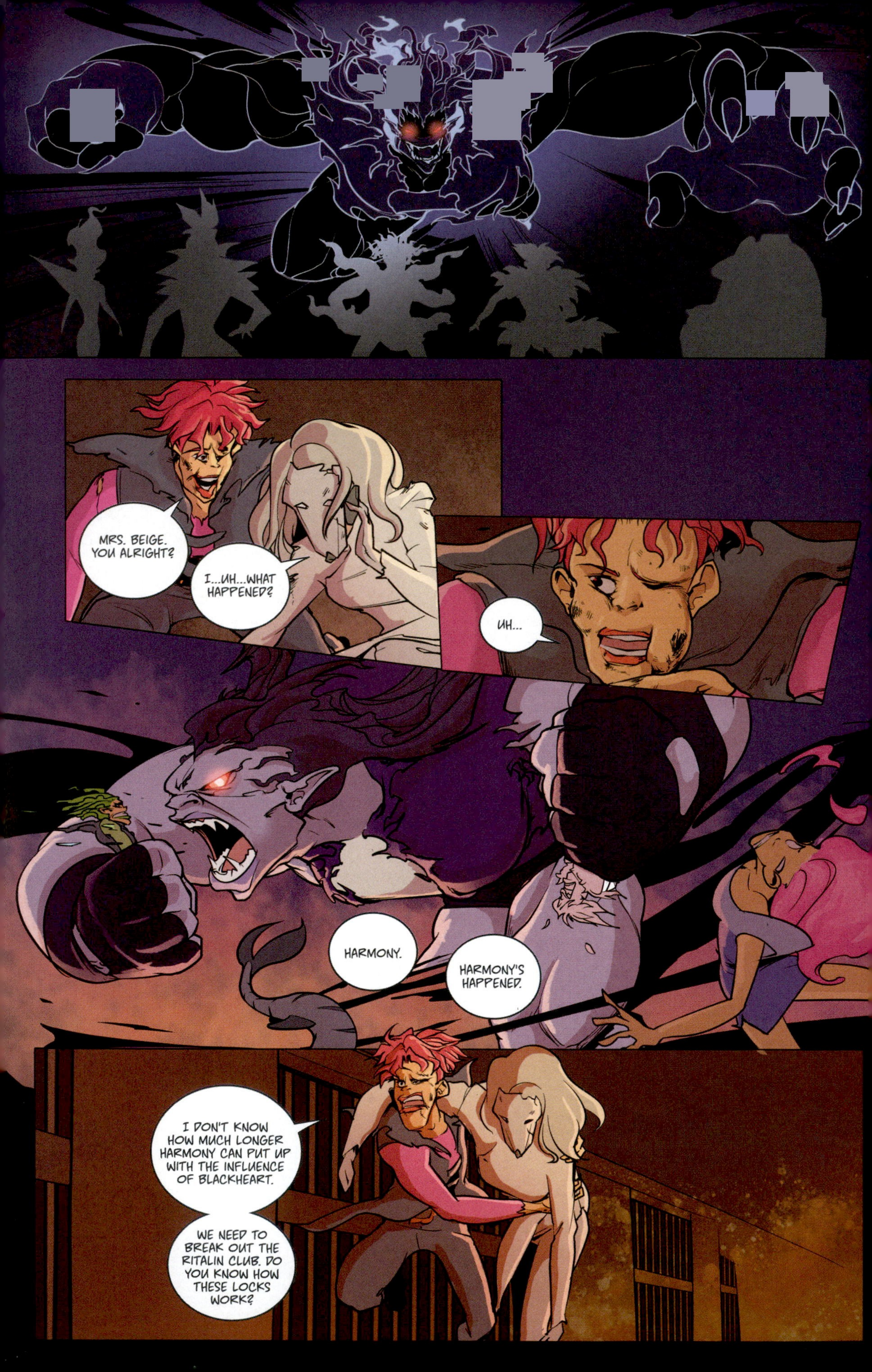
MRS. BEIGE. YOU ALRIGHT?
I...UH...WHAT HAPPENED?
UH...
HARMONY.
HARMONY'S HAPPENED.
I DON'T KNOW HOW MUCH LONGER HARMONY CAN PUT UP WITH THE INFLUENCE OF BLACKHEART.
WE NEED TO BREAK OUT THE RITALIN CLUB. DO YOU KNOW HOW THESE LOCKS WORK?

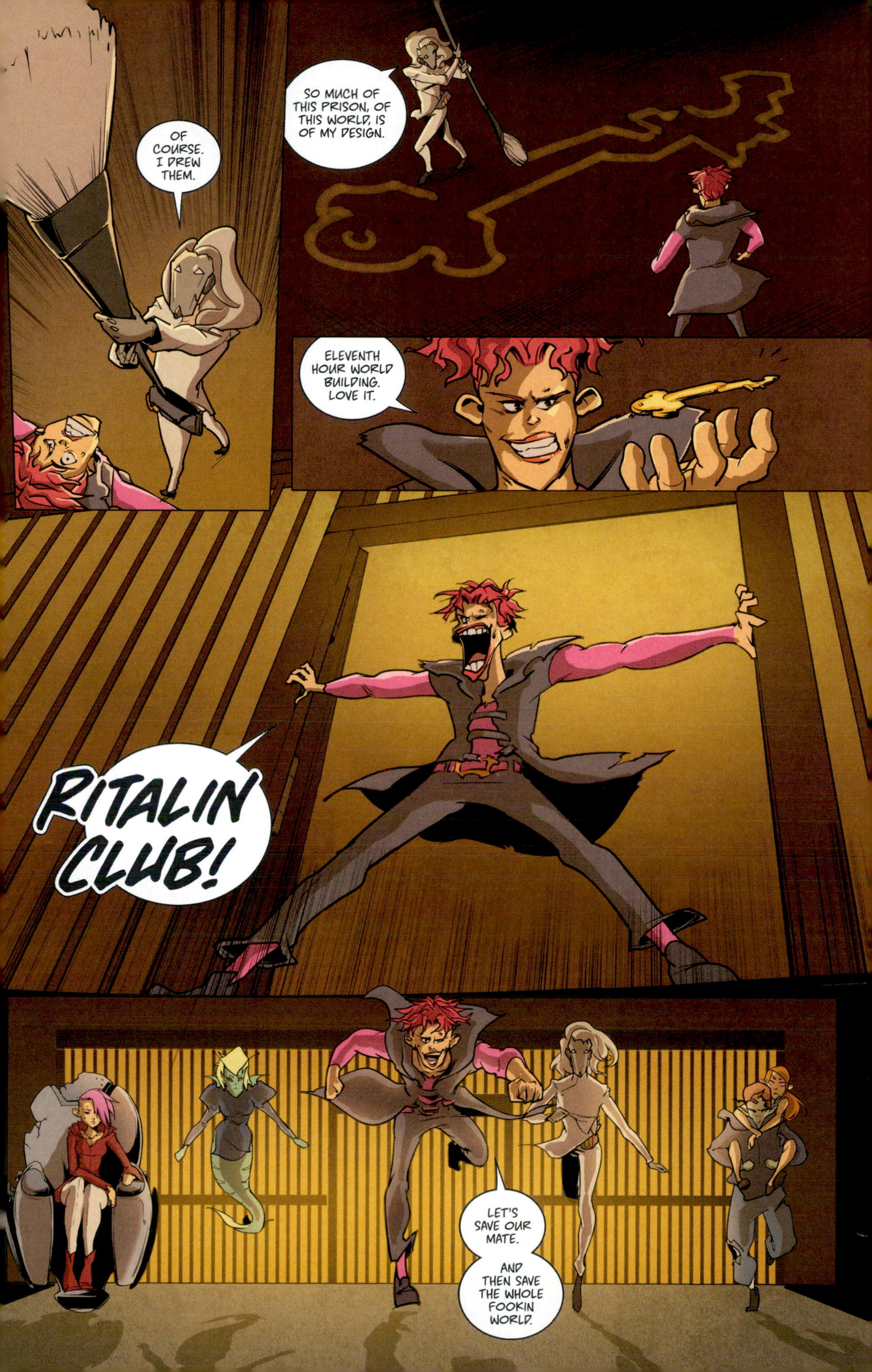
OF COURSE. I DREW THEM.
SO MUCH OF THIS PRISON, OF THIS WORLD, IS OF MY DESIGN.
ELEVENTH HOUR WORLD BUILDING. LOVE IT.
RITALIN CLUB!
LET'S SAVE OUR MATE.
AND THEN SAVE THE WHOLE FOOKIN WORLD.

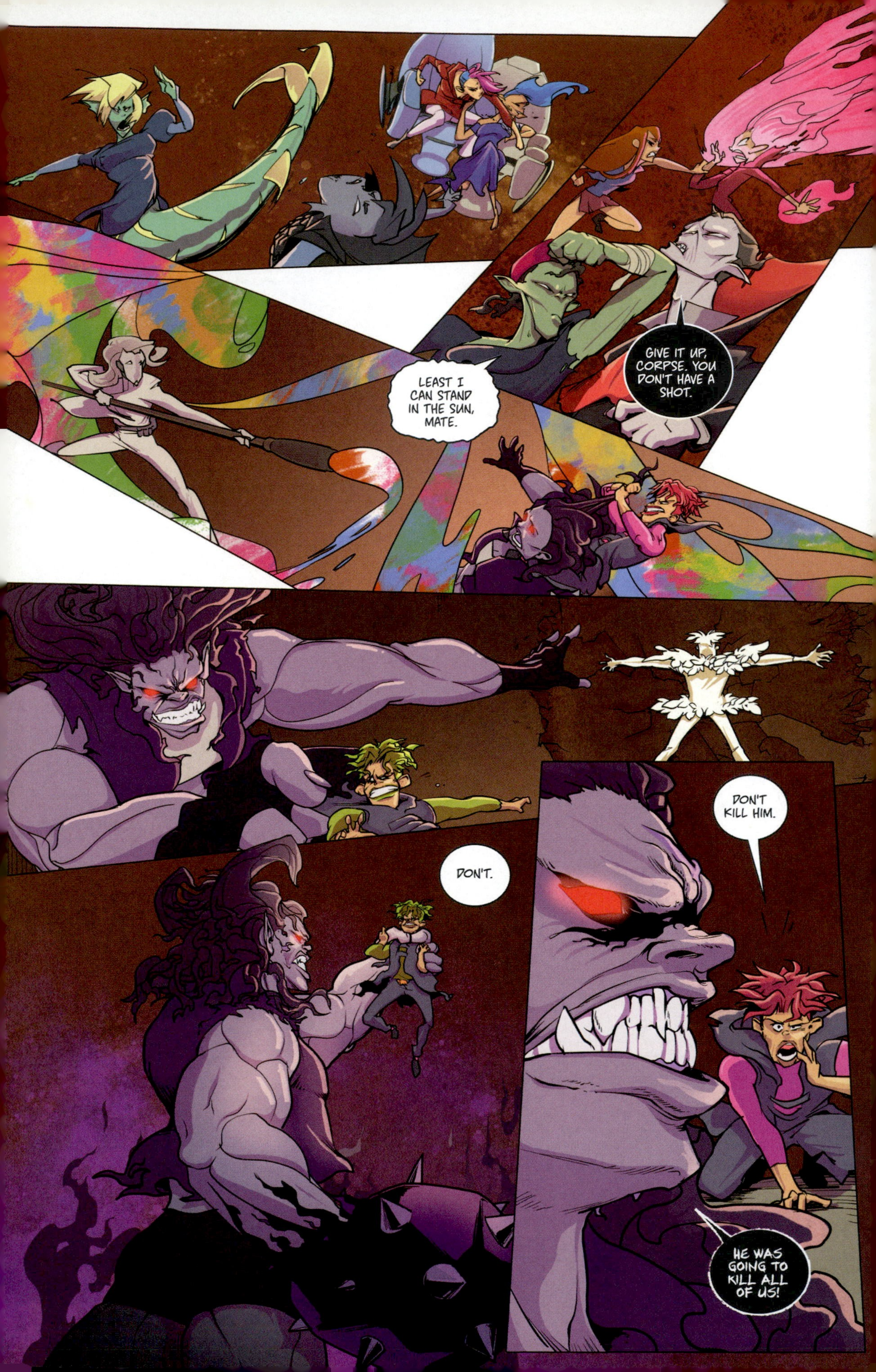
LEAST I CAN STAND IN THE SUN, MATE.
GIVE IT UP, CORPSE. YOU DON'T HAVE A SHOT.
DON'T.
DON'T KILL HIM.
HE WAS GOING TO KILL ALL OF US!

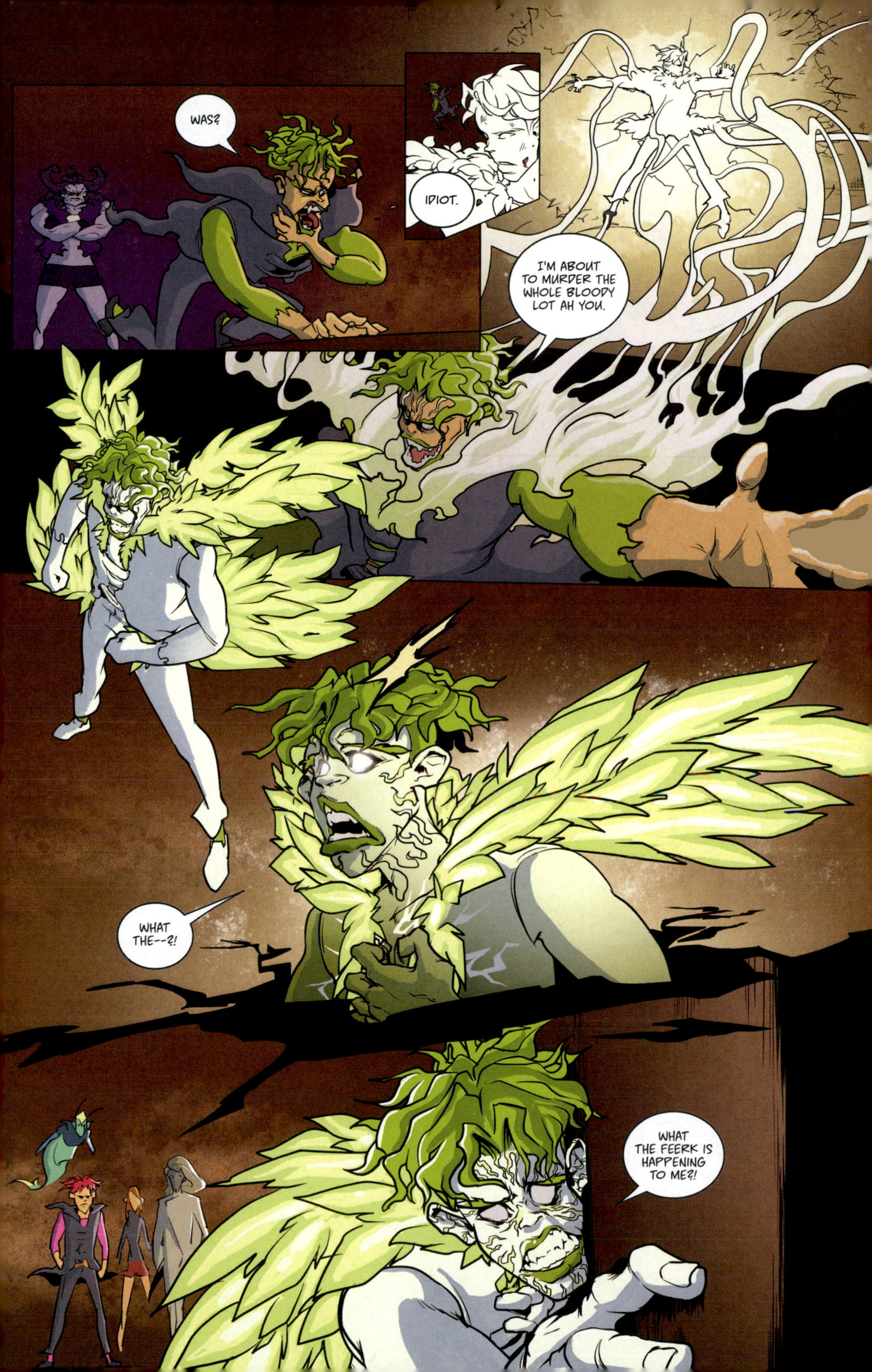
WAS?
IDIOT.
I'M ABOUT TO MURDER THE WHOLE BLOODY LOT AH YOU.
WHAT THE--?!
WHAT THE FEERK IS HAPPENING TO ME?!

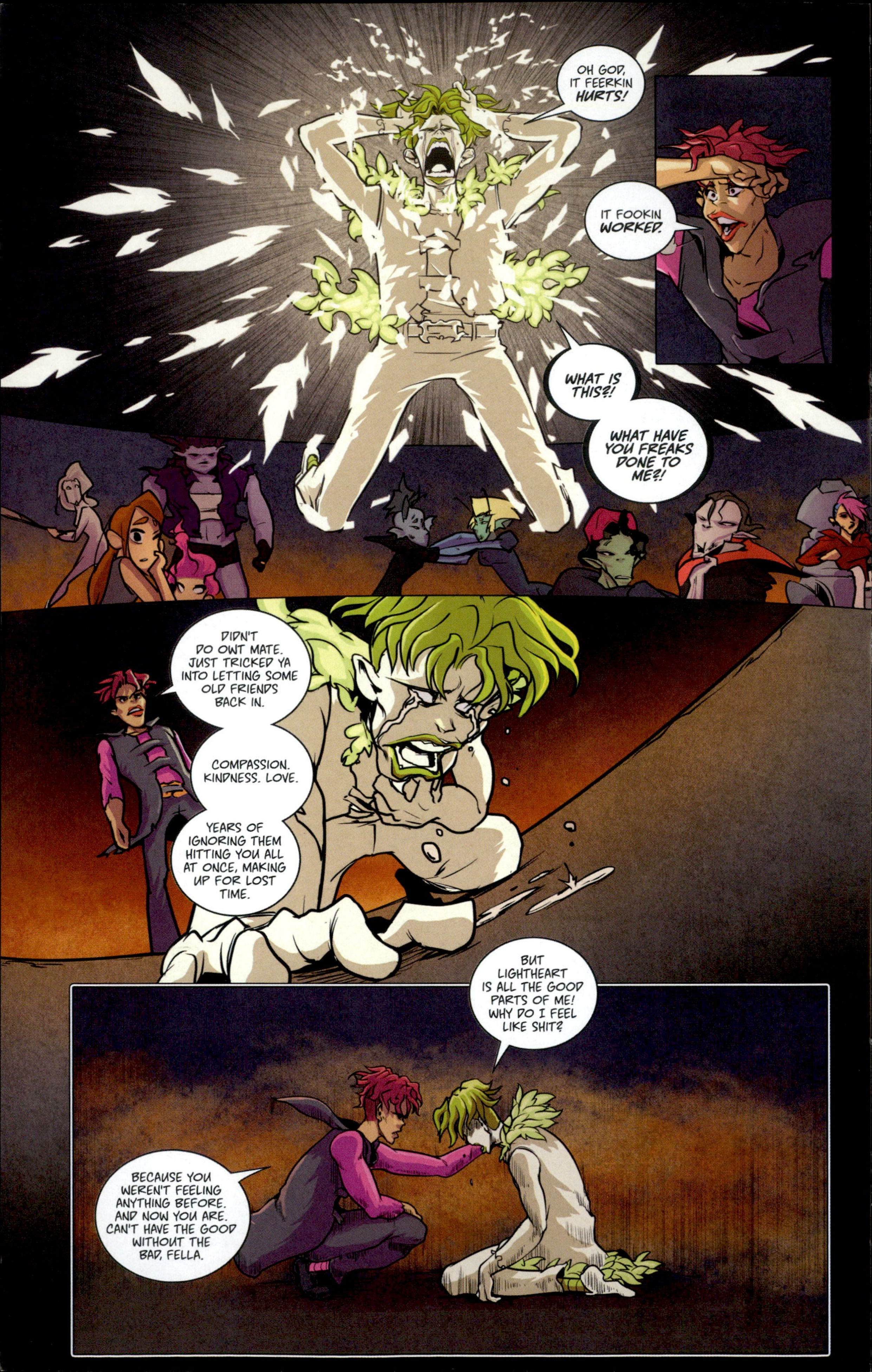

OH GOD, IT FEERKIN HURTS!
IT FOOKIN WORKED.
WHAT IS THIS?!
WHAT HAVE YOU FREAKS DONE TO ME?!
DIDN'T DO OWT MATE. JUST TRICKED YA INTO LETTING SOME OLD FRIENDS BACK IN.
COMPASSION. KINDNESS. LOVE.
YEARS OF IGNORING THEM HITTING YOU ALL AT ONCE, MAKING UP FOR LOST TIME.
BUT LIGHTHEART IS ALL THE GOOD PARTS OF ME! WHY DO I FEEL LIKE SHIT?
BECAUSE YOU WEREN'T FEELING ANYTHING BEFORE. AND NOW YOU ARE. CAN'T HAVE THE GOOD WITHOUT THE BAD, FELLA.

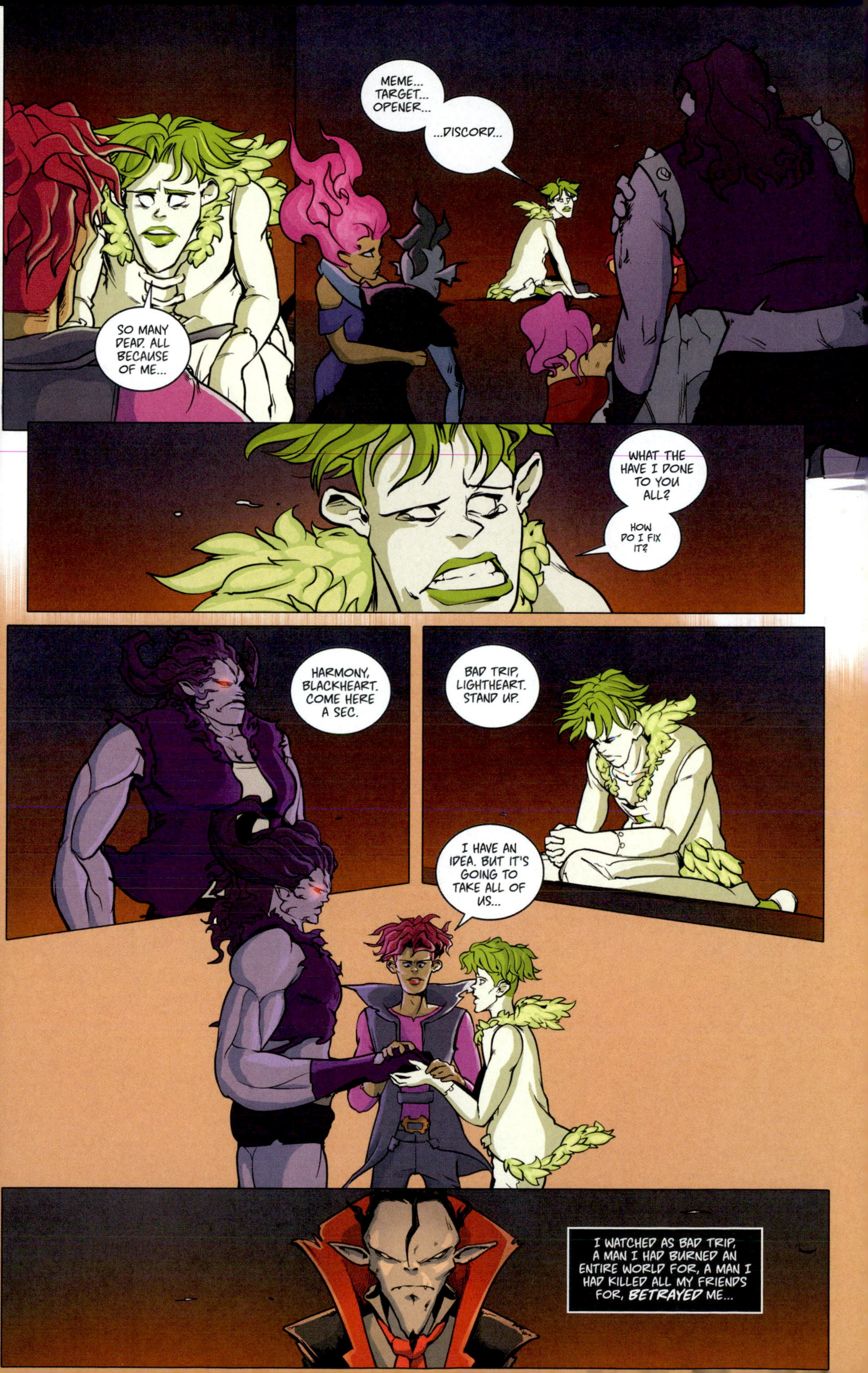
SO MANY DEAD. ALL BECAUSE OF ME...
MEME... TARGET... OPENER...
...DISCORD...
WHAT THE HAVE I DONE TO YOU ALL?
HOW DO I FIX IT?
HARMONY, BLACKHEART. COME HERE A SEC.
BAD TRIP, LIGHTHEART. STAND UP.
I HAVE AN IDEA. BUT IT'S GOING TO TAKE ALL OF US...
I WATCHED AS BAD TRIP, A MAN I HAD BURNED AN ENTIRE WORLD FOR, A MAN I HAD KILLED ALL MY FRIENDS FOR, BETRAYED ME...

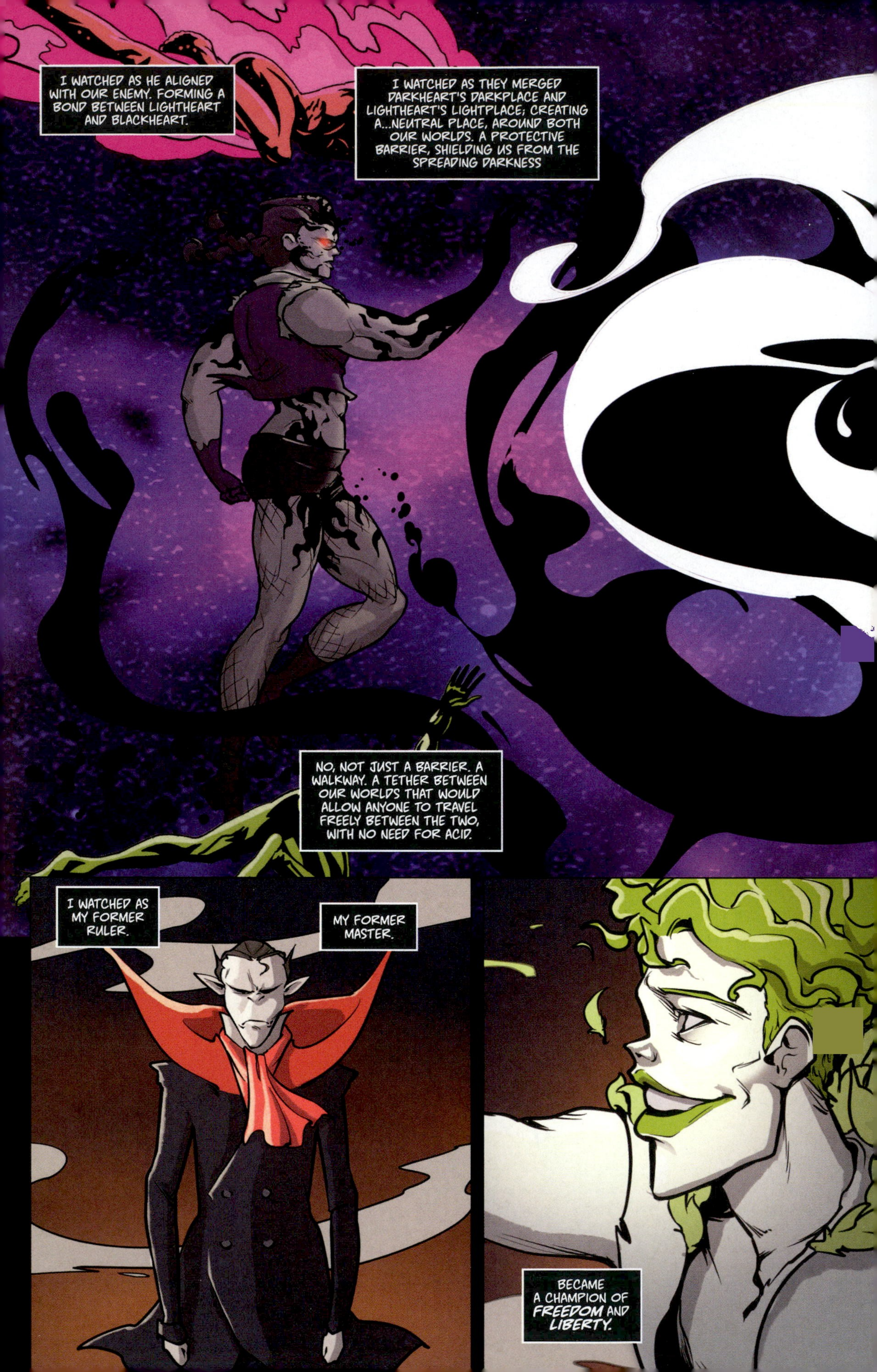
I WATCHED AS HE ALIGNED WITH OUR ENEMY. FORMING A BOND BETWEEN LIGHTHEART AND BLACKHEART.
I WATCHED AS THEY MERGED DARKHEART'S DARKPLACE AND LIGHTHEART'S LIGHTPLACE; CREATING A...NEUTRAL PLACE, AROUND BOTH OUR WORLDS. A PROTECTIVE BARRIER, SHIELDING US FROM THE SPREADING DARKNESS
NO, NOT JUST A BARRIER. A WALKWAY. A TETHER BETWEEN OUR WORLDS THAT WOULD ALLOW ANYONE TO TRAVEL FREELY BETWEEN THE TWO, WITH NO NEED FOR ACID.
I WATCHED AS MY FORMER RULER.
MY FORMER MASTER.
BECAME A CHAMPION OF ***FREEDOM*** AND ***LIBERTY***.

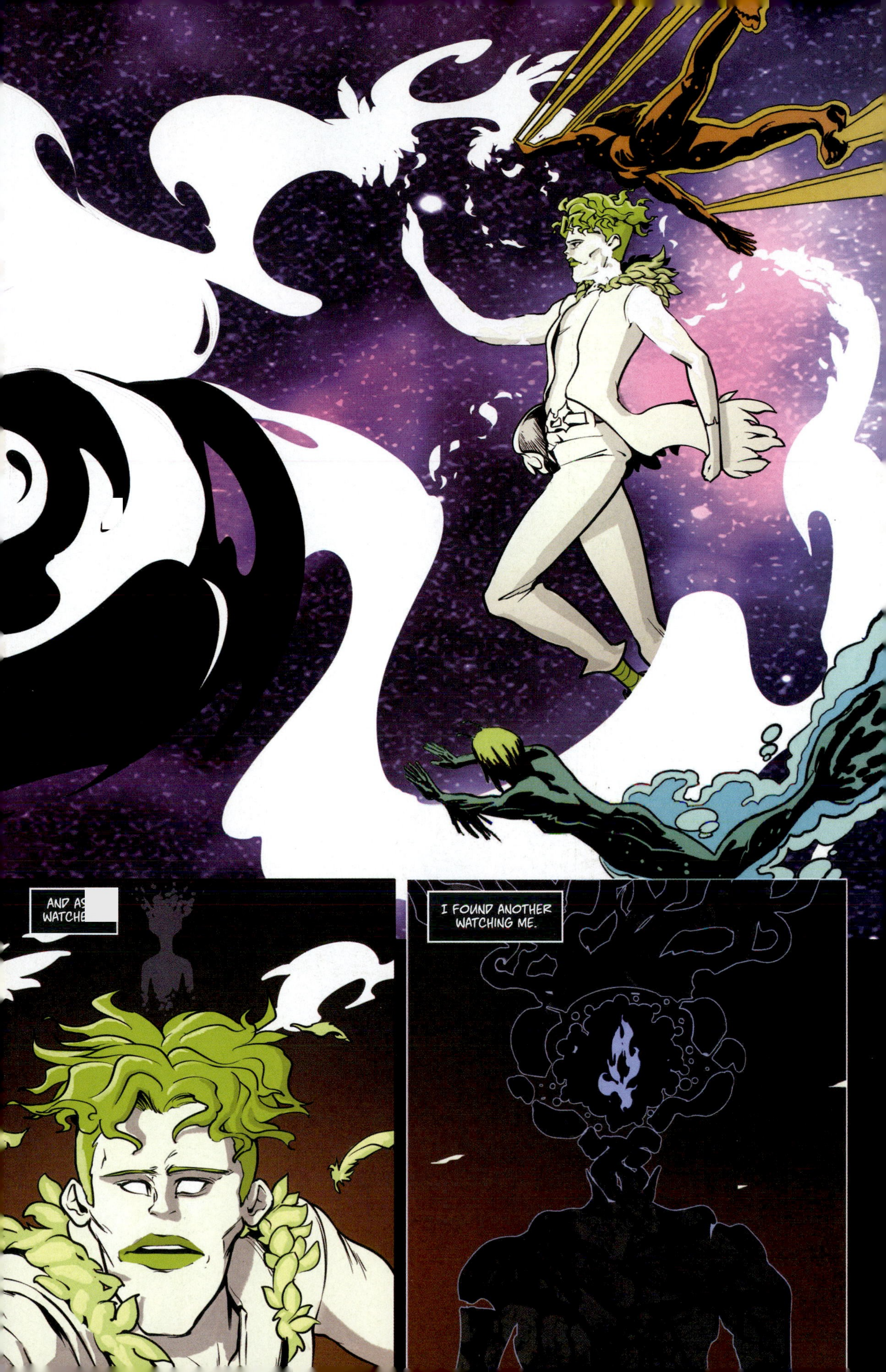
AND AS
WATCHE
I FOUND ANOTHER WATCHING ME.

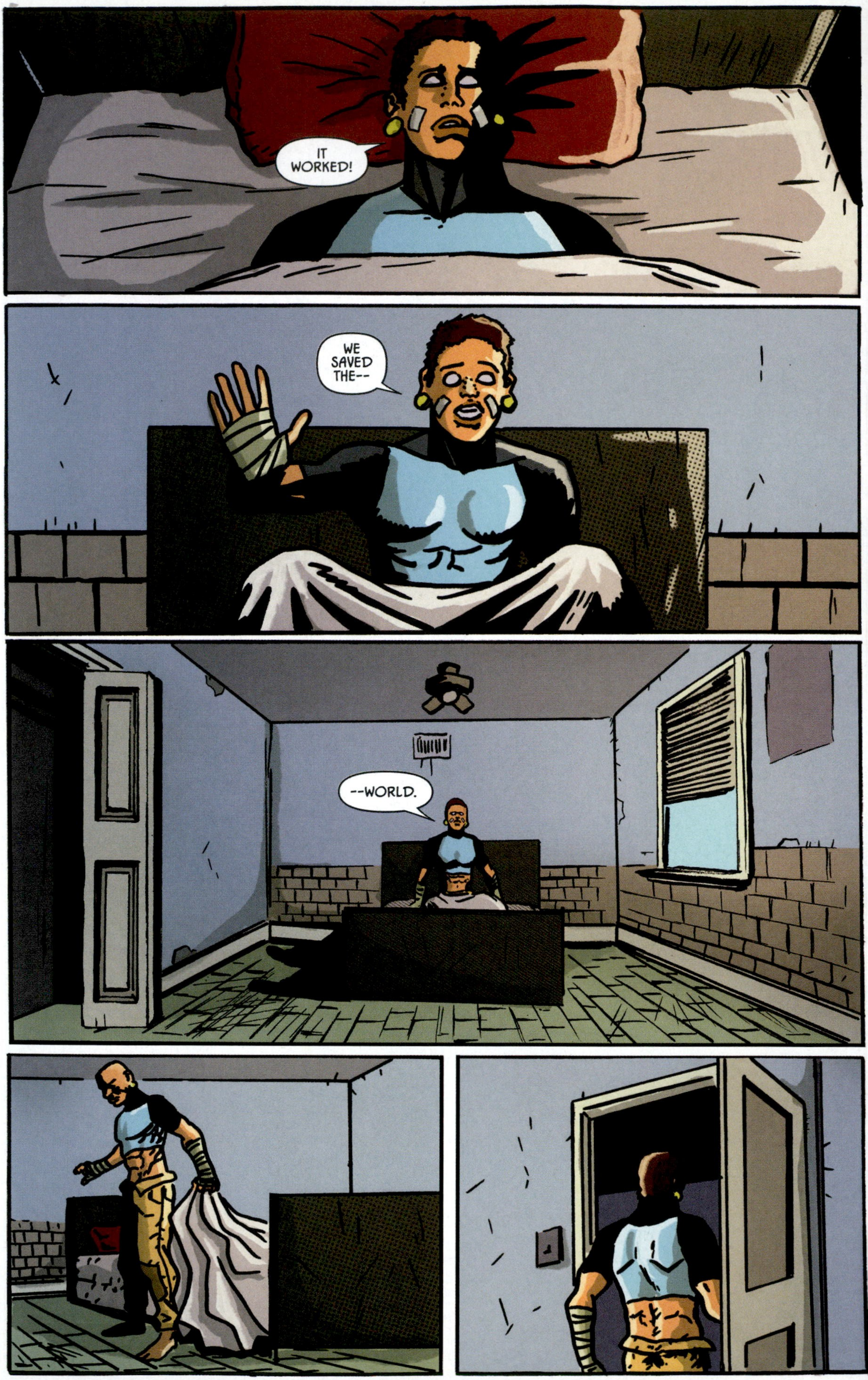
IT WORKED!
WE SAVED THE--
--WORLD.

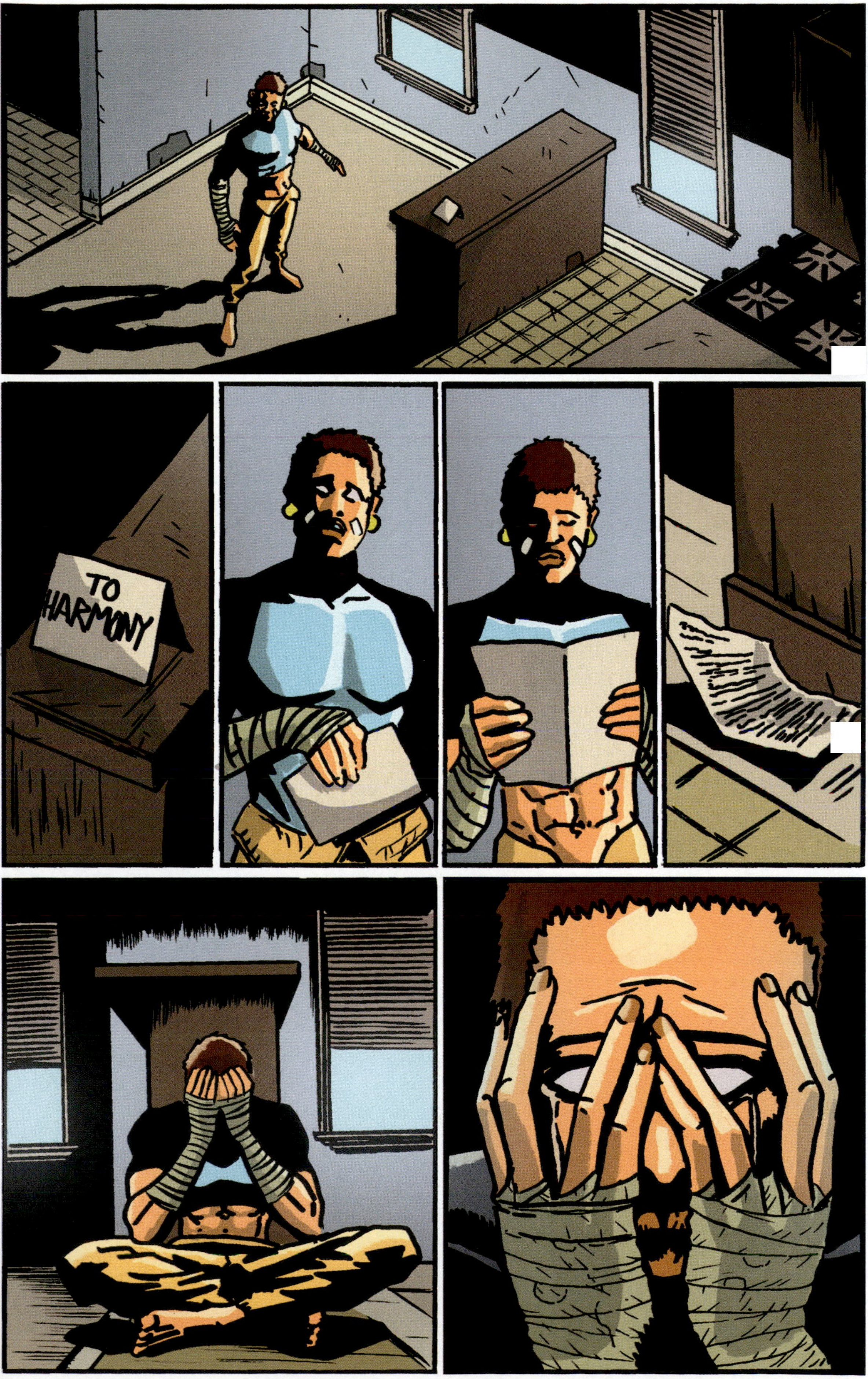
TO HARMONY

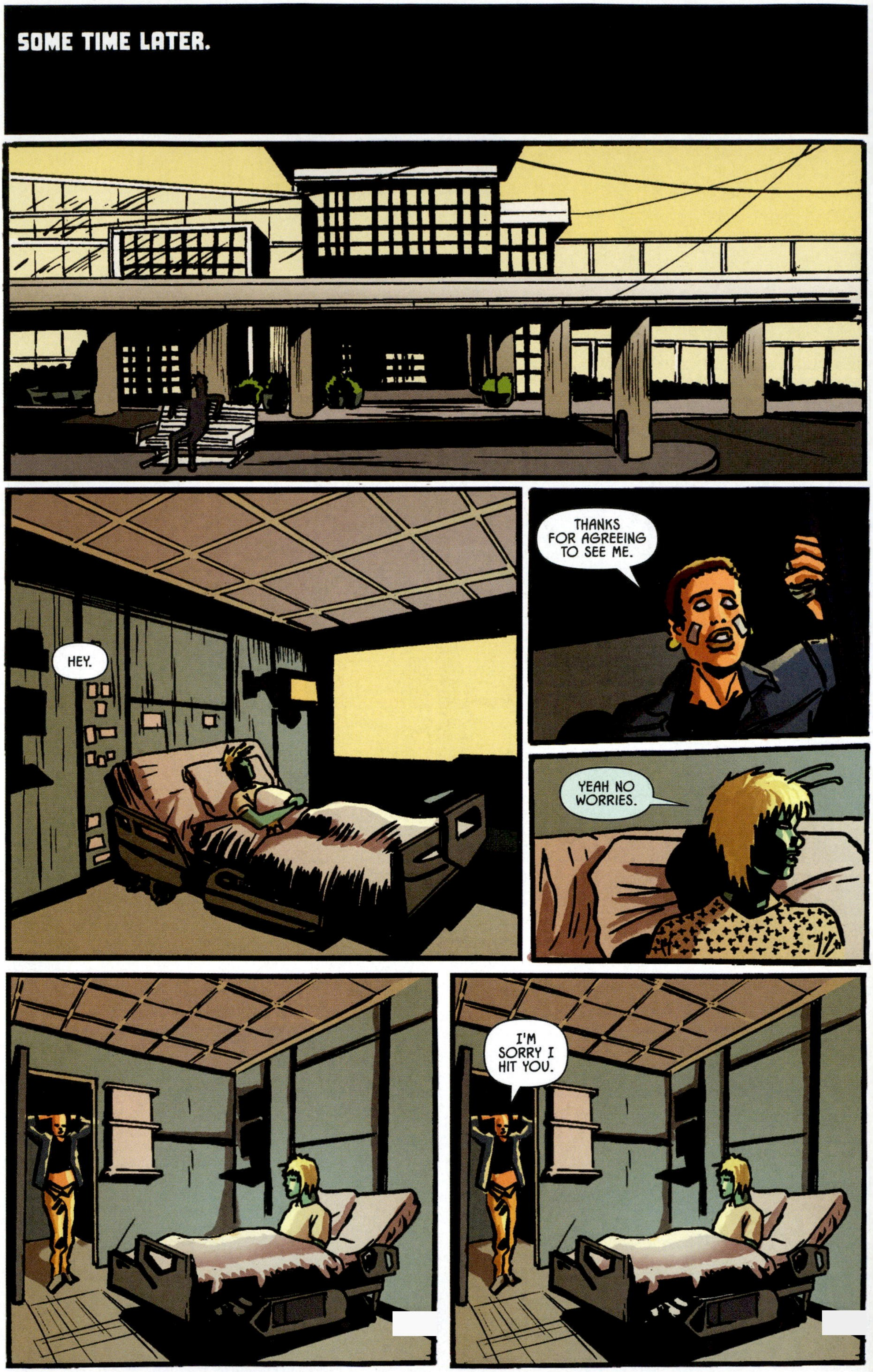
SOME TIME LATER.
HEY.
THANKS FOR AGREEING TO SEE ME.
YEAH NO WORRIES.
I'M SORRY I HIT YOU.

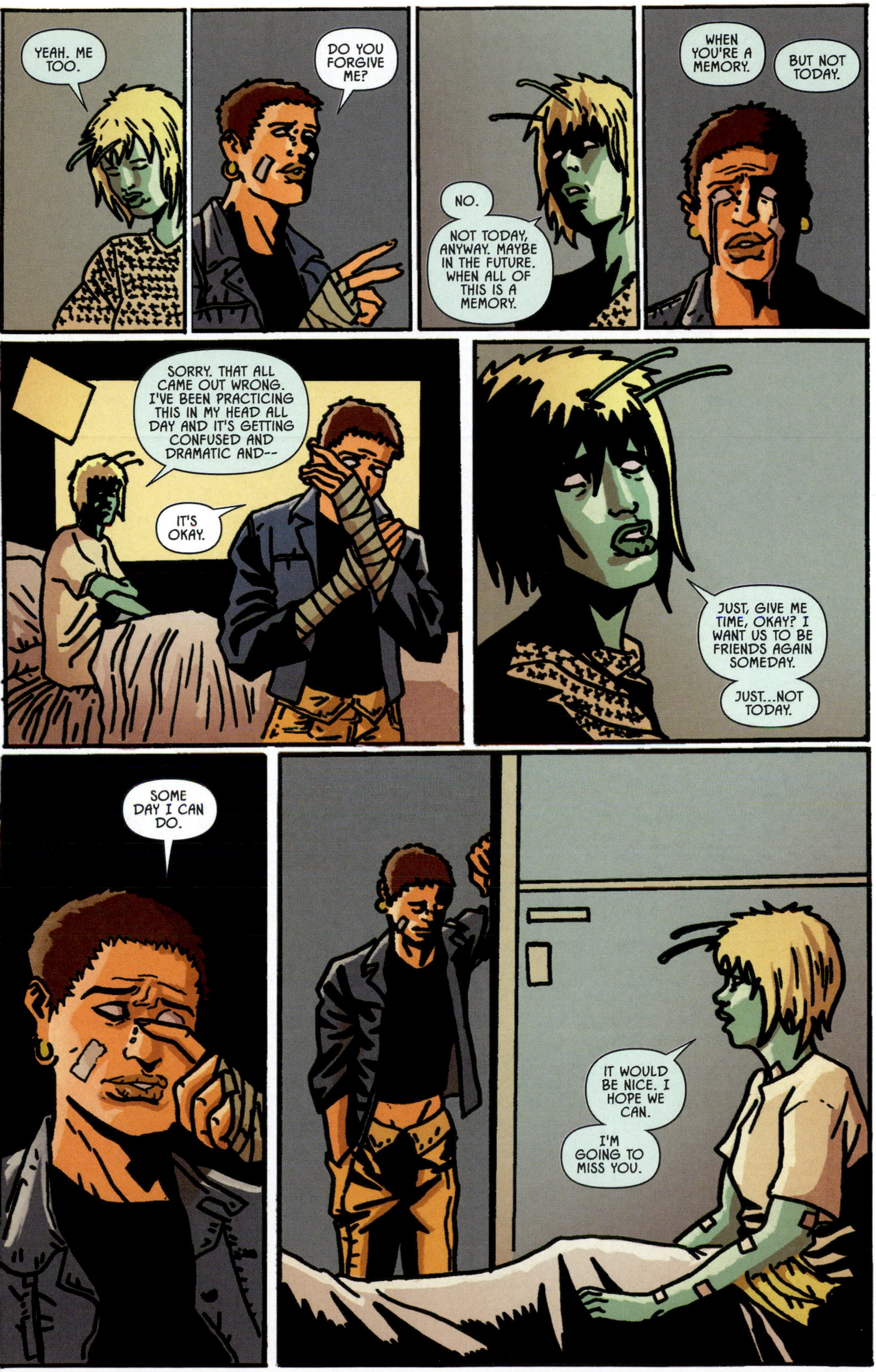
YEAH. ME TOO.
DO YOU FORGIVE ME?
NO.
NOT TODAY, ANYWAY. MAYBE IN THE FUTURE. WHEN ALL OF THIS IS A MEMORY.
WHEN YOU'RE A MEMORY.
BUT NOT TODAY.
SORRY. THAT ALL CAME OUT WRONG. I'VE BEEN PRACTICING THIS IN MY HEAD ALL DAY AND IT'S GETTING CONFUSED AND DRAMATIC AND--
IT'S OKAY.
JUST, GIVE ME TIME, OKAY? I WANT US TO BE FRIENDS AGAIN SOMEDAY.
JUST...NOT TODAY.
SOME DAY I CAN DO.
IT WOULD BE NICE. I HOPE WE CAN.
I'M GOING TO MISS YOU.

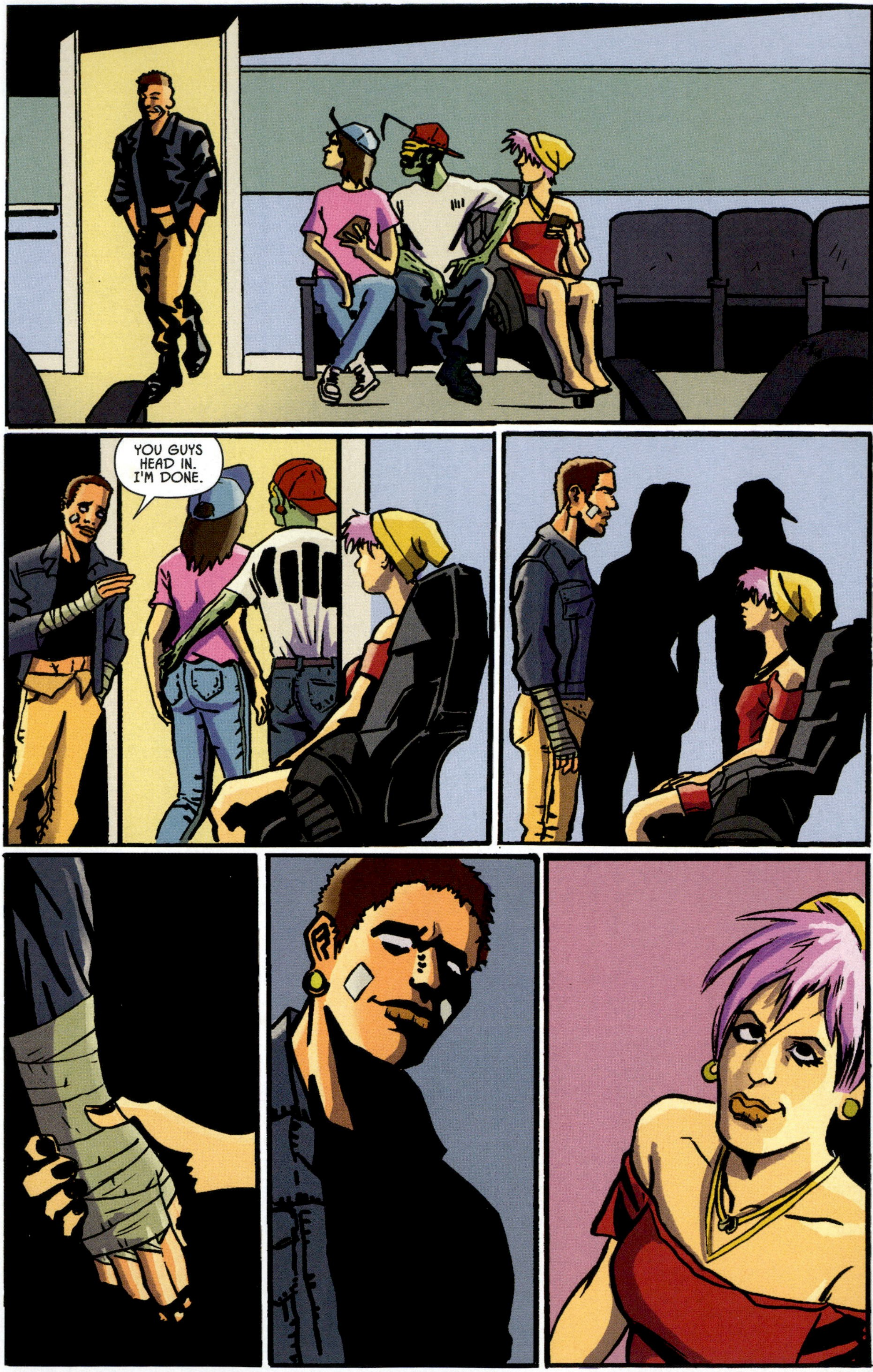
YOU GUYS HEAD IN. I'M DONE.

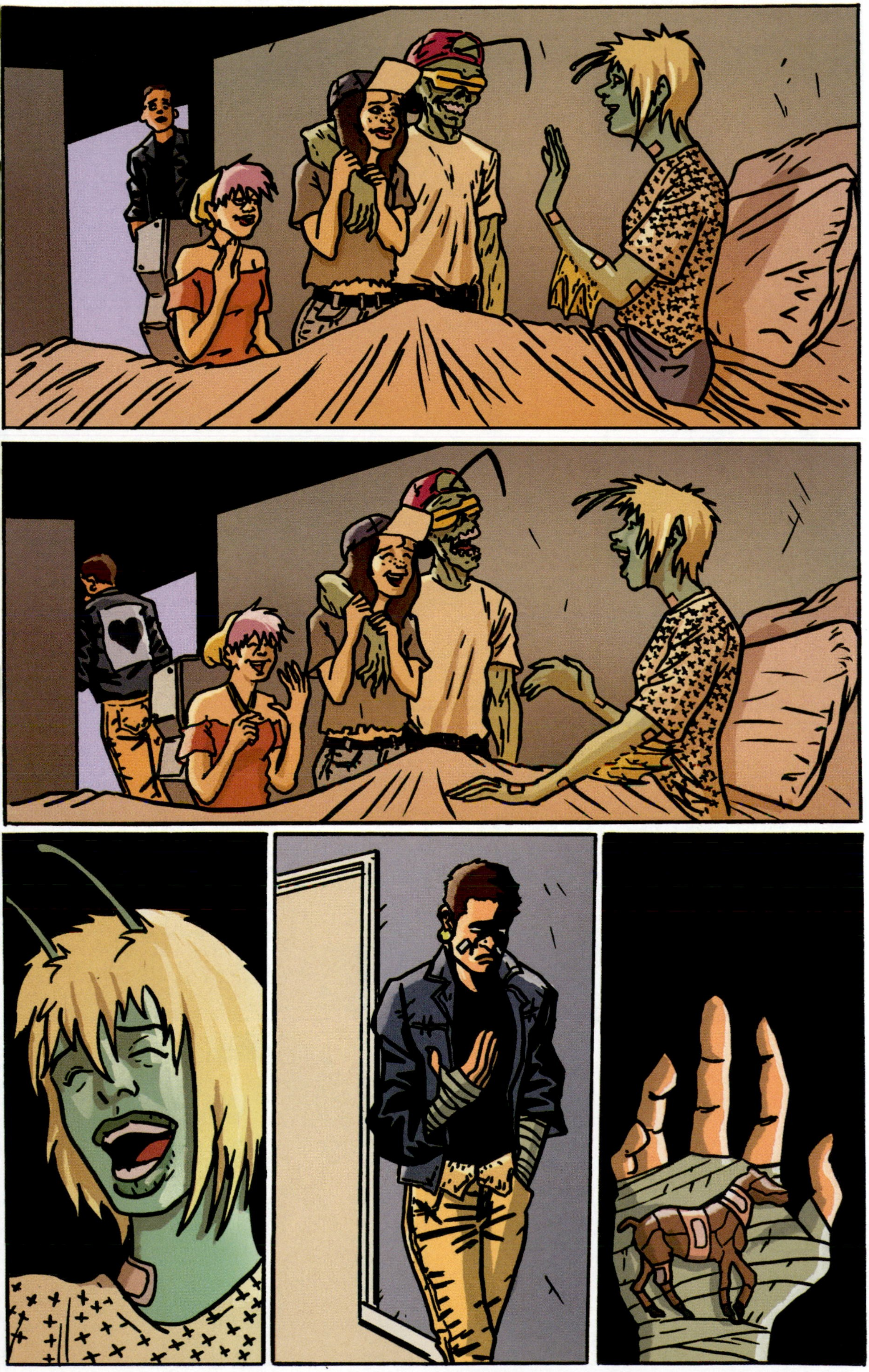

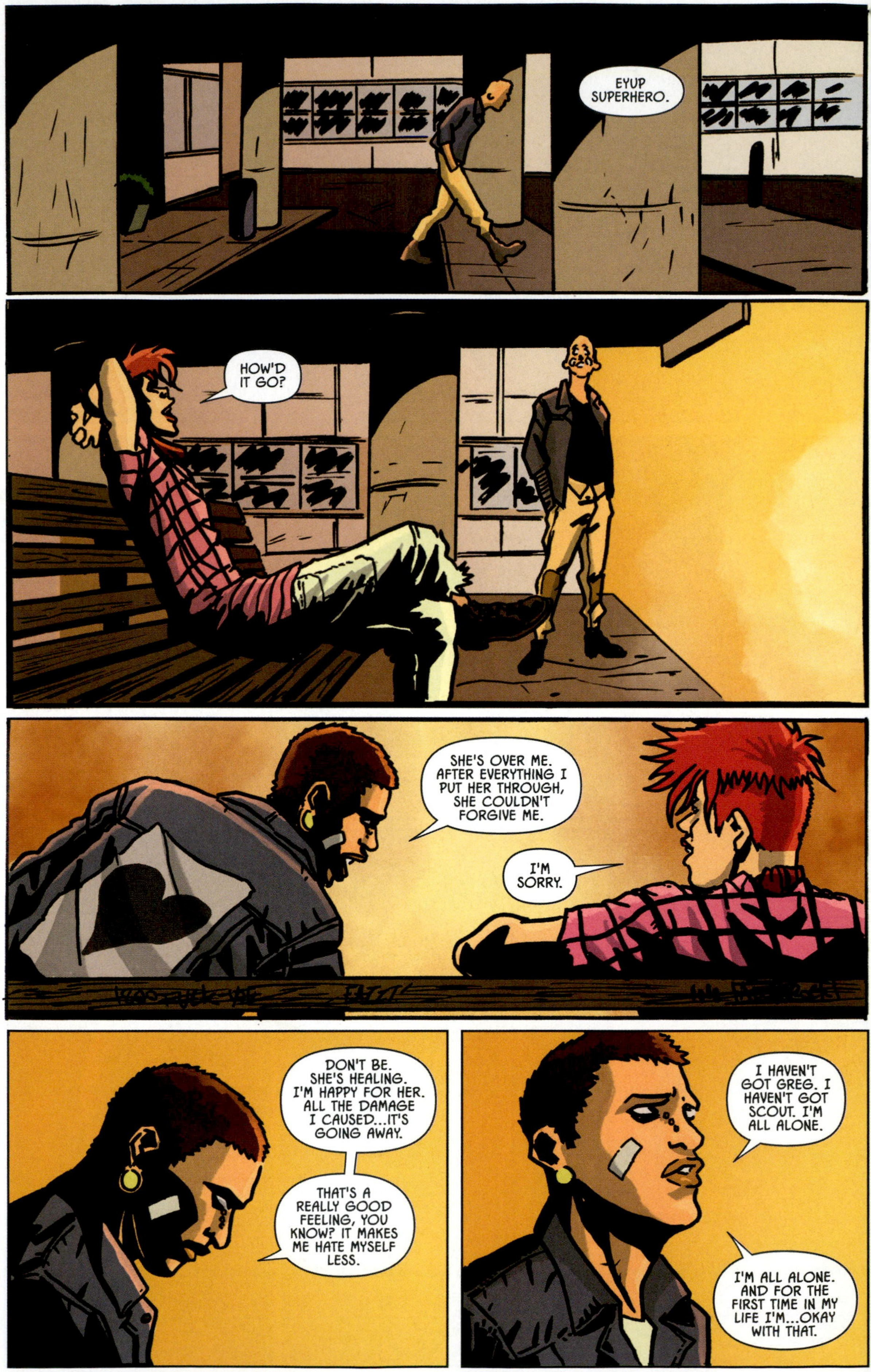

EYUP SUPERHERO.
HOW'D IT GO?
SHE'S OVER ME. AFTER EVERYTHING I PUT HER THROUGH, SHE COULDN'T FORGIVE ME.
I'M SORRY.
DON'T BE. SHE'S HEALING. I'M HAPPY FOR HER. ALL THE DAMAGE I CAUSED...IT'S GOING AWAY.
THAT'S A REALLY GOOD FEELING, YOU KNOW? IT MAKES ME HATE MYSELF LESS.
I HAVEN'T GOT GREG. I HAVEN'T GOT SCOUT. I'M ALL ALONE.
I'M ALL ALONE. AND FOR THE FIRST TIME IN MY LIFE I'M...OKAY WITH THAT.

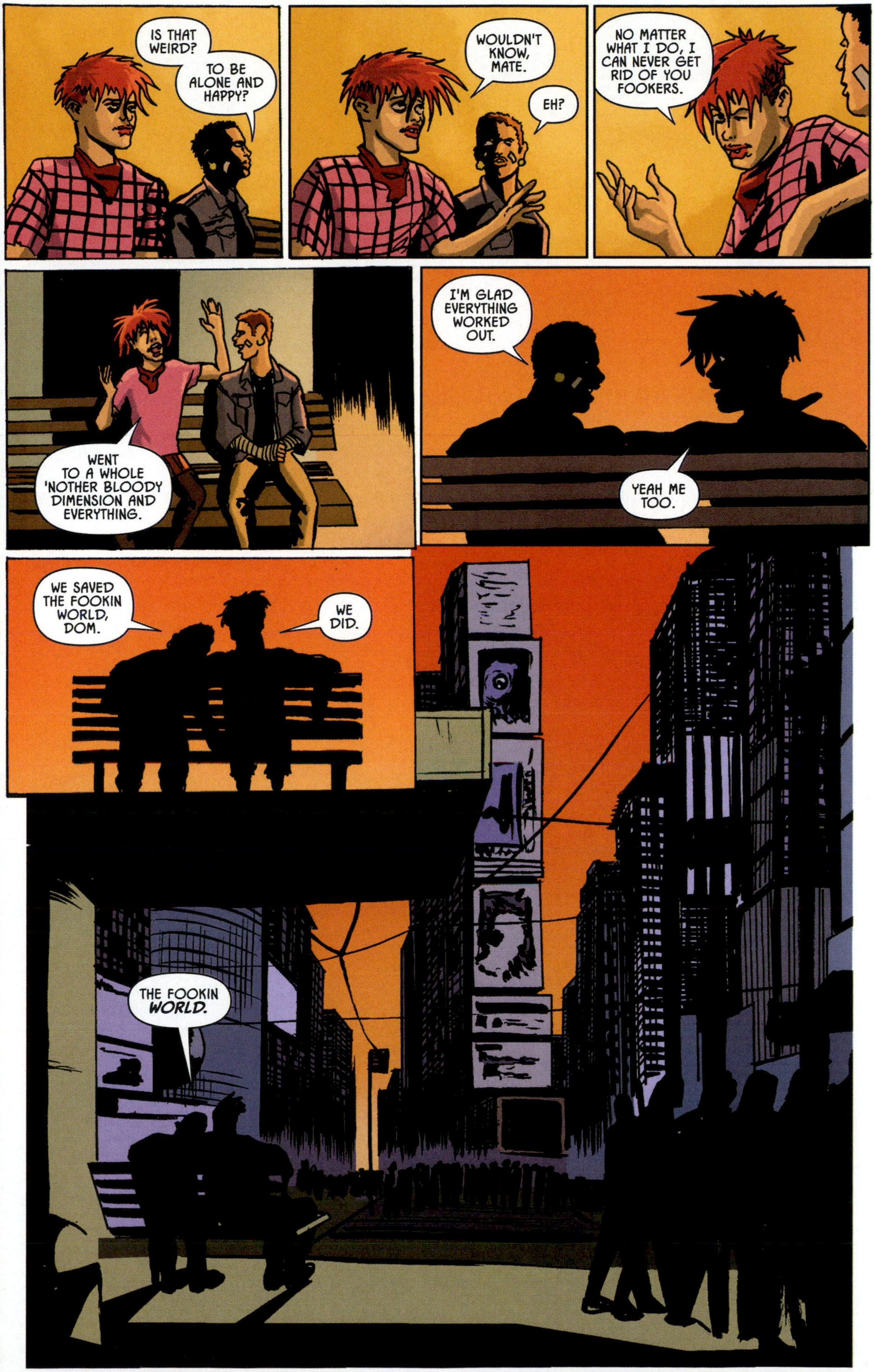
IS THAT WEIRD?
TO BE ALONE AND HAPPY?
WOULDN'T KNOW, MATE.
EH?
NO MATTER WHAT I DO, I CAN NEVER GET RID OF YOU FOOKERS.
WENT TO A WHOLE 'NOTHER BLOODY DIMENSION AND EVERYTHING.
I'M GLAD EVERYTHING WORKED OUT.
YEAH ME TOO.
WE SAVED THE FOOKIN WORLD, DOM.
WE DID.
THE FOOKIN *WORLD.*

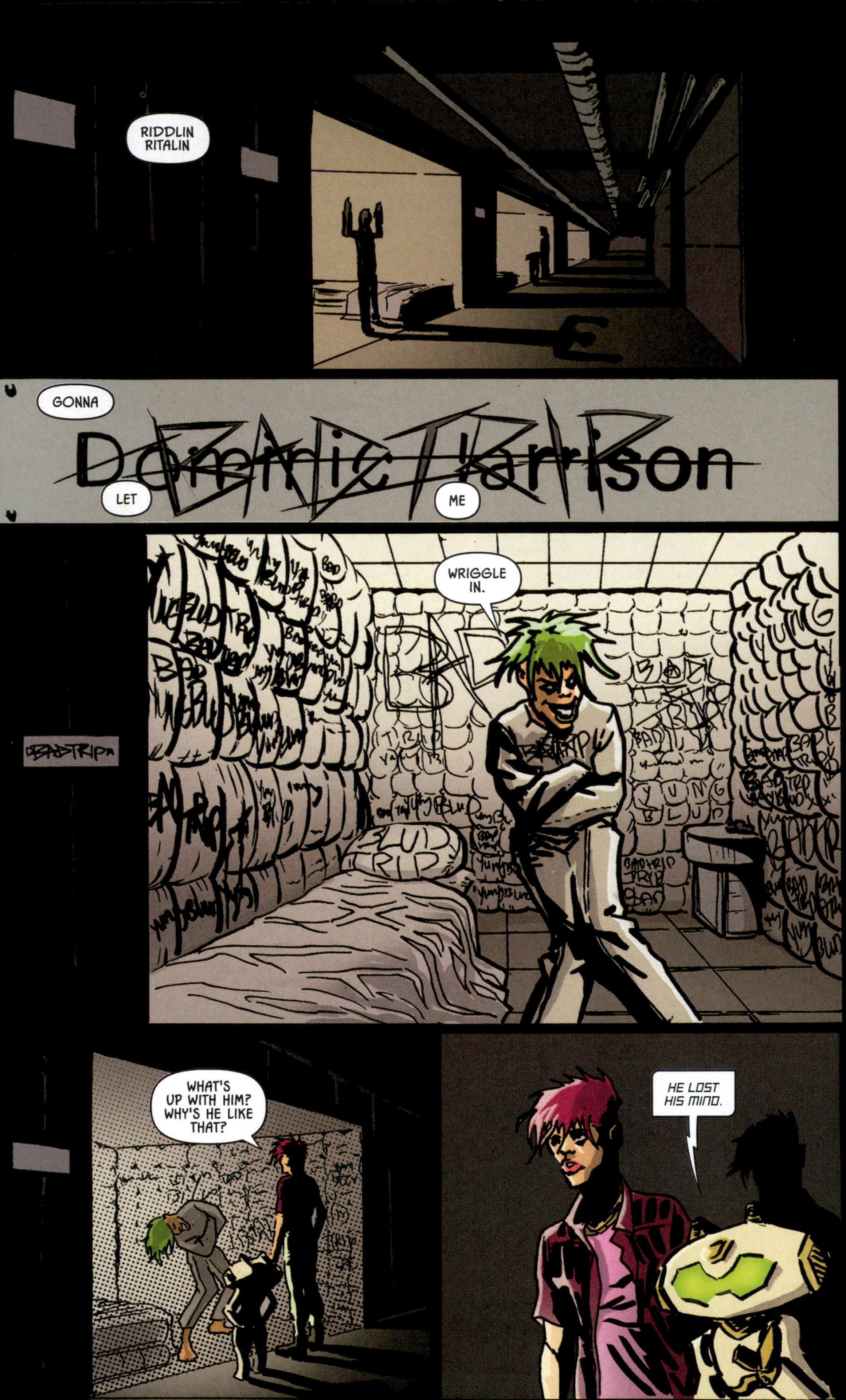
RIDDLIN RITALIN
GONNA
Dominic Harrison
BAD TRIP
LET
ME
WRIGGLE IN.
BAD TRIP
WHAT'S UP WITH HIM? WHY'S HE LIKE THAT?
HE LOST HIS MIND.

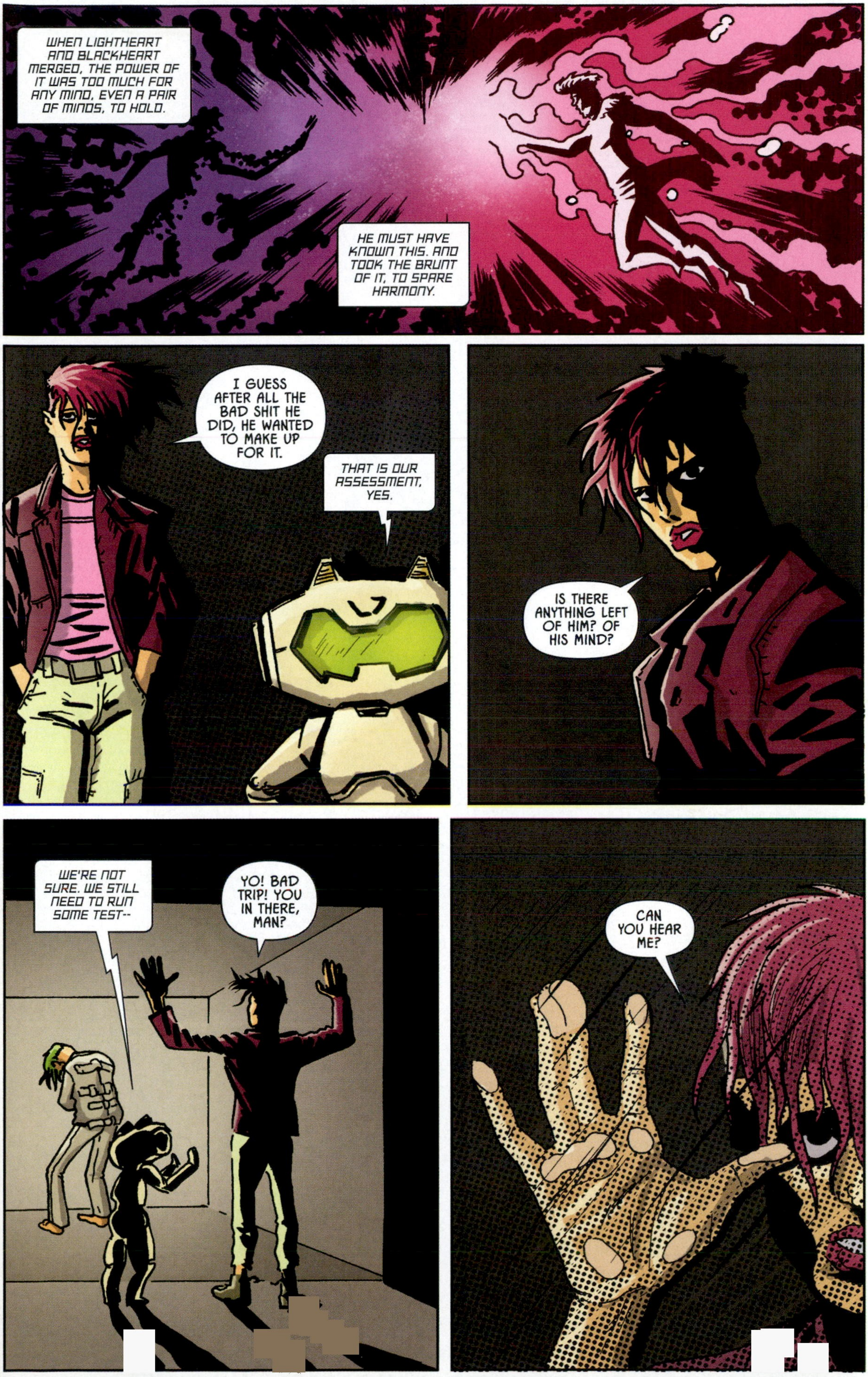
WHEN LIGHTHEART AND BLACKHEART MERGED, THE POWER OF IT WAS TOO MUCH FOR ANY MIND, EVEN A PAIR OF MINDS, TO HOLD.
HE MUST HAVE KNOWN THIS. AND TOOK THE BRUNT OF IT, TO SPARE HARMONY.
I GUESS AFTER ALL THE BAD SHIT HE DID, HE WANTED TO MAKE UP FOR IT.
THAT IS OUR ASSESSMENT, YES.
IS THERE ANYTHING LEFT OF HIM? OF HIS MIND?
WE'RE NOT SURE. WE STILL NEED TO RUN SOME TEST--
YO! BAD TRIP! YOU IN THERE, MAN?
CAN YOU HEAR ME?

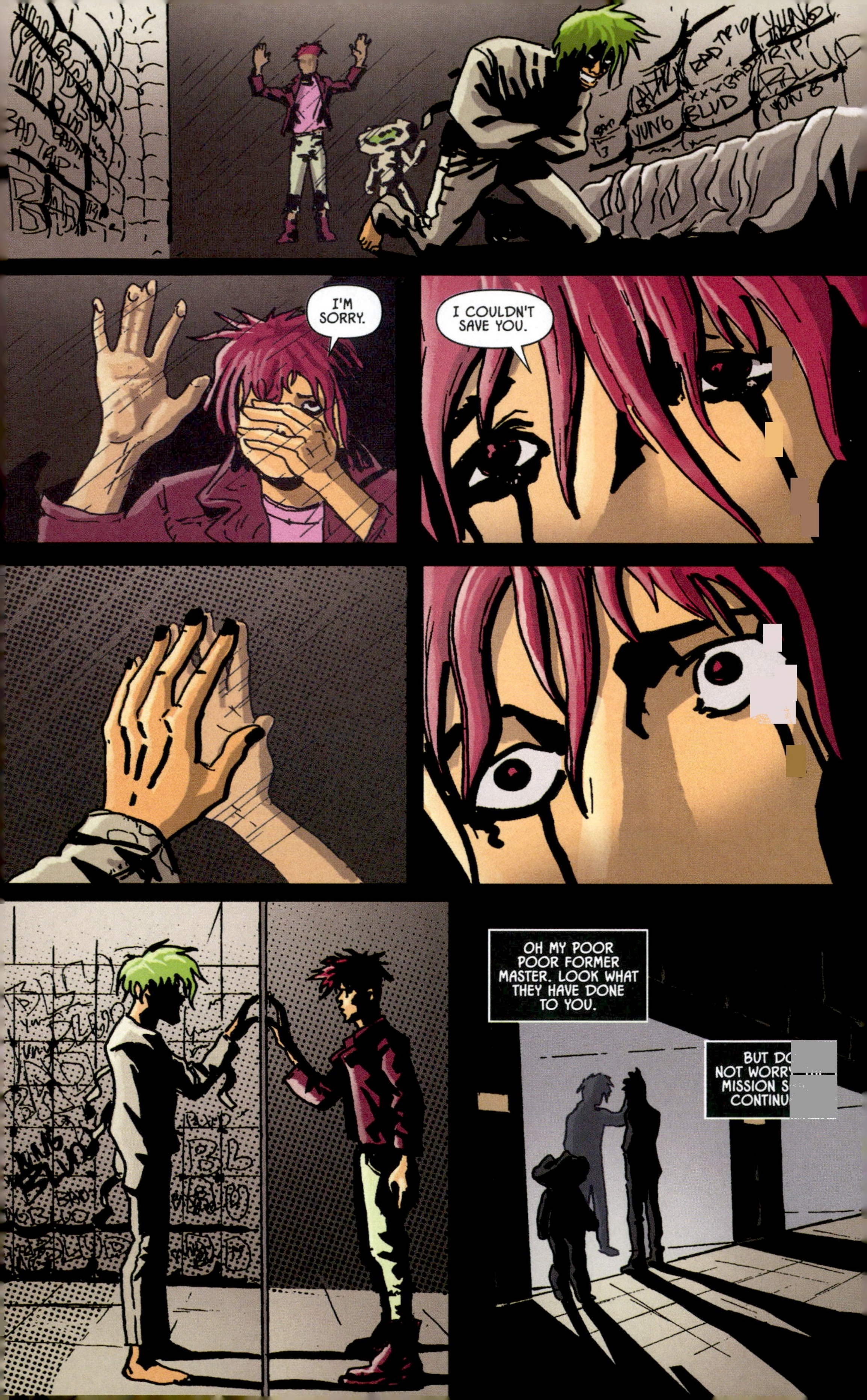
I'M SORRY.
I COULDN'T SAVE YOU.
OH MY POOR POOR FORMER MASTER. LOOK WHAT THEY HAVE DONE TO YOU.
BUT DO NOT WORRY

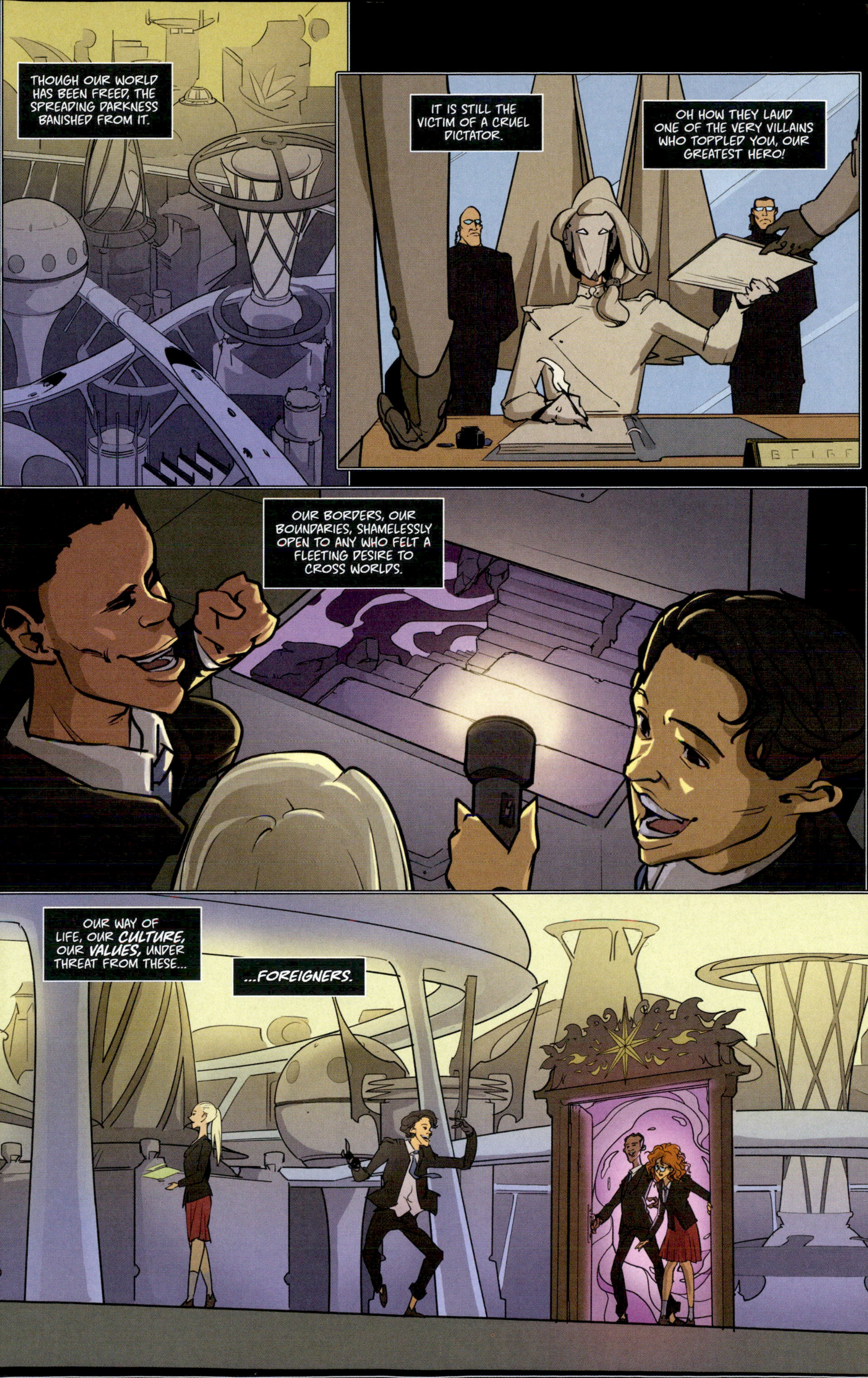
THOUGH OUR WORLD HAS BEEN FREED, THE SPREADING DARKNESS BANISHED FROM IT.
IT IS STILL THE VICTIM OF A CRUEL DICTATOR.
OH HOW THEY LAUD ONE OF THE VERY VILLAINS WHO TOPPLED YOU, OUR GREATEST HERO!
OUR BORDERS, OUR BOUNDARIES, SHAMELESSLY OPEN TO ANY WHO FELT A FLEETING DESIRE TO CROSS WORLDS.
OUR WAY OF LIFE, OUR CULTURE, OUR VALUES, UNDER THREAT FROM THESE...
...FOREIGNERS.

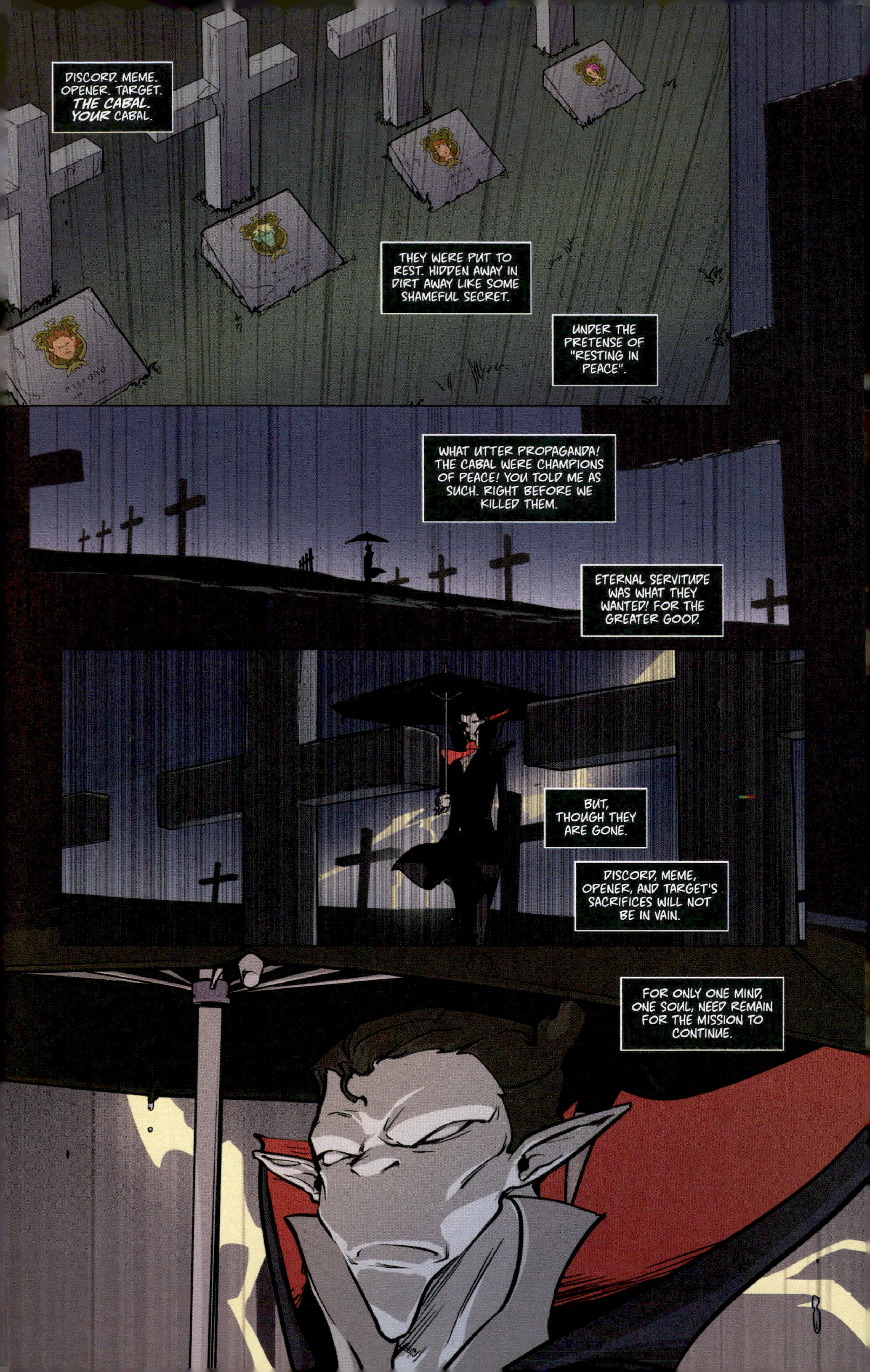
DISCORD. MEME. OPENER. TARGET. **THE CABAL. YOUR** CABAL.
THEY WERE PUT TO REST. HIDDEN AWAY IN DIRT AWAY LIKE SOME SHAMEFUL SECRET.
UNDER THE PRETENSE OF "RESTING IN PEACE".
WHAT UTTER PROPAGANDA! THE CABAL WERE CHAMPIONS OF PEACE! YOU TOLD ME AS SUCH. RIGHT BEFORE WE KILLED THEM.
ETERNAL SERVITUDE WAS WHAT THEY WANTED! FOR THE GREATER GOOD.
BUT, THOUGH THEY ARE GONE.
DISCORD, MEME, OPENER, AND TARGET'S SACRIFICES WILL NOT BE IN VAIN.
FOR ONLY ONE MIND, ONE SOUL, NEED REMAIN FOR THE MISSION TO CONTINUE.

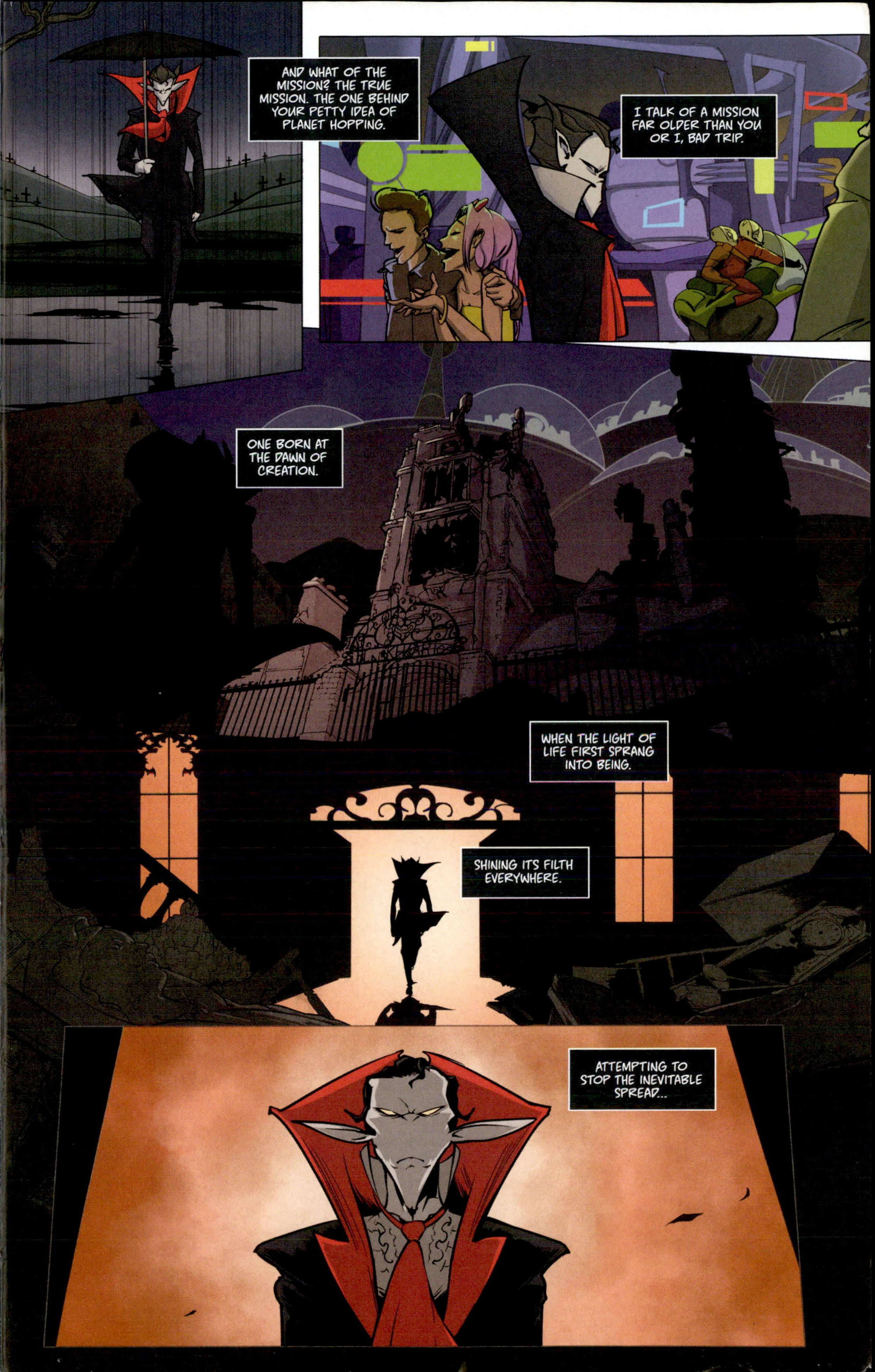
AND WHAT OF THE MISSION? THE TRUE MISSION. THE ONE BEHIND YOUR PETTY IDEA OF PLANET HOPPING.
I TALK OF A MISSION FAR OLDER THAN YOU OR I, BAD TRIP.
ONE BORN AT THE DAWN OF CREATION.
WHEN THE LIGHT OF LIFE FIRST SPRANG INTO BEING.
SHINING ITS FILTH EVERYWHERE.
ATTEMPTING TO STOP THE INEVITABLE SPREAD...

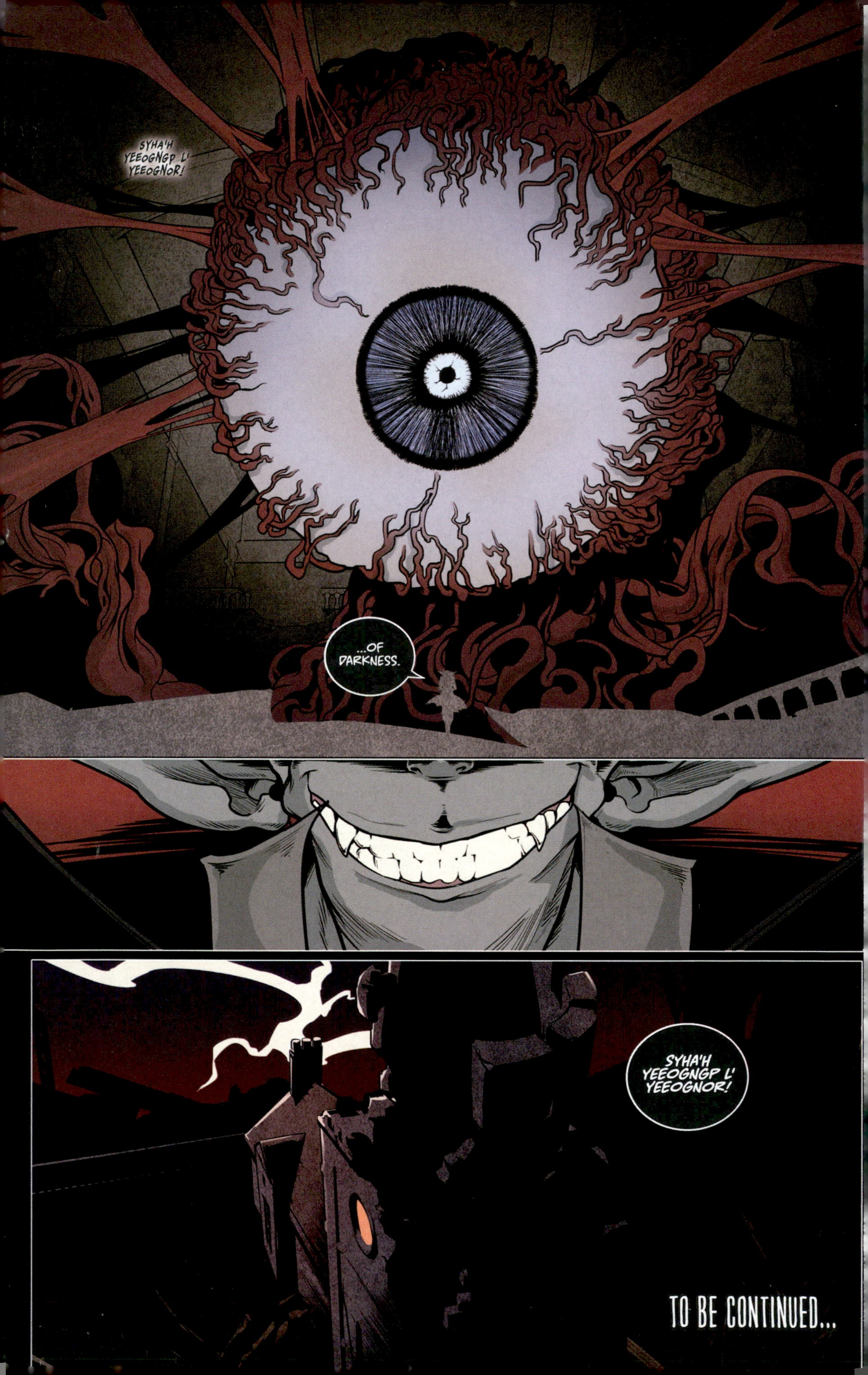
SYHA'H YEEOGNGP L' YEEOGNOR!
...OF DARKNESS.
SYHA'H YEEOGNGP L' YEEOGNOR!
TO BE CONTINUED...